AF813635

THE RADICAL UNPRESENT

THE RADICAL UNPRESENT

CULTURAL RESISTANCE IN A FRACTURED WORLD

GREGORY SHOLETTE

THE MIT PRESS
CAMBRIDGE, MASSACHUSETTS
LONDON, ENGLAND

The MIT Press
Massachusetts Institute of Technology
77 Massachusetts Avenue
Cambridge, MA 02139
mitpress.mit.edu

The MIT Press would like to thank the anonymous peer reviewers who provided comments on drafts of this book. The generous work of academic experts is essential for establishing the authority and quality of our publications. We acknowledge with gratitude the contributions of these otherwise uncredited readers.

This book was set in Arnhem Pro and New Frank by New Best-set Typesetters Ltd.
Printed and bound in the United States of America.

Library of Congress Cataloging-in-Publication Data is available.

ISBN: 978-0-262-05411-9

10 9 8 7 6 5 4 3 2 1

EU Authorised Representative: Easy Access System Europe, Mustamäe tee 50, 10621 Tallinn, Estonia | Email: gpsr.requests@easproject.com

In Solidarity with the Future

CONTENTS

LIST OF FIGURES

INTRODUCTION
ENTERING THE UNPRESENT

No matter how one looks at the year 2022, when my last book on artistic activism first appeared in print, it seemed to be a watershed moment for progressive-left culture.[1] Striking museum staff organized themselves into labor unions; celebrated photographer Nan Goldin's group P.A.I.N. targeted the Sackler family's cultural funding over their involvement in mass pharmaceutical addiction; environmental activists tossed cake, soup, and mashed potatoes at artworks or Krazy-Glued themselves to paintings by Vermeer, Van Gogh, and Monet; demonstrators condemned art-collecting Russian oligarchs for backing Putin's war against Ukraine; and the protest group Decolonize This Place occupied the Whitney Museum over links between its board members and the munitions industry. It was also a time when the tactics of Black Lives Matter and the #MeToo movements were being incorporated into the programming of high culture, as the air itself seemed electrified with a surge of protest aesthetics and activist art practices unlike anything since the 1960s.[2]

But if 2022 was the culmination of unprecedented left political dissent in the streets and in the arts that had built steadily for years, something else is taking shape less than four years later as I write this introduction. It is a sudden cultural shift that has done more than push all such progressive developments into retreat; it is actively reversing them. With large areas of the globe embracing conservative nationalist or even autocratic political values—Argentina, Chile, El Salvador, Turkey, Serbia, Slovakia,

FIGURE 1

In Mykola Ridnyi's *Blind Spot Series* (2014–), a C-print covered with ultra-black nitrocellulose paint, most of an apartment building in eastern Ukraine is obscured, leaving only a limited view around the edges, simulating visual disorders like scotoma. This work creates "a parallelism between the ways in which disease affects human vision and how media propaganda destroys our ability to reflect on social and political reality"—particularly relevant given Russia's ongoing war against Ukraine since 2014, as much as it is for an age of ultra-surveillance. As Ridnyi asserts, "Any war is a war of images" that challenge how "the more we see the more we are blind" in our media-saturated environment (Anna Remešová, "Mykola Ridnyi: Any War Is a War of Images." *Blok*, October 28, 2022). Image courtesy of the artist.

Hungary, India, Russia, Belarus, Georgia, Iran, Israel, and the US, all on a miserable and growing list—it is now progressives who confront the rapid ascension of a very different cultural movement. What this book hopes to accomplish is to provide a framework for understanding this mutating sociopolitical landscape while speculating on ways of differentiating and negating the rise of what I will generally refer to as *the nationalist right* or simply *MAGA*: Make America Great Again. Once again, I write from the perspective of cultural theory and practice, informed by decades of research and progressive social and political organizing primarily in the visual arts. But this time, unlike in the past, I recognize the possible risks my candor might invite. Such is our current moment, such is the Unpresent.

WHEN TIME BECOMES UNCANNY

While, certainly, any attempt made now at offering a definitive understanding of these still-unfolding political and cultural circumstances risks inaccuracy, the hazard of not attempting an analysis is even more formidable. For example, we are already witnessing self-censorship spreading across the art world, as well as overt cancellation of controversial or topical exhibitions and performances.[3] We are watching the US government intervene in the arena of culture by challenging, renaming, and even replacing leadership of cultural institutions in Washington, DC, while seeking to impose a preferred aesthetic style on the construction of new monuments and buildings in the nation's capital. It is unlikely that the transformation of life MAGA seeks to bring about will remain restricted to federal institutions only. Just how long will it be before other established museums, university art galleries, or even the private, commercial art market begins to question certain types of exhibitions and art, including the vibrancy of an inclusive and democratic artistic activism which they have only recently begun to fully embrace? Will this progressive-leaning vitality soon be shunned in favor of less confrontational content, more placid aesthetic forms, or even advocacy for antiprogressive or nationalist-oriented cultural trends?[4] These are among a cluster of questions and concerns animating this study, which nonetheless proposes a still broader framing of this fast-moving fundamental transformation of art, culture, and politics. And yet it seems as if the faster things move, the more they remain stuck in the present, or even the past. My argument is that we are in a moment when time is itself under singular duress as our sense of past, present, and future flatten into an uncanny condition where any familiar sense of space and time is out of joint. A central contention of this book is that social routines, cultural institutions, economic and political protocols still outwardly look the same, but are in fact being fundamentally hollowed out from within. The resulting consequences appear like a spreading social delirium. I will call this condition the *Unpresent*.

Let me offer two examples of my claim. The first illustrates this condition at a personal scale, the second shows how the evisceration of familiar structures operates as a political project. In early 2025, I visited the Northeast Philadelphia suburbs where I grew up before leaving for New York City to attend art school in the late 1970s. While there, I stopped by the Neshaminy Mall, a local shopping center built in 1968 whose very name was an act of symbolic theft. Neshaminy is a Lenape word for the double creek that ran through Indigenous land appropriated centuries earlier, the tribe having been dispossessed from the region as early as the mid-eighteenth century. My teenage memory of this colonially branded, commodity-filled space was of its scale and allure to an upwardly mobile working-class public. The Mall, as it was generally referred to, was many times larger than all of the surrounding buildings, and always teeming with shoppers browsing merchandise, devouring fast food, or waiting in line to watch *The Godfather*, *Planet of the Apes*, or *Jaws*, well before such blockbusters returned as recursive franchises. So massive and alluring was this artificial world that still today I recall having to park far from the entrance due to the high volume of customers. All in all, the Mall encapsulated a thriving consumer universe with its own sense of time, space, and aura, however abbreviated, including that of community, such as it was in the era of postwar upclassing.

On my recent visit, the encircling parking lots (there are several) were virtually empty. Once inside, I found many of the retail shops long-shuttered, and only a handful of individuals, some who looked as if they had possibly moved into the building, roaming about languidly or plopping themselves down on benches. A once sparkling fountain ringed with luxuriant foliage was dry, the plantings now dead or synthetic replacements. Squatting in this broken-down arcadia sat the familiar bronze statue of a romanticized "Neshaminy Indian," a tribe that never existed, commissioned by a bygone Philadelphia-based department store in 1970. The entire facility appeared now as a sprawling ghost town of the neoliberal era. It was an utterly unsettling experience for me to try to reconcile my memory of the place with its current desolation. No doubt locals had adjusted to these changes over time, but I was confronting them as if everything had happened overnight. And here is the key takeaway: had Neshaminy Mall simply been shut down or perhaps made over into some other enterprise altogether, the haunted ambience would have been missing. But as a space physically identical in most ways to my memory of what it once was, only now with its internal existence and operations practically terminated, the entire complex was both present and not-present, identical and radically different, all at once. In addition, this encounter raised another possibility: that my own memory was faulty or even fictitious. It is this level of experiential shock and downright weirdness that I suspect many people feel today, although scaled up to the level of society as a whole.

EVISCERATING LIBERAL DEMOCRACY: THE HUNGARIAN TEMPLATE

If the mall story demonstrates what it feels like when the familiar is gutted from within, can this condition be politically weaponized? The answer, disturbingly, is yes. My second example comes not from the United States but from Hungary, a former socialist nation long considered to be the cultural and political template for the American MAGA movement, or what Gábor Erlich calls "the semi-core of the Illiberal International."[5] After solidifying power in 2010, President Viktor Orbán and his far-right Fidesz party rapidly transformed Hungary's cosmopolitan and once internationally oriented liberal society into a version of my uncanny shopping mall in Pennsylvania. As one mainstream journalist put it after visiting Budapest in 2025, "there are no tanks in the streets; there are [still] elections, and public protests, and judges in robes. But the more closely you look at its core civic institutions, the more you see how they've been hollowed-out from within."[6] That sense of eviscerated reality is well under way today, including in the United States. And there are precedents. Ernst Fraenkel's analysis of the Nazi "dual state," in which a seemingly normal "normative state" masked a "prerogative state" operating by arbitrary power, provides an earlier template for understanding how authoritarian regimes preserve institutional facades while gutting their substance.[7] Yet what distinguishes the current moment is how this hollowing-out operates not merely within familiar legal and governmental structures, but as a broader temporal, cultural, and even ontological disembowelment of reality, affecting our very experience of time and space. Welcome to what I am calling the Unpresent.

Readers of this book may see in this description of Hungarian politics, as I do, a situation eerily similar to that of the United States following Donald Trump's return to the White House in 2025. (Orbán and his Fidesz Party's celebrated 2026 electoral defeat may signal the first significant shift in the global rightward political tide, or it may be more of an anti-corruption correction, leaving much of the ethnonationalist repurposed cultural terrain standing.) The first convicted felon to be elected president, Trump let loose a rapid-fire cannonade of executive orders, memoranda, and proclamations that have sought to expunge a range of allegedly liberal targets including environmental legislation, DEI (diversity, equity, inclusion) programs, liberal global trade (via tariffs), higher education and student visas at major universities, as well as immigration policy. He has also canceled federal grants to the sciences and arts, and in an executive order on January 20, 2025, sought to "[Promote] Beautiful Federal Civic Architecture," ostensibly eliminating new brutalist and modernist government building designs.[8] Trump's pardoning of January 6 rioters (including those convicted of violence and weapons possession), his embrace of imperialist military policy in Latin America, and the unleashing of ICE (Immigration and Customs Enforcement) across city neighborhoods have shattered any remaining sense of social normality. The killing of Minnesotans Renee Nicole Good and Alex Pretti in January 2026—two US citizens caught in ICE raids on immigrants—and the White House's subsequent description of homicides as self-defense against leftists and terrorists has only crystallized the inherent climate of state-sponsored menace. For those on the liberal-to-left side of the political and cultural spectrum, including the majority of contemporary artists, the visceral sense of being under attack has become undeniable, whether or not they consider themselves politically active. These ICE "invasions" of blue cities including Los Angeles, Portland, Chicago, and Minneapolis/St. Paul represent not merely authoritarian overreach but evidence that the United States has already entered a new civil war, one that is becoming increasingly impossible to deny. Federal troops operating against American cities, citizens killed in raids, military occupation of neighborhoods: these are the tactics of internal conflict, not democratic governance.

What is important to note is that many within MAGA itself are also suffering from what some call cognitive dissonance, with the bombardment of Iran beginning February 28, 2026 greatly intensifying this discord. This is what is unique about the condition that I am calling the Unpresent: the uncertainty spreads in all directions. For, without a perception of society's moving toward an improved future reality, the immediate sensation of time is dully repetitive, but also stirringly edgy and anxious. When it becomes impossible to envision any tomorrow, but especially one that advances living conditions for the majority, the present becomes haunted by a past grounded in divisive fantasy, including once-discarded historical narratives such as Manifest Destiny, or ostensibly abandoned policies of hemispheric military dominance like the Monroe Doctrine, or even imagined versions of past decades including the postwar 1950s and Reagan's 1980s. This is also what makes the Unpresent different from George Orwell's well-known dystopian vision in which the past is overwritten by a centralized authority. The vertiginous uncertainty we experience is a direct result of a disturbance in our perception of time, regardless of whether some Big Brother figure seeks to impose a top-down counternarrative. Indeed, Trump and his administration seem eager to continuously undermine all sense of stability. And yet, while the Unpresent is certainly radically disruptive, it also discloses possibilities of resistance precisely due to its untimely feverishness. I will address this critical prospect in the third and fourth sections of this book by addressing the spectral surplus of resistance made accessible as a phantom archive.

Therefore, along with addressing the likelihood of a regressive backward turn toward a less inclusive, officially sanctioned and politically guarded cultural environment, this book also aims to comprehend and attempts to confront the haunting, disabling condition of the radical

Unpresent itself, that uncanny time and space that have become severely out of joint.

THE STRUCTURE OF THE BOOK

This study unfolds in four parts, each addressing different aspects of our current cultural and temporal crisis. Part I consists of five chapters and establishes the theoretical framework for understanding how we arrived at the Unpresent. It begins by revisiting my earlier concept of artistic *dark matter*—the necessary cultural labor and imagination that are contributed by the majority of creative producers who invisibly sustain the mainstream art world—and traces how these once-suppressed activities have become illuminated thanks to neoliberalism's extractive networks that seek to harvest value from every conceivable corner of life.[9] Crucially, this brightening of what was hidden in plain sight has revealed not only progressive forces but also resentful and reactionary energies long festering in the shadows. The 2026 midterm elections offer a case in point. Should Democrats retake the House, there is reason to expect a check on the most aggressive elements of the MAGA legislative program—and that matters. But the risk is that electoral reversal becomes a substitute for confronting the temporal condition this book describes. The Unpresent does not dissolve with a shift in congressional majorities. Its hollowed-out institutions, its weaponized nostalgia, its flattened horizons persist regardless of which party controls a single chamber. To invest the midterms with redemptive finality is itself a symptom of the very temporal crisis at stake: the desperate search for a decisive turning point within a condition defined by the absence of such turns.

I next examine how the century-old ambitions of the artistic avant-garde to merge art with everyday life while disrupting bourgeois normalcy has found its realization not through revolutionary socialism but through capitalism's total aestheticization of human existence as it incorporates vanguard tactics into its endless pageantry of consumer pleasures. While both resistant art and the avant-garde have other possibilities when time itself is conspicuously interrupted, as I will propose, it is this general condition of spectacularized and commodified reality that sets the stage for understanding MAGA as our new retro-vanguard. By this I mean that MAGA is a contemporary movement that employs culturally disruptive tactics not to rush toward an emancipated future, as the historic avant-garde—or most of it—once intended, but instead to restore an imaginary past in place of a liberated tomorrow. It does so even as it uneasily thrives upon the upended time and space of the Unpresent.

Part I culminates with a detailed theorization of the Unpresent itself, tracing its immediate genealogy from Mark Fisher's "capitalist realism" through the temporal disruptions of recent years including Brexit, Trump's first presidency, the Covid lockdowns, and the surreal spectacle of January 6, 2021, or hereinafter simply J6.[10] What emerges is a condition of capitalist *unrealism* or simply the Unpresent, where time, and often space, appear flipped inside-out, leaving us suspended in a doubly unsettling present that feels simultaneously familiar and utterly transformed.

Part II deepens the backstory of the Unpresent via Sigmund Freud's interpretation of *das Unheimliche*, or "the uncanny," and its derivations over time by the Frankfurt School and contemporary anthropologist Rebecca Bryant. It also addresses the phenomenon of the radical nationalist right's attack on higher education by way of Stefano Harney and Fred Moten's concept of the "fugitive undercommons," followed by a similar critique of museums raised by conservative artist and critic Alexander Adams, who alleges that institutions of high culture are subjugated to a broad leftist intrigue.[11] In these two chapters we confront the paradoxes of institutional critique at a moment of institutional besiegement.

Parts III and IV pivot to examine possibilities for resistance to MAGA culture and the disquieting time of the Unpresent. Moving beyond a discussion of paralysis, these parts examine how certain socially engaged art practices attempt to repair our fractured relationship with time through what I term "the phantom archive," a surplus repository of unrealized possibilities that haunts our current moment. Or as Michiko Akiba describes this archive, it comprises "the accumulated efforts throughout history aimed at social transformation—some of which were partially successful, though many ended in failure."[12] Thus, she writes, it is made up of "immaterial elements—memories, ideas, aspirations, metaphors, and tactics from past movements—that, though intangible, still carry the potential to influence the present."[13] This is why the artworks highlighted in this volume include works involving reenactment, repurposing, and conspicuous repair with regard to historical narration and political agency. Put differently, this is a type of cultural repair that *declares itself as repair*, with the phantom archive's surplus materials and ideas serving as the warehouse for this conspicuous repurposing. Paradoxically, however, this commitment to conspicuous repair generates its own predicament: the same brightening that reveals suppressed cultural possibilities also renders them available for extraction, manipulation, and control. Under conditions of expanding technological surveillance, visibility increasingly can lead to vulnerability. The tension between making visible and remaining operative—between conspicuous repair and what I will call tactical opacity or strategic redarkening—also runs as a structural contradiction throughout this study, surfacing most fully in my conclusion.

Between the first two parts and the second two parts is an experimental interlude that, in the spirit of Russian theorist Mikhail Bakhtin's carnival, explores the entanglement of the artistic avant-garde with MAGA's J6 insurrection.[14] It moves sideways across time while drawing on the phantom archive in a crablike scuttle revealing unexpected connections and divergences. At the back of the book, you will find a glossary of terms used in this study. And strategically inserted throughout its chapters is a parallel curated visual presentation consisting of fifty reproductions of works by a wide range of contemporary artists which serve to amplify, contrast, and perhaps at times challenge the book's claims. Think of the illustrations, therefore, as a rhythmical counterpoint to the body of the text.

EXIGENCIES

It is my conviction that the questions driving this investigation extend well beyond art world concerns and into the broader sphere of a rapidly shifting cultural paradigm. MAGA and the nationalist right's political wins across the globe demonstrate that reactionary forces have proven more adept than progressives at mobilizing voting blocs, including in working-class sectors of the world population. With these wins has come an equally animated aesthetic strategy. A primary argument of this volume is that MAGA's cultural approach must be taken seriously. It is a cultural movement that relies upon the totally spectacularized environment of neoliberal capitalism, even as it seeks to curtail or terminate many aspects of that same socioeconomic model. Rather than dismissing MAGA as merely appropriating countercultural and left-progressive forms and ideas, or dismissing it as mere nostalgic regression, we must recognize it as a genuinely contemporary phenomenon, one now in the process of establishing its own counterhegemony against established liberal democracies. Only by understanding how the cultural programs of the nationalist right operate in opposition to but also in alliance with the effects of the Unpresent can we begin to formulate effective counterstrategies.

A word of caution. Perhaps what I describe here actually stems from nostalgia following years of socially engaged art activity, research, and teaching, mixed with personal anxiety about changing cultural and political circumstances. In a decade, all of this moment may appear merely transitional. While I doubt it, I leave that judgment to readers now and in the future. For the duration of this study, I aim to resist what might be called a wide-awake narcolepsy—a conscious paralysis where time is so severely dislocated that familiar metaphors like sociopolitical sleepwalking fail to capture our actual condition. This book proceeds from the conviction that adequate description precedes effective action: if we cannot name our predicament, we cannot confront or change it.

PART I

DIAGNOSIS

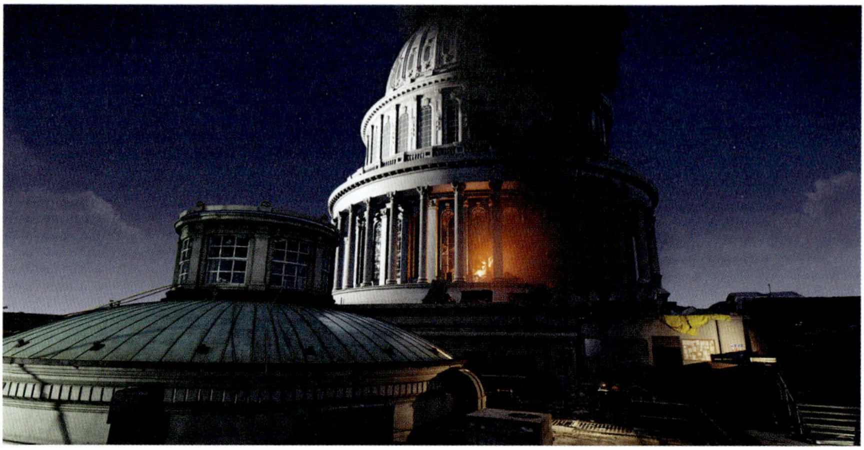

FIGURE 2

Sons & True Sons, a screen grab from a 2025 performance involving a repurposed video game altered by the Viennese art collective Total Refusal, who describe themselves as "pseudo-Marxist media guerrillas" (https://totalrefusal.com/). The work explores disturbing parallels between the video game *Tom Clancy's The Division 2* and the real-life storming of the US Capitol on January 6, 2021. In this live gaming lecture format, the collective scrutinizes how the game's narrative "inadvertently anticipated" events of January 6 and examines MAGA theorist Steve Bannon's strategic engagement with male gamers. Image courtesy of the artists.

1

DARK MATTER REVISITED

The three concluding sentences of my 2010 book *Dark Matter: Art and Politics in the Age of Enterprise Culture* were ominous yet ironically upbeat: "the archive of dark matter has split open. We are its dead capital. It is the dawn of the dead."[1] What I had hoped to announce was the inevitable illumination of a multitude of cultural laborers and creative practices long relegated to the margins and shadows of the mainstream art world. This missing creative mass included, above all, the throngs of program-certified art graduates who serve as project fabricators, gallery managers, museum staff, and art movers. Their overlooked labor is essential for sustaining the minuscule number of celebrated artists who enter the illuminated spotlight of the global art scene. They were, and still are, invisible in plain sight, even as the industry of high culture depends on their muted participation, not as artists but as essential workers. Still, what I identified foreshadowed something more troubling than I anticipated, for clearly any theory of systemic invisibility is both inherently complex and potentially paradoxical. But let me first recap the concept of artistic "dark matter," or the missing mass of the art world.

MAPPING ART'S INVISIBLE UNIVERSE

The dark matter hypothesis was intended to affirm the overlooked activism of politically engaged artists and art collectives, many of whom

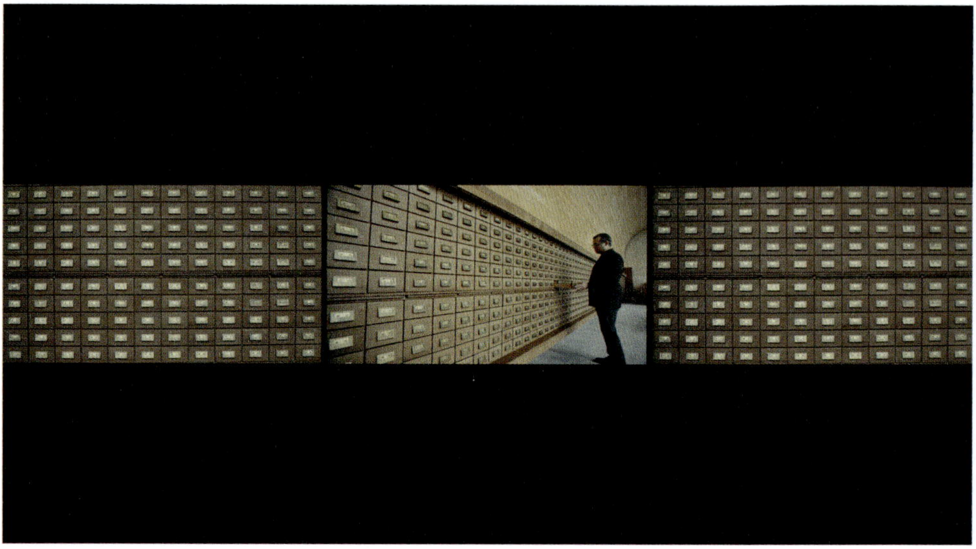

FIGURE 3

Naeem Mohaiemen's three-channel film installation *Two Meetings and a Funeral* (2017) examines how institutional memory systems both preserve and erase history. Mohaiemen's interest in questions of visibility and evasiveness extend back to the security panic following the attacks of September 11, 2001 with his collective project *Disappeared in America* (2004–2007) that focused on the government detention of shadow citizens: immigrants who drive taxis, deliver food, sell newspapers disappeared by state authorities. *Two Meetings and a Funeral* demonstrates that archives are also like living entities wrestling with the contradictions of recognition and suppression, while challenging established narratives about who controls our collective historical memory. Image courtesy of the artist.

intentionally distanced themselves from the mainstream art world both as a critique of its hegemony and out of a desire for autonomy. But this category represents the smallest of three types of artistic dark matter. The second includes the multitude of MFA, BFA, and increasingly PhD-credentialed practitioners statistically destined for career invisibility. Those who continue producing art years after graduating do so while juggling other paid employment including teaching, but also fabricating, transporting, installing, or studio managing for their more successful colleagues. When all is said and done, these professionals remain no more visible than the third and largest mass: informal nonprofessional artists engaged in live action role play, P2P (peer-to-peer) file sharing of drawings, music, and videos, or informal hobbyists and Sunday painters. Yet this latter group is distinguished by having no expectation of art world recognition. They do what they do for pleasure, "personal development," or to "fill up" or simply to "kill" time in a world demanding constant productive participation.

This admittedly schematic triad of miscellaneous practitioners supports the mainstream industry of high culture in varying ways (with activist art collectives exempted until fairly recently, as we shall see). If pre-failed art school graduates function as the art world's semiemployed workforce, then the realm of informal artists becomes a dark backdrop of everything that a successful artist is not. At the same time, they indirectly add value to the art world by purchasing art supplies, taking classes taught by professionals turned part-time instructors, and perhaps paying for museum memberships and art journals. Think of the trajectory of graffiti writers from streets and subways to art galleries and museums, all the while adding considerable value to spray paint manufacturers, many of whom also produce professional art supplies.[2] Is it possible, I asked a quarter-century ago, that the majority of creative activity in our postindustrial society is invisible to the institutions and discourses—the critics, art historians, collectors, dealers, museums, curators, and arts administrators—who manage and interpret contemporary culture? In the decades since, an abundance of scholarly citations to the dark matter hypothesis suggests the answer is resoundingly yes. Briefly restated, the informal artist, the credentialed art graduate, and the blue-chip celebrity artist all exist on a continuum. This is quite unlike how the mainstream art world portrays what are essentially class differences within its province, preferring to imagine all three forming discrete spheres of solitary activity. Nevertheless, the political economy of high culture requires all of these laborers, even as it rolls on, continually rewriting its own narrative to exclude this inconvenient reality.

HIDDEN IN PLAIN SIGHT

In response to these hard-edged realities, I proposed the need to map what appeared to be an artistic universe made up of a small patch of light surrounded by a far larger realm of darkness. I turned to a favorite passion: the hard sciences and, in particular, a theory proposed by astrophysicists that the known universe of visible matter and energy—the stars, planets, illuminated gases, and so forth—is surrounded by a far larger quantity of unknown *dark* matter and *dark* energy. And it is this missing mass, according to scientists, that anchors everything in physical existence, preventing it from expanding into a cold, dissipated void. But if we only inhabit about 5 percent of what is known and is visible, what does this tell us about the reality we take for granted?

Notably, this celestial dark matter and energy are detectable only by measuring their knock-on effect upon visible galactic bodies. This simple but productive metaphor worked well because the dark matter of the art world is also apprehensible only by way of its veiled absence, a ghostly archive detectable only through gaps in the official inventory. And yet, once bumped into, this newly noticed presence forces us to question the very space and time, interior and exterior, of high culture. Of course, there is one crucial difference between scientific investigators and their art world counterparts: the former want to uncover what cosmic dark matter consists of, whereas the latter prefer to keep it off the record in the dark. More importantly, this disregard by the institutional art world regarding its missing mass was about to be disrupted, as dark matter was becoming increasingly less dark, with consequences both overdue and unsettling.

CAROL DUNCAN'S GLUT OF CREATIVITY

I was by no means the first scholar to reflect upon this phenomenon of a missing artistic mass. As early as 1983, the American art historian Carol Duncan pinpointed a fundamental though typically overlooked feature of high culture: that most professionally trained artists make up a vast surplus of producers whose redundancy is "the normal condition of the art market."[3] Beyond the recognized boundaries of the established art world, Duncan added, lies an even larger pool of individuals whose talents never had a chance to develop. Building from Duncan's observation, I wondered if these many (allegedly) superfluous cultural producers played a necessary and affirmative role in upholding the same art institutions that systematically excluded them by casting their labor into the shadows.

My question was elementary: what would it mean for creative dark matter to become illuminated? Yet this question led to other concerns. How could the contemporary art world even manage the highlighting of its own obscured sources of propagation? Might this not expose the often arbitrary and porous gatekeeping mechanism that determines what is "serious" art and what is not? Consider also the volume of what is obscured, compared to what is endorsed and visible. Class politics also seemed to play a role here as well, leading to issues within contemporary society more broadly. For example, could this illumination of art's missing mass also serve to spotlight other precarious and disregarded laborers, such as janitorial custodians, caregivers, and similar essential though typically devalued workers?

Far from purely theoretical musing, these questions carried urgent practical implications as the inquiry into art's missing mass became significant in two distinct ways. First, as stated above, the investigation builds an argument in support of socially engaged and activist art. Significantly, at the time I wrote *Dark Matter* (2010), these activist practices were still a relatively marginalized, even intentionally muted cultural phenomenon, unlike today. This was also the case, surprisingly, among many self-defined leftist and Marxist art critics, historians, and curators who often ignored such work in favor of artists with existing gallery representation or with museum or international biennial status. In addition, this divide also pivoted on practitioners with a familiar studio-oriented practice as opposed to those embedded in social movements making posters, street stencils, art for demonstrations, and other ephemeral work. The dark matter hypothesis was therefore an intervention aimed at challenging these dichotomies, while providing efficacy to socially engaged and collective artists, professionals and nonprofessionals alike.

Second, and most significantly I would argue, these invisible anchoring forces within and around the margins of the art world were undergoing a rapid metamorphosis: *dark matter was getting brighter*. This growing visibility was not primarily due to its internal dynamism, although art's missing mass certainly has its own agency, especially when self-organized into groups and collectives. Instead, this transformation was driven by a more dominating jurisdiction of power that had become interested in these less visible shoals and archipelagos of human labor power for its own extractionist purposes. Briefly stated, dark matter was being illuminated by the inherently predatory forces of neoliberal capitalism as it vacuumed up assets in the social and cultural realm, all of those spheres of reproduction and everyday life previously considered outside its formal economic, but also observational, purview. The introduction of the Internet accelerated this extractive process even as it opened new channels for communicative action and resistance. However, one other aspect of this mining and illuminating process often sidelined by enthusiastic early cyberactivists was the magnified panoptic capability of these same technologies. The recoil of that oversight, what those techno-utopian enthusiasts failed to anticipate, now saturates the Unpresent as unrelenting surveillance.

NEOLIBERALISM'S PREDATORY BRIGHTENING EFFECT

To understand this shift, we need to briefly recount how the deregulated neoliberal marketplace of the late 1970s broke with what immediately preceded it. For at least the century prior, capitalist value, and ultimately surplus value, had been generated within industrial factories. But by the postwar era, and especially by the 1980s, Fordist assembly line manufacturing was replaced by decentralized, spatially dispersed forms of global production. Italian Marxist theorist Mario Tronti famously described the concurrent transformation as the emergence of a social factory, in which the boundaries between productive labor and everyday life began to dissolve.[4] Feminist theoretician Silvia Federici later added that women's unwaged work, always present in the background of industrial capital, was now being overtly incorporated into this postindustrial model of production.[5] The feminist and Marxist thinker Angela Dimitrakaki has neatly summarized this economic-social relation with regard to women's labor: "Capitalism requires unstoppable growth—this is what generates such levels of competition and environmental devastation—and its logic spills into society, exceeding what is more narrowly defined as the economy. Capitalism as a social relation is thus the unavoidable terrain of the feminist struggle."[6]

What capital was in search of was profits, a prize becoming increasingly difficult to extract under regimes of regulation and social welfare. It found new territory in both the deregulation of public institutions and a wholesale annexation of spaces and times previously reserved for nonproductive activity, including eating, sleeping, sex, learning, and unpaid leisure. Public wealth was privatized, precariousness and debt normalized, as something more experiential was also happening to the working classes in the West. By the 1990s, post-Fordist neoliberalism introduced new forms of communications technology via mobile cellular networks and the public rollout of the Internet. Beginning in the developed Global North, but soon spreading to most other parts of the world, networked capitalism called upon the multitude to mobilize their collective capacity of imaginative labor as a new source of surplus value.[7] As these networks permeated all layers of society, the capacity for developing horizontal circuits of resistance expanded—but so too did the possibilities for monitoring them. CEOs and business theorists grasped the extractive and surveillance potential of such developments far sooner than either official state security apparatus or the vanguard art world. As regards the latter, artist and scholar Dave Beech has shown that the production of high culture remains something of an economic anachronism, operating by different rules than contemporary capitalism—which may be the very reason why it became such an attractive target for financial markets.[8]

What business leaders recognized was that both distributed cultural labor and the social networks through which it circulated could be monetized. The booming private surveillance industry is one outcome; platform capitalism's colonization of creative production is another. What early cyberactivists heralded as a new commons of communicative action and resistance was simultaneously, and less visibly, becoming an apparatus of extractive visibility from which no networked activity could escape. Most importantly, the dark matter thesis only proposed that this process of brightening held out a *potential* for a more inclusive and equitable democratic cultural practice (and by "equitable," I mean here a redistribution of art world assets downward, where they belong). Inspired by the dark matter concept, theorist John Roberts called this cultural shadow zone art's secondary economy.[9] Still, while much emphasis has been placed on this radical possibility by myself and others, a far less welcome form of dark matter was always waiting in the wings.

NETWORKS, CREATIVITY, AND UTOPIAN BLIND SPOTS

Consequently, for the enthusiastic proponents of the then still-emerging, digitally connected techtopia of the post-Cold War universe, the notion of cyberspace networks charged with right-wing bitterness and rancor simply never crossed their minds. Instead, such key figures of the 1990s and 2000s as Yochai Benkler, Lawrence Lessig, and Francis Fukuyama spoke of greater freedom and equity, flourishing creativity and innovation, as well as, remarkably, people becoming "less susceptible to manipulation by others than they were in the [old] mass-media culture."[10] However, as I cautioned in 2010—but did so all too summarily as it turns out—nothing assures us that "this increasingly visible social productivity, this materializing missing mass, will be a force of liberty, as some neoliberal proponents of the new economy insist. What is described in these pages as 'dark matter,' therefore, is not intrinsically progressive, not in the typical liberal or radical senses of that term. Instead, it possesses at best a potential for progressive resistance, as well as for reactionary anger."[11]

FROM DARK MATTER TO DARK TIME

What I did not consider in 2010 was just how rapidly and violently this darkest of dark matter would begin to materialize and assert itself in both unforeseeable and ultimately triumphal ways over the next fifteen years. Similarly, it is inevitable that any perforation of a once-suppressed archive of shadowed cultural activity will expose the wounds of political exclusions, both real and imagined. It was just such repeated acts of blockage and offense that had wholly or partially shaped dark matter social production in general. As radical-left theologian Cornel West has argued: "subversive memory and other-regarding morality are the principal weapons for the wretched of the earth and those who fight to enhance their plight."[12]

However, a quite similar Nietzschean *Ressentiment*[13] was already developing and expanding among those on the far right who identified such things as the United Nations, the European Union, and even the US federal government as oppressive, liberal-globalist regimes. In 2026, these assertions have regrettably become far more commonplace. Still, we first began to see mainstream media and social consciousness more broadly starting to react to this phenomenon in the lead-up to Brexit and the first Trump presidential election, as will be discussed in chapter 3. At present, I have been obliged to return to these metaphors of light and dark, visible and invisible, in this new book, many years later, although now without irony, and with a decidedly less upbeat assessment for the progressive reanimation of this missing mass. Unquestionably, a darker realm of dark matter has arisen, forcing itself into view, and thus thrusting itself into the very ambit of this project. Assuredly, this book could not have been written prior to this moment when neoliberal capitalism is itself entering a death spiral as the new ethnocentrist and nationalist right advances into this worsening sociopolitical terrain. Think of the trajectory of this book, therefore, as one in which the previously marginalized spaces of culture's missing mass now impact our imperiled sense of past, present, and future. If dark matter named the invisible labor that anchors the art world, dark time names the temporal disruption that now anchors our social reality, the Unpresent itself.

The archive of dark matter has split open. We are its dead capital. It is the dawn of MAGA culture.

2

MAGA: OUR NEW (RETRO) AVANT-GARDE

On January 6, 2021, a chanting, angry throng of no-longer-obscured dark matter marched directly into the inner sanctum of the US liberal-democratic system, the Capitol building in Washington, DC. They claimed to be taking their home back from occupying wealthy liberal elites. Something had indeed arrived that day, but it would be four more years before it could be seen for what it was. With the return of Donald J. Trump to the White House, this darkest of newly enfranchised dark matter has ascended to become a cutting-edge cultural movement, except that its fervent tip of the spear points decidedly into the past, or, more accurately, it is aimed wistfully toward a simulacrum of America that never was. At the same time, MAGA people, like the Brexit voters in the UK, are not homogeneous, an important discernment for developing opposition to the ascendency of the new nationalist right. Consider British art historian Kim Charnley, who explains that the 2008–2009 financial crisis and credit crunch prepared the ground for Brexit and a nostalgia for a long-gone Empire, but "the social upheaval that became crystallized in the Brexit debate is many-sided, and . . . it has its origins both in long-term economic tendencies and deep-seated cultural narratives. Any attempt to represent this situation finds itself faced with the inadequacy of routine accounts of social agency, of class and identity."[1]

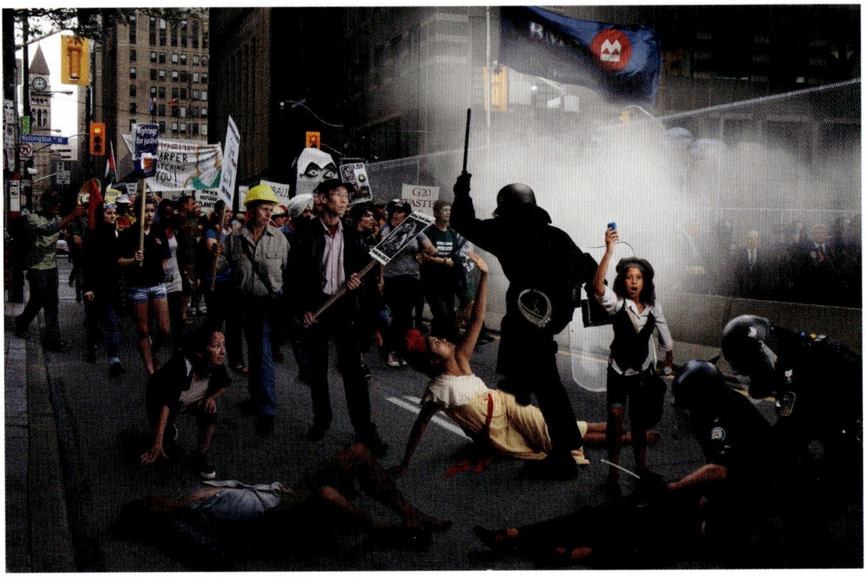

FIGURE 4

This staged and digitally modified photograph by Carole Condé and Karl Beveridge, titled *Liberty Lost* (2010), is their artistic response to the events surrounding the G20 summit in Toronto in 2010, in which 1,100 people were detained in the largest arrest in Canadian peacetime history. The work emerged from left antiglobalization protests against neoliberal policies and corporate power, a political orientation distinctly opposed to the right-wing antiglobalism that would surface in movements like MAGA several years later. Along with progressive activists, many of those arrested were peaceful journalists and bystanders simply in the area at the time. The image represents Condé and Beveridge's collaborative approach involving theatrically composed scenes that dramatize social justice issues, particularly labor struggles and political protests. In their five-decade partnership, Beveridge and his late partner Condé "challenge the cultural conventions of the union movement as well as those of the arts," while transforming perceptions of working-class experiences through sophisticated visual storytelling. ("Karl Beveridge Reflects," *Labor Art Review*, October 2, 2025.) Image courtesy of the artists.

THE RETRO-VANGUARD THESIS

At its base, this new nationalist-right movement is appreciably composed of mostly white working-class and middle-class elements who have long felt invisible to the exceedingly educated cosmopolitan urbanites, such as myself (although my class and ethnic background started out the same as theirs). It is also a cultural phenomenon trying to radically break with the disruptive impact of neoliberalism's globalizing economic model. After some forty-five years of ultra-free-market dominance, the right, even more than the left, is genuinely seeking a way out of the numbing, alienating effects of a total capitalist aesthetic of consumer spectacle, fragmentation, and derealization. This is true even though this very same culture of estrangement has served as the new nationalist right's cultural midwife. Wendy Brown has argued that movements like MAGA represent "not neoliberalism's intended spawn, but its Frankensteinian creation"—the unintended consequence of neoliberal rationality's "imminent failures and occlusions."[2] Furthermore, has not MAGA's own feral progeny currently occupying the Oval Office maximized the potential of disruptive performance at a scale unimaginable to previous vanguard artists?

What strikes me as necessary for progressives to come to grips with is that movements such as MAGA are best understood as our newly arrived, twenty-first-century cultural retro-vanguard. Of course, it is many more things as well, including a crusade for xenophobic cleansing, ethnonationalism, and the dismantling of hard-won trans and nonbinary rights. It is also a prime beneficiary of both dark and light money from deep-pocketed ultracapitalist families, oligarchs, and tech bros. But even if MAGA has not yet bloomed into a full-fledged fascist movement with all the unifying symbolic paraphernalia, military control, and other trappings, it does share with past forms of right-wing authoritarianism an obsession with one charismatic figure. It was his name that was frequently invoked in chants and slogans by the J6 insurrectionists. Meanwhile, MAGA has successfully reassembled a variety of cultural meanings and values into one semicohesive form for its members at a moment when all such normalcy has been spectacularly inverted. And it has robust variations around the globe in the form of ultranationalist movements in other nations, including Hungary, as will be discussed ahead.

Consider these examples of the new ethnonationalist right's cultural profile: During recent French elections, a smiling frog meme topped with wavy blond hair circulated online, standing before the tricolor with the name Le Pen flanking this repulsive yet mesmerizing Lovecraftian caricature. In Hungary, functionally designed, communist-era bus stop shelters are rebuilt as folkish cottages complete with tile roofs, wood siding, and stone foundations—what anthropologist Kriszti Fehérváry calls "Hungarian Organicism," an aesthetic that emerged from the state-socialist period in opposition to the "'ugly' and 'unnatural' aesthetics of Soviet-style modernist architecture."[3] As a retro-vanguard movement, factions of this movement are even recycling reactionary futurisms from the past.

THE QUESTION OF CULTURAL OWNERSHIP

Some progressives will contend that the cultural right merely co-opts ideas, tactics, and practices of the left, including aspects of 1960s counterculture. It is time to acknowledge the weakness of this argument. Surely there have been reactionary political movements in the past that generated their own cultural forms and tendencies. Think of Italian and German fascist aesthetics of Novecento or Führer Architecture set in opposition to modernist ideas of historical progress as defined by universal equivalence and social justice.[4] Marco Baravalle reports about Italy under the hard-right government of Giorgia Meloni that "despite its meaningless weight in the world arena, Italy is . . . becoming a globally recognized laboratory for the postfascist right," but he quickly and significantly adds: "it is up to us to analyze it with a fresh gaze and to make it into a laboratory of alternatives, resistances and lines of flight."[5] Indeed.

But even if MAGA and other strands of the new nationalist right do at times mimic what is considered progressive cultural property, are not such parodic tactics fully in keeping with such left-identified practices as tactical media from the 1990s and 2000s? Clearly, there is also a logical contradiction in seeking to claim a pure form of mimicry in the first place, given that mimicry is itself an "impure" action involving pilfering or counterfeit production. The left must do better than reduce the new right to mere copyists or appropriationists. Accepting the fact that there is no such thing as "ownership" of the forms and methods of imaginative production is one step toward recalibrating where things are at and what must be done.

Obviously, it is now the aspiring restorationists of the hegemonic right who argue otherwise by claiming to possess cultural authenticity today, as will be discussed in chapter 8. Neither was everything about our fondly remembered, youthful 1960s counterculture progressive or emancipatory. Far from it. Racial and gendered hierarchies were far too present and persistent, as were varying degrees of condescension toward the working classes, who were considered unhip, nonurbane, or "square." Ironically, it was the emerging "spirit" of neoliberalized capitalism that, according to sociologists Luc Boltanski and Ève Chiapello among others, handily appropriated the radical chic internationalism of the counterculture into its so-called outside-of-the-box management style.[6] These considerations should also give pause to those who simply charge the right with theft of left culture. Proposing that a given protest aesthetic is an effective maneuver of resistance only when used by certain individuals or cultural practitioners, and not by others, is a defective argument turned into an assertion. That stated, if we set aside notions of abiding proprietorship, certain consequential differences can be teased out of a comparison between how at this moment the right and the left make use of art and culture. But first, what exactly do I mean when I suggest that MAGA is our new true (retro) vanguard? Am I being facetious? No, not in the least.

A primary aim of every artistic avant-garde has been to merge its particular and typically disruptive vision with everyday social life—think of the militaristic aesthetics of Italian futurism, the otherworldly free associations of surrealism, the absurd tumult of Dada, or the utopian designs of constructivism, productivism, and suprematism, discussed in chapter 14. The MAGA movement and its global kindred represent a definite variation of this impulse. But rather than envisioning an emancipated, inclusive, and environmentally harmonic future, these movements seek to restore, or reveal, this or that past that liberalism supposedly buried. But the pasts they invoke operate on radically different temporal scales. The far-right media pundit Tucker Carlson states tersely: "I liked America in 1985," longingly conjuring up his own childhood and, with it, the very year

Ronald Reagan began to consolidate the neoliberal privatization of American society.[7] (Of course, this was just before neoliberal free-market policies became a target of the ultraconservative right.) Other MAGA actors reach further back. During the January 6 assault on the Capitol, gatherers intoned "1776" in unison, alternating it with roars of "USA! USA! USA!"—invoking not a lived past but an idealized mythic origin story. And their global kindred reach further still. Hungarian *népies* nationalism draws on pre-Christian Magyar origins; Germany's neo-*völkisch* revival invokes a golden age it cannot fully name without confronting the Nazi period; Russia's Eurasian and Orthodox Christian turn claims not restoration but civilizational eternalism—a past that was never lost, only temporarily obscured by Western contamination; and India's Hindutva nationalism positions the subcontinent as a civilization older than any of its colonial conquerors. Each of these is a different kind of temporal refusal, a different way of attempting to opt out of the Unpresent.[8]

THE GLOBAL RIGHTWARD SHIFT: FROM REAGAN TO ORBÁN

As a cultural movement, MAGA represents the leading edge of a global rightward political shift that has been coming on in fits and starts for several decades. But its genealogy reaches further back. As Franco "Bifo" Berardi observes, "the year 1977 can be seen as a turning point: this was the year when the punk movement exploded, whose cry, 'No Future,' was a self-fulfilling prophecy that has slowly enveloped the world."[9] This transformation began tentatively at the policy level with the anti-welfare state policies of Reagan and Margaret Thatcher in the early 1980s, and then this rightward drift enlarged and armed itself in the 1990s with the US militia movement, which grew to 370 groups in 1996.[10] This was followed by strong, anti-Islamic sentiments in the aftermath of the 2001 attacks in the US and Europe, helping to boost such figures as the late Jean-Marie Le Pen and his National Front into the second round of the 2002 French presidential elections. Le Pen is quoted as stating, "I am not a xenophobe. I am a Francophile," while insultingly describing the burqa that devout Muslim women wear as a garment that "protects us from ugly women."[11]

Next, the 2008–2009 financial collapse helped give birth to the fiscally conservative US Tea Party movement, even as the increasingly extreme right-wing militia movement resurged under President Obama's tenure, while anti-EU sentiments proliferated in the UK. Over the next few years, far-right populist politicians in the US and Europe began to have increased electoral success. In 2010, Viktor Orbán's extreme nationalist Fidesz party, previously ousted from power in 2002, reasserted itself in a center-right power-sharing arrangement in Hungary. This political resurfacing gained Fidesz a two-thirds governmental supermajority. Orbán immediately consolidated his newly attained state power by undermining the independence of the Hungarian judiciary and initiating a systematic counterhegemonic approach to culture and the arts. Notably, and not surprisingly, Orbán and his cadre of extreme ethnonationalists have provided much of the template for nationalist-right efforts at parliamentary takeover in nearby liberal democracies. This includes most of the Yugoslavian successor states of Serbia, Croatia, North Macedonia, Montenegro, and Slovenia, but also the Philippines when ruled by Rodrigo Duterte, the Brazil of former president Jair Bolsonaro, and Poland under the Law and Justice Party whose founder, Jarosław Kaczyński, also began a state takeover of cultural institutions while promising to create an Orbán-style "Budapest in Warsaw."[12]

Meanwhile, on this side of the pond, Trump and MAGA have faithfully adopted much of this antiprogressive ideology, using it so far to manage containment of what has been for many decades a fractious pastiche of autocratic ultranationalists, old-fashioned American Manifest Destiny-style conservatives, and Silicon Valley libertarians. The result is a potentially combustible confederation of populist antiliberal counterrevolutionaries like Steve Bannon and the late Andrew Breitbart seated beside traditionalists from the Heritage Foundation with their moralizing Project 2025 White Christian jingoism, accompanied by hipster new right tech bros Curtis Yarvin and Peter Thiel, alongside the ultrasurveillance entrepreneur Alex Karp. But above all else, Orbán's ultranationalist counterhegemonic template forms the armature for this acrimonious federation. MAGA, much as with Orbán, Bolsonaro, and others, is the beneficiary of those who have been spurned both culturally and economically by the managerial professionals who have benefited from neoliberal globalization, especially following the downfall of twentieth-century socialism. In the US, the new nationalist right builds on decades of disparagement from liberals as well as from much of the left.

With Trump's first presidential victory in 2016, a cluster of anti-deep-state groups, including the Three Percenters and Oath Keepers, began to move from the dark margins into greater prominence. They were soon followed by QAnon in 2017, a still unidentified figure who issued cryptic ultraright conspiracy posts via the alt-right internet message boards 4chan, then 8chan. That same year witnessed the Unite the Right rally in Charlottesville, Virginia, bringing together sundry ultranationalist, far-right, and overtly neofascist and racist groups within the US. But it was Trump and his supporters who soon replaced the traditional Republican party. And then came the "Stop the Steal" campaign against the duly elected incoming president, Joe Biden, which brings us to the events on January 6, 2021, in Washington, DC. In the words of Grant Kester, MAGA has also been shaped by a long-standing conservative strategy involving "figures such as George Wallace, Ronald Reagan, Paul Weyrich, Lee Atwater, Patrick Buchanan, David Duke and many others."[13] All of this underscores one certainty above all others: the new nationalist right may be jingoistic, but it is not entirely new; it too has a backstory, one it is ardently idealizing into a new counterculture. To cite Fisher again, "*Repetition and doubling*—themselves an uncanny pair which double and repeat each other—seem to be at the heart of every 'uncanny' phenomenon."[14]

J6: A DARK CARNIVALESQUE INSURRECTION

In preparation for this chapter, I submerged myself in this antagonistic MAGA worldview by watching dozens of the phone videos created by rioters on January 6, 2021. Many are currently archived on the website of ProPublica, the nonprofit, Pulitzer Prize-winning investigative journalist organization, while other sources are found on the Internet Archive and PBS.[15] What I observed over the course of many hours was troubling but also more complex than I had expected, and certainly more so than the way the Democratic Party and liberal-oriented mass media have portrayed the events of that day. The video archive reveals MAGA as something more passionate and searching than a mindless mass of spellbound Trump yes-men and women—and many women were present and led some of the crowd's most aggressive actions. Neither did they appear to have been whipped into a disciplinary commando force by the tactical brilliance of a few alt-right factions such as the Oath Keepers, Proud Boys, Boogaloo Movement, or Three Percenters, though the presence and organizing efforts of these groups were significant, particularly in the assault on police lines and building entry. Instead, what I perceived, as the hours of often shakily recorded events unfolded, was far more in keeping with Occupy Wall Street's collective swarming a decade earlier. It was at one and the same time a carnival of distractions and self-defined loyalist sloganeering, backed up by bursts of colored smoke, rhythmical drum banging, punctuating air-horn tooting, and vociferous crowd-stimulating hoots, hollers, and whistles. It was, in brief, as zealous a profusion of protest aesthetics as anything produced by the left. And by midafternoon the festive nationalist fanfare began to give way to actual bursts of bellicose populist violence.

"Whose house? Our house!" and "1776, 1776, 1776!" and "We the people!" "We the people!" complemented the visual cacophony of the day, which reflected a diverse range of symbolism from anticommunist signs, homemade Trump flags, and White Christian religious imagery to bizarre faux Indigenous hats, spears, and Revolutionary War-era garments. One man, wearing an eighteenth-century tricorn hat, tapped on a snare drum, his cosplay fully in keeping with the day's overall nostalgic reimagining of America's past. Scattered among the sea of Stars and Stripes, some flipped upside-down, the MAGA hats and Trump banners, Gadsden flags, Christian standards, and a farcical 3D-printed Trump bust held aloft, I glimpsed a Guy Fawkes mask on one protester as well as the flags of South Korea, Japan, and Canada, and a prerevolutionary Iranian Lion and Sun flag—a banner of monarchist exiles carried by some opponents of the Islamic Republic. Perhaps most curiously, at 1:06, 1:28, and 2:59 PM we clearly see a rainbow Pride flag on display. Still, what truly caught me off guard were the looks of startled dissociation on the faces of many in the crowd, a visible gap between the material reality of their actions and the affective experience of those actions. It would not be too far a stretch to say that they exhibited a dual consciousness, one part entranced like a video game player in a flow state, the other part startled to arrive at a destination previously imagined as unattainable, even forbidden.

ENTERING THE CAPITOL

Just before breaking into the Capitol, one participant—John Sullivan, a self-described activist filming under the alias "Jayden X"—exclaims breathlessly to a man beside him, "I can't believe this is reality! We accomplished this shit, together!"[16] The irony of Sullivan's exclamation would only become apparent later: though he claimed to be documenting the riot as a journalist, federal prosecutors successfully argued he was actively inciting it, leading to his conviction on five felonies in 2023 (though later pardoned by Trump on his return to the presidency on January 20, 2025). Yet this contradiction between observing and participating, between documenting reality and constructing it, captures something essential about the J6 events. The collectively unreal, but simultaneously hyperreal, nature of the day's actions was repeatedly brought home to me as I watched hours of these brief, real-time recordings. Along with other expressions of phantasmagoria and spectacle, the crowd revealed a genuine yearning to experience meaningful agency in a society that had allegedly stolen their political empowerment and their history, while rendering them powerless observers. Sullivan's footage, shot as he moved with the mob through police lines and into the building, exemplifies this collapse of observer and participant, of reality and performance.

The most surreal scenes were revealed inside the Capitol building itself, the primary objective of the crowd's momentum, even as the most contradictory emotions were also on display. I watched as MAGA insurrectionists wandered the rotunda like dazed tourists, taking selfies against the backdrop of national architecture and art. "I always wanted a tour of the Capitol," remarks one man, adding, "I didn't think it would be like this."[17] With language alternating between scatological expressions about breaking taboos and moments of awe and reverence, one theme unfolded most clearly to me: the rioters' desire to exorcise what they perceived to be a diabolic force occupying "their" house, the Capitol. That demonic presence was, of course, liberal elites.

Pushing deeper into the building, a mixture of resentment and intimidation was evident. In one loud exchange, a man exclaimed, "We're in the fucking Capitol, bro!," and another MAGA insurgent shouted back, "Our tax money paid their salaries—freaking $40K of furniture in their offices, and we have families starving in the street." Still others expressed a desperate desire to reaffirm their collective identity, caroling, "We the people!," only this time more restrained than when they had been outside in the open air. The "we," however, consisted almost exclusively of white, Anglo-American-looking individuals. And once inside the national temple to which they had spent most of the day seeking to gain entrance, most appeared dazed and in awe, as if they were audience members from a reality television show who suddenly found themselves up on stage.

GOTHIC HORROR AND THE HAUNTED PRESENT

This drive to purify the rioters' "home," the epicenter of political power and the forum of the nation's lawmakers, was especially striking during the culminating moments of January 6, around 3:00 PM. As MAGA members explored the vacated Capitol's corridors, an eerie mist of tear gas drifted across its marble floors. I watched in wonder at what now appeared to be scenes from a low-budget Gothic-style horror film or image grabs of the haunted structures from video games, such as the Finch House, Croft Manor, or Mount Holly.[18] Yes, of course, "I can't believe this is reality," because of course it is not reality, at least not as it was only years before. And it was this eerie image that, for me, illuminated something unexpected as well as essential. On January 6 MAGA was attempting an exorcism of the Capitol building, as well as an exodus out of the haunted time and space of the Unpresent, but doing so by conjuring up an equally unreal, Disneyesque version of America's glorious, ethnically homogeneous past. Yes, the house was indeed haunted. But not by what the J6 rioters imagined.

This radical and uncanny temporal disorientation is not entirely unprecedented. As Alexis de Tocqueville observed regarding the historical imaginary of nineteenth-century America, "as the past has ceased to throw its light upon the future, the mind of man wanders in obscurity."[19]

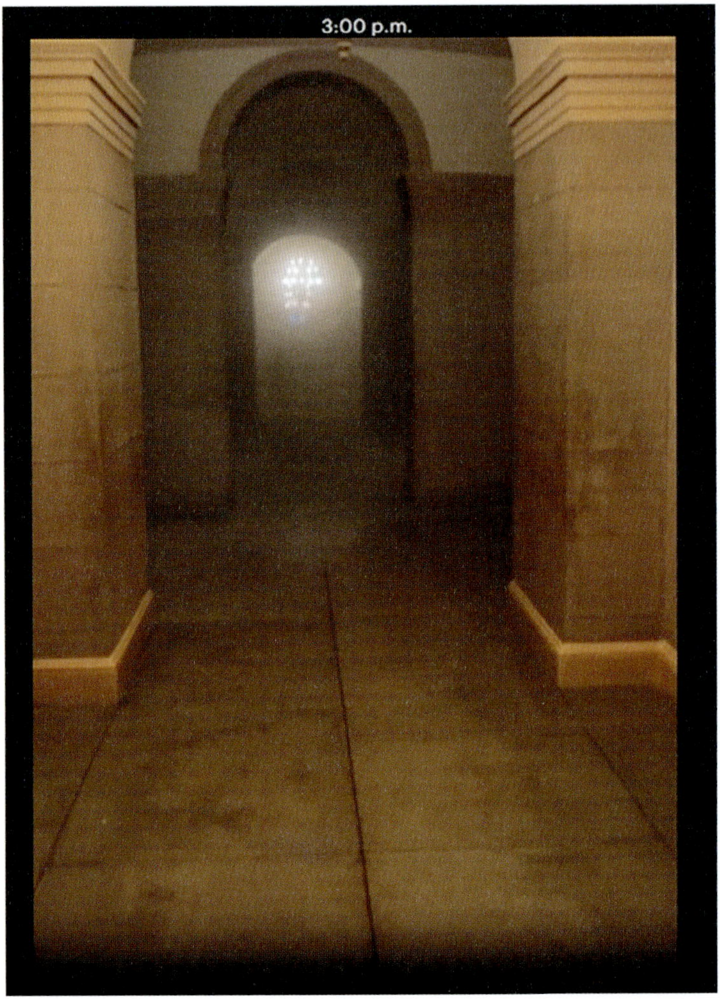

FIGURE 5

Screenshot from Parler video inside Capitol, January 6, 2021, 3:00 PM.

More recently, Mark Fisher proposed that "when the present has given up on the future, we must listen for relics of the future in the unactivated potentials of the past."[20] Today, MAGA agrees but inverts the formula. It searches not for a future by way of the past, but for a past that is satisfactory to the present, or, if you permit me, satisfactory to the Unpresent. And yet the J6 rioters were no less a part of the haunting than that which they dreaded. Theorist Max Haiven offers a way of framing this entrapment by explaining that after forty years of neoliberalism and financialization everyone has been transformed into competitive game players "where cheating is normalized," adding trenchantly that "if we are all players, most of us cannot win."[21] Systemic and structural failure, a need to expunge its imagined cause, a desire to escape the cabin fever of capitalist unrealism: the ingredients for sedition await only a prime instigator.

I was now seeing the events of January 6, 2021, as an urgent, even frantic attempt not only to regain something lost, but to vanquish something else that had taken its place like an uncanny doppelgänger. Whatever existential anguish MAGA might be undergoing, it is certain that the actual leadership of the movement, which has now returned to the White House, is taking full advantage of this sense of loss and sensation of being haunted. The political utility of maintaining the Unpresent, with its unsettling wide-awake narcolepsy, is clear enough when we examine Viktor Orbán's powerful sixteen-year grip on Hungary and the way legal, cultural, and educational institutions there have been hollowed out from within, leaving them seemingly the same on the outside yet entirely transformed. In the words of Hungarian-born scholar Kristóf Nagy, "civil society does not disappear in authoritarian regimes," but rather we find a systemic "cooptation and orchestration of pre-existing civic forms."[22] We will return to this phenomenon of hollowing out and repurposing in the chapters ahead. Meanwhile, in the breach of this uncanny transformation, MAGA became ecstatic and at times startled to discover itself rapidly growing into a full-throttle political and cultural power. Indeed, MAGA manifests as the turbulent underbelly of Oskar Negt and Alexander Kluge's counterpublic sphere, a realm where fantasy operates as both "libidinal counterweight to alienation" and a previously clandestine mode of production.[23] In any event, can we affirm that MAGA, especially in its post-2024 "2.0" manifestation, has become fully emergent as it erupts from its far-right chrysalis like a mass of formerly dark matter? If so, the consequences are more far-reaching than merely the rise to prominence of an odious ideology. Now, only several years after the J6 insurrection, that day is chronicled as both violent insurrection and patriotic celebration. The very warp and weft of time are being unraveled as two (or more) realities are represented as true at the same time.

That stated, my focus on the day's surreal, carnivalesque dimensions must not obscure another brutal reality, the approximately 140 police officers who were injured, the fact that at minimum 20 participants carried firearms, and that factions within MAGA undeniably sought to stage a violent coup against the federal government. Let us also recall that Trump urged supporters that day to "fight like hell" at the Ellipse. And in the video documentation of that afternoon some chanted that they had been "invited" to the Capitol by the president. A few years later, Trump reframed the J6 attack as a "day of love." After returning to the presidency he immediately pardoned convicted participants, installing several insurrectionists in the Department of Justice, including Jared Wise, who had urged rioters to "kill" cops.[24] This systematic overwriting of recorded events exemplifies the Unpresent's most pernicious operation: hollowing out historical meaning while preserving its recognizable shell, which is not Orwellian replacement, but uncanny evacuation of veracity itself. Likewise, it represents the collapse of Fisher's capitalist realism where, as baffling as it was, at least one could find a depressive orientation within a single oppressive reality. The Unpresent fractures space and time into a state of multiple competing unrealities, as time goes to war with itself and reality itself becomes, in the words of Trump's White House, "flexible."[25]

As early as February 2016, still many months before Trump's first electoral victory, the German artist Hito Steyerl commented alarmingly that "history seems to have morphed into a loop."[26] Steyerl's concern was directed at the role museums once played in establishing a sense of the past, upon which any concept of the future must depend. But the rising dismay at a world fractured in both time and space was also present in mainstream media, far from the exclusive world of fine art. Mapping out the growing shock of journalists as they confronted what I propose is the dawning of the Unpresent is the aim of the following chapter. It begins by paying homage to the remarkable acumen of an even earlier cultural figure, Philip K. Dick, the well-known mid-twentieth-century author of speculative fiction. Perhaps more than any other writer, Dick captures the queasy sensation of temporal displacement that my own book seeks to describe, explain, and confront. Significantly, but also insignificantly, it all starts with the most negligible of incidents.

3

THE UNCANNY VALLEY OF MAGA 2.0

"I can't find the light cord," cries Vic, a central character in Philip K. Dick's 1959 book *Time Out of Joint*.[1] Vic is reaching for something remembered and yet now absent as he tries to turn on the bathroom light just as he has done so many times before. After a moment of increasing anxiety, he realizes that "there was no light cord."[2] Instead, there was "a switch on the wall, at shoulder level, by the door."[3] Later reflecting on his mistake, Vic wonders, "why did I remember a light cord? For after all it was a specific cord, hanging a specific distance down, at a specific place. I wasn't groping around randomly . . . I was hunting for a light cord I had pulled many times. Pulled enough to set up a reflex response in my involuntary nervous system."[4]

Despite all appearances, or the response of his own muscle memory, Vic was no longer standing in the same space or time he had occupied many times in the past. What he had encountered was a glitch in time revealed by a routine and relatively minor action in a seemingly familiar space. What this chapter hopes to demonstrate is the early appearance of the Unpresent as mainstream media journalists and outlets grappled with the growing deformation of familiar reality. Focusing on the rising use of such adjectives as "surreal," "unreal," and especially "uncanny," I uncover traces of this glitch in time and space through four keyword searches in the Nexis Uni information database of news, business, and law records dating back to the 1970s, with some document types earlier still.

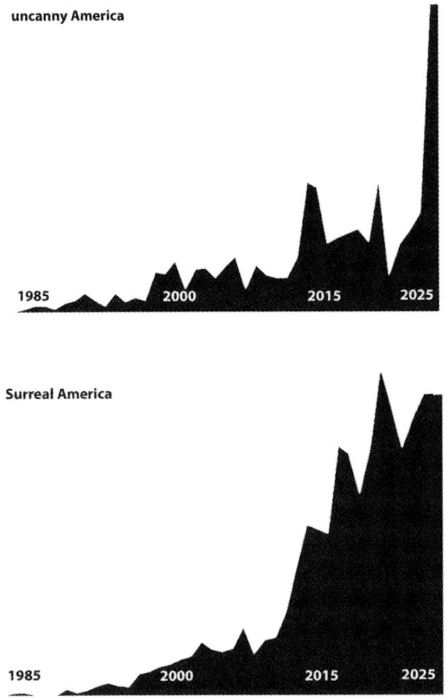

FIGURE 6

Data visualization graphic charts tracking frequency data generated from Nexis Uni, a comprehensive news database aggregating major US and UK newspapers, magazines, and newswires. Searches conducted for "uncanny America" (1,507 results), "Surreal America" (8,469 results), "uncanny UK," and "uncanny reality" across the period 1980–2025. Accessed December 14, 2025.

VISUALIZING THE ARRIVAL OF THE UNPRESENT

Four data visualizations (figure 6) derived from Nexis Uni searches carried out in December 2025 reveal telling patterns. While I do not present this data as hard empirical proof of my thesis, the strong impression they provide is compelling. Using 1985 as a starting point, we see the search terms *uncanny America*, *uncanny UK*, *Surreal America*, and *uncanny reality*, all with similar results. In every case, the closer the search gets to the present, the higher the peak usage of each word or phrase by media. The strongest uptick takes place around 2015, the year leading up to both Brexit in the UK and the first election of Donald J. Trump as US president. Zooming in on details from these searches, we might infer that what at first seemed to be a mere glitch in the media's ability to describe events using familiar language becomes steadily more prevalent and then fully dominant. Think of Vic's encounter with the absent light cord which starts as a mere annoyance or snag in his routine, before taking on the permanent condition of a new and unsettling irreality.

THE VOCABULARY OF TEMPORAL DISRUPTION

Consider this selection of media responses starting with the emergence of Trump and Brexit:

March 2016:

> Trump is not a populist, but a half-populist. He shows an uncanny knack for tapping public discontent over elite hypocrisies. (*States News Service* citing Hoover Institution on War, Revolution and Peace)

June 2016:

> Most of these stories were closer to science fiction than reality. (*i-news* on the UK Brexit)
>
> The demographics of the "leave" camp had an uncanny similarity with the supporters of Donald Trump. (*South Asia Monitor* on Brexit)

November 2016:

> It was upsetting on so many levels. I was deeply saddened to realize that a person who has targeted specific groups of people, that reality is not

what things really are, but what people perceive and want them to be. (*University Wire*)

December 2016:

The surprise ending has long been one of cinema's most unsettling tricks, but 2016 was the year reality joined in. (*The Telegraph*, London)

April 2023:

Trump's empire of unreality, a world of untruth, an infinite universe of bullshit. (*Sunday Independent*, Ireland)

May 2024:

The weirdness of this nightmare is striking compared to the actual reality. (*Creators Syndicate*, California)

January 2026:

To me, the past decade has been an often surreal and always disturbing rupture in the flow of normal political life. For my students in their mid-20s, it is simply life in America. (Attorney Paul Campos, *Lawyers, Guns & Money*)

This shifting terminology of bewilderment—from *uncanny* to *unreal* to *surreal* to *weirdness*—to which we might add the somewhat less feverish terms *unprecedented* and *unimaginable*, traces the deepening of temporal displacement and efforts to put a name on it. What began as an unsettling sense that something was slightly off has evolved into a comprehensive breakdown of reality's coherence. But the most dramatic manifestation of this linguistic crisis occurred on January 6, 2021, which becomes a switching point between the arrival of what is merely uncanny and the astonishment of a visceral encounter with the Unpresent that refuses to fade away. Headlines from that consequential day reveal the media's desperate struggle to find adequate language for describing the day's events:

One of the Most Unreal Moments in American History (*CBS Minnesota*)

A Surreal Scene Unfolds in Washington as Donald Trump Tries to Undo the Election (*Time*)

Capitol Complex Secure after Surreal Scene in Washington D.C. (*Washington AP*)

12 Surreal Photos of Violence, Chaos at U.S. Capitol (*Patch, Washington DC*)

'Unreal' Scene as Pro-Trump Mob Invades U.S. Capitol (*Connecticut Mirror*)

America's Anti-democratic Chaos Looks Surreal from Abroad (*CNN*)
Surreal, Terrifying Photos of the Capitol Under Siege (*The Cut*, New York)

The repetitive use of *surreal*, *unreal* and uncanny across dozens of outlets reveals a collective linguistic short-circuiting of normal press coverage; it also mirrors the temporal disruption of the Unpresent itself. But the apparent calm of a generation that has never known anything else should not be mistaken for normalization. Normalization implies a process in which the abnormal is absorbed, adjusted to, eventually accepted as ordinary. The Unpresent operates differently. It does not normalize disruption; it eliminates the temporal ground from which disruption could be recognized as such. What looks like acceptance is closer to temporal dispossession: not learning to live with the earthquake, but never having known the ground to not be constantly shifting. This is also why it is unlike Orwell's world of double-speak.

THE QUEST FOR REALITY CZARS

The response from liberal commentators to this crisis has been equally telling. In his February 2021 op-ed "How the Biden Administration Can Help Solve Our Reality Crisis," *New York Times* technology columnist Kevin Roose asked: "How do you unite a country in which millions of people have chosen to create their own version of reality?"[5] Roose blames a "muddled, chaotic information ecosystem" for this divisiveness, suggesting that President Biden should appoint a "reality czar" who would run a task force to centralize data on misinformation and conspiracy theories.[6] Written over a year before the advent of ChatGPT, Roose's earnest editorial already seems dated, as if any response to a growing sense of unreality would be hopelessly too slow for unreality's rapid expansion. He concluded with the plaintive proposal that "if President Biden wants to bring extremists and conspiracy theorists back to reality, he can start by making that reality worth coming back to."[7] Put differently, isn't it the responsibility of elected officials to affirm our collective right to reality as a basic entitlement?

If we approach this same demand from MAGA's point of view, we can see that it represents the flip-side response to a mutual sense that a known reality has been taken away. Liberals and MAGA alike look toward a powerful authority figure who can bring them back to normal, to a familiar space and time. What is really at stake here is a desire to time-travel out of the Unpresent rather than confront a reality that is dissolving into thin air.

CULTURAL STAGNATION IN THE UNPRESENT

Two years after Roose's op-ed, another *Times* piece took a different approach to the temporal stagnation of the radical Unpresent. In "Why Culture Has Come to a Standstill," commentator Jason Farago maintains that "cultural production no longer progresses in time as it once did."[8] Contrasting the twentieth century's drive to discover artistic novelty with our own twenty-first century, where culture "loses that velocity," Farago lamented our inability "to deliver step changes for quite some time."[9] Unlike Roose, Farago explicitly linked this floating reality with capitalism, noting that the US had had "the slowest productivity growth of any decade" in the 2010s, suggesting that cultural innovation's slowdown "might just be part and parcel of a more generally underachieving century."[10] Farago's proposal was to submit to capitalist realism, arguing that "surely it would be healthier—and who knows what might flower—if we accepted and even embraced the end of stylistic progress, and at last took seriously the digital present we are disavowing."[11] Farago's image-rich but emptied-out world is better understood as capitalism's total aesthetic morphing into the Unpresent.

DIAGNOSING THE CRISIS

Whether blame for the mental delirium and artistic atrophy of the Unpresent falls to failed father figures, pick either Biden or Trump, or results from more general cultural ennui linked to digital devices, there is no doubt about the uncanniness of this impossible-to-wake-up-from moment. But we must move beyond a liberal interpretation. The media's repetitive invocation of "uncanny," "unreal," "surreal," and occasionally "nightmare" reveals not just a crisis of vocabulary, but a fundamental inability to process temporal experience in disarray. This phenomenon emerges from neoliberal capitalism's thoroughgoing aestheticization of reality into a spectacle of commodities, brands, and their endless circulation as images. Yet that same neoliberal system's current crisis now withdraws the debilitating but familiar coordinates by which we had learned to orient ourselves. Mark Fisher captured this condition with precision: "The slow cancellation of the future has been accompanied by a deflation of expectations."[12] Or, as anthropologists Jeff Maskovsky and Sophie Bjork-James summarize the situation at the socioeconomic level:

> With US-led globalism in decline, liberalism itself, and neoliberalism in particular, have weakened in several senses. The neoliberal orthodoxies of unfettered international competition, flexible and deregulated labor markets, and the noninterventionist state, for example, no longer hold sway even if the global economy continues to be organized with a neoliberal architecture. At the level of policy and ideology, neoliberalism has become a form of zombie economics, a set of dead ideas and policies that walk the earth in search of vulnerable people to feed on.[13]

No wonder MAGA's bewildered J6 insurgents grasp for familiar symbols in an unfamiliar unreality, while a liberal pundit calls for "reality czars" to restore normalcy and cultural critics lament the end of progress, all representing different responses to the same underlying condition: the collapse of coherent temporal experience into the suspended animation of the Unpresent. But this very breakdown also contains the seeds of its own negation. Meanwhile, the liberal press, from Roose's call for "reality czars" to Farago's resigned embrace of cultural stagnation, frames our current crisis as either an information problem requiring technocratic management or a productivity slump demanding acceptance. Both responses mistake symptoms for structure. When Roose asks "how do you unite a country in which millions of people have chosen to create their own version of reality," he frames the Unpresent as an epistemological failure—people choosing wrong information in a fixable "muddled information ecosystem."[14] His proposed solution reveals liberalism's reflex:

appoint an authority figure, centralize data, restore normalcy through better management.

The temporal vertigo evident in MAGA's appeal is not unique to the far right. Media theorist Douglas Rushkoff has diagnosed what he calls "present shock," the condition where "everything is live, real time, and always on," producing a "diminishment of anything that isn't happening right now."[15] This reorientation affects material reality: when "people stop looking to the future, they start looking at the present," economic behavior shifts accordingly, as "investments begin to matter less for what they might someday be worth."[16] The widespread nature of this temporal crisis creates political opportunities across the spectrum. As Rushkoff observes about the right vs. the left, "whether looking back or looking ahead, both sides promise relief from the shock of the present."[17] Still, these promises do in fact diverge fundamentally. MAGA offers restoration of a mythic past, filling the Unpresent with nostalgia for 1776, 1985, or whatever bygone era resonates with its constituents. The progressive cultural response this book explores works differently by not denying temporal disruption but learning to actively resist *within* it through such practices as conspicuous repair, reenactment, and repurposing explored ahead.

The Unpresent is not merely an information crisis (liberal media analysis) brought about by fake news and the introduction of artificial intelligence, nor is it the result of technological acceleration (Rushkoff), or solely due to post-pandemic cultural exhaustion (as Claire Bishop proposed and as discussed in chapter 5). Furthermore, the Unpresent is reflected in, but not strictly the same as, the "dead zones" of our imagination as outlined in David Graeber's bureaucratic dystopia.[18] Nor is it fully encapsulated by what Anton Jäger—following Jean Baudrillard's diagnosis of American simulacral politics—labels "hyperpolitics," an extreme form of politicization without actual political consequences.[19] Instead, taken together, these varied and astute analyses underscore the presence of our deepening ontological crisis in space and time, of our Unpresent.

Crucially, as a working hypothesis, the concept of the Unpresent builds upon, while also extending, Fisher's idea of capitalist realism in which we lose our ability to imagine any alternative to current circumstances.[20] Which is why I refer to this phase of the crisis as capitalist *un*realism. Crucially, it is taking place as capitalism's ultra-free market project of the past fifty years disintegrates around us. Which is also why no "reality czar" can restore us to normalcy. There is no stable reality to return to, no familiar or conventional authenticity to be recovered. What liberal commentators perceive as chaos or delusion, but also what the frantic MAGA minions grasp for via a mythical past, are genuine responses to actual conditions: the collapse of futurity, the erasure of emancipatory past exemplars, the hollowing-out of institutions from within, and the evacuation of meaningful temporal experience under capitalism's total aestheticization.

Where Farago counsels submission to capitalist realism and Roose dreams of managerial restoration, this study pursues a third path: understanding how the contradictions of neoliberalism itself generated these conditions, and how practices of conspicuous repair—drawing on the phantom archive of blocked potential futures and unrealized pasts—might forge resistance not through nostalgia or technocratic fixes, but through marking what was obstructed while refusing to abandon what persists.

The media's desperate search for adequate descriptors reveals that we are living through a profound sense of temporal disruption. But recognizing this disruption as structural rather than informational is the first step toward developing effective counterstrategies. If we cannot adequately name our condition, we will remain trapped within it. We must now turn our attention to the backstory of the radical Unpresent.

4

TOTAL CAPITALIST SPECTACLE

The illumination of cultural dark matter outlined in chapter 1 and the emergence of the Unpresent have not occurred in a social or political vacuum. Rather, they are fully part of a specific historical condition we can identify as a total capitalist aesthetic—a circumstance in which the century-old ambitions of the artistic avant-garde ultimately found their realization not within revolutionary socialism or technological utopia, but as consumerist spectacle—becoming a key driver of neoliberal capitalism's comprehensive colonization of life itself. Understanding this condition is essential for grasping how reactionary movements like MAGA emerged within our current moment as both progeny and opponent of this spectacularized condition. However, this pageantry of copious imagery also has a definite impact on the activist culture of left social movements.

A series of recent essays, books, and conferences have focused on the artistic attributes of twenty-first-century political protests and demonstrations: collective bodies choreographed in coordinated public movements, bold graphic protest imagery, exclamatory slogans, space and time galvanized by visual and aural rhythms as well as eruptions. The motley and multifarious forms of activist culture will be taken up again in the second half of the book. For now, I want to explore the foundational conditions for this phenomenon, which I have previously likened to a

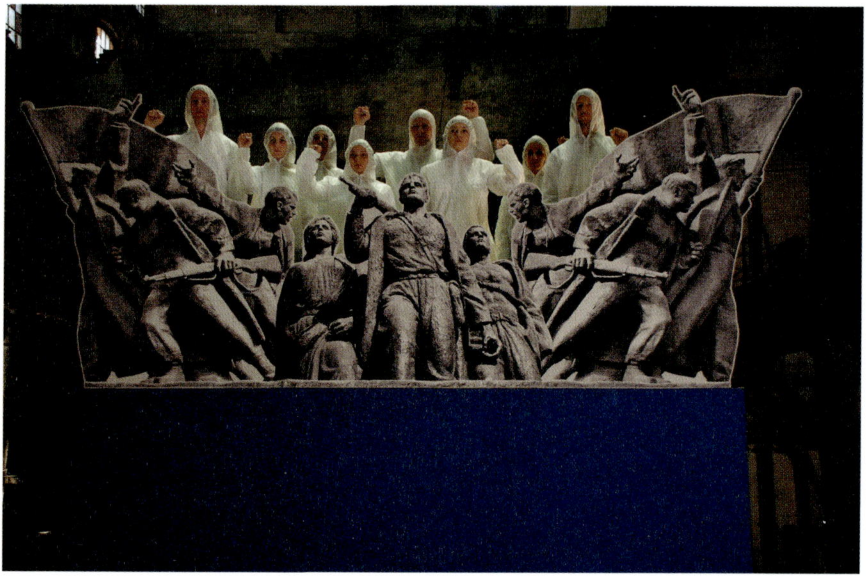

FIGURE 7

Chto Delat (What Is to Be Done), video still from the Russian collective's Brechtian *Partisan Songspiel* (2009). Performers in white hooded garments enact choreographed gestures reminiscent of Soviet choral traditions, positioned before a projection of the Freedom Monument (Споменик Слобода), a 1951 Yugoslav partisan memorial incorporated into a stage set by Serbian artists Rena Rädle and Vladan Jeremić. This layering exemplifies Chto Delat's critical approach to Soviet avant-garde heritage, while simultaneously embodying and interrogating revolutionary aesthetics through Brechtian *Lehrstücke* (learning play) techniques that reactivate historical forms of collectivity for contemporary political engagement. Image courtesy of the artists.

"Diagram flipped and reflected backwards, as if in a looking glass."[1] Allow me to explain.

THE AESTHETIC TURN IN ACTIVISM

Two years before Brexit and Donald Trump's first election as US president, philosopher of art Boris Groys offered a complex yet cautiously affirmative take on what a thoroughly spectacularized world might mean for critical and political cultural practices. Activist art, he proposed, had undergone such a rapid rise in stature that it was now an entirely new phenomenon. This followed upon curator Peter Weibel's suggestion that activist art "may be the first new art form of the twenty-first century."[2] Earlier still, theorist Marc James Léger described activist art as unquestionably "the most interesting development in contemporary art."[3] Arguably, cultural practices engaged in politically assertive protest are not a new development but have their own backstory and archive, something further debated in the second half of this book. However, what is new and unprecedented is the degree to which these once-separate spheres of human labor and social agency have become inextricably superimposed, a phenomenon made possible, as I will contend below, by capitalism's total aestheticization of reality.

Evidence of this hybrid integration is found in the number of academic publications based in non-art-oriented disciplines—anthropology; urbanism; gender, postcolonial, globalization, and immigration studies; political science—that approach public protests and demonstrations as if these were aesthetic practices. For example, the editors of *The Aesthetics of Global Protest* tell us that protest aesthetics consist of a material culture made up of visual and performative "slogans, art, symbols, slang, humor, graffiti, gestures, bodies, color, clothes, and objects."[4] These protest performances, they write, invoked anticolonial resistance and sought to generate a space of democracy in otherwise oppressive political circumstances.

In the words of Judith Butler, the aesthetic dimension of these events is broader still, involving "a complex interplay of performance, images, acoustics and all the various technologies engaged in those productions."[5]

It is, namely, a fully sensorial *aisthēsis* at play, to apply the ancient Greek term for sensory perception, as distinct from the general interpretation of aesthetics defined as involving the pleasing, beautiful, or artistic. The integration of sensory playfulness can also repurpose aspects of capitalist spectacle for anticapitalist purposes. Or as Weibel puts it, various "'cultures of repair' are in search of ways out of a far larger social crisis" that he describes as "the partial inability of politics to act."[6] The concept of repurposing and repair will return in the latter part of this book, but for now, consider that the aesthetics of protest can also be thought of as a substitute for the failure of politics to truly shape and transform reality. Simply put, notions such as prefigurative politics and temporary autonomous zones, popularized by contemporary activist artists and such events as Occupy Wall Street, could be viewed as the migration of utopian hopes tentatively linked with past political vanguards into the cultural sphere. It is this point of convergence involving time and memory and the archive that defines the art of activism and the activism of art and its paradoxes. Perhaps this is one reason Groys proposes that the new phenomenon of activist art is unprecedented, and it also pivots on a form of annihilation.

BORIS GROYS AND THE DEATH OF THE STATUS QUO

Groys agrees that we have entered a totally spectacularized social condition, one where the realm of commodities, brands, and lifestyle options has come to dominate an all-encompassing reality. Nevertheless, the philosopher sees within it a way forward, arguing:

> Total aestheticization means that we see the current status quo as already dead, already abolished. And it means further that every action that is directed towards the stabilization of the status quo will ultimately show itself as ineffective—and every action that is directed towards the destruction of the status quo will ultimately succeed. Thus, total aestheticization not only does not preclude political action; it creates an ultimate horizon for successful political action, if this action has a revolutionary perspective.[7]

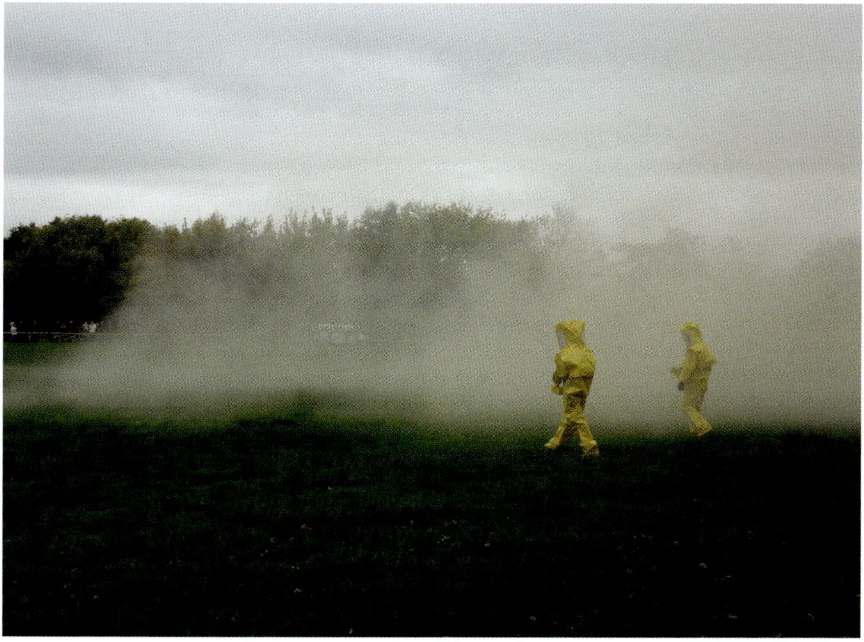

FIGURE 8

Critical Art Ensemble (CAE) performs *Radiation Burn: A Temporary Monument to Public Safety* in Halle/Saale, Germany, October 15, 2010. As the late Steve Kurtz wrote, "the dirty bomb is a near perfect propaganda weapon to produce fear [which in turn] drives the wheels of politics and profit" (Critical Art Ensemble, "Radiation Burn: A Temporary Monument to Public Safety," project description). Here, members of CAE perform in hazmat suits, casually navigating a simulated contamination site as a facetious commentary about public anxieties fueled by the "war on terrorism." Image courtesy of the artists.

Let's unpack this assertion. First, Groys's statement that the aesthetic status quo is dead is less strange than it may initially seem when observed from the vantage of art history. Representational images rendered in classically graphic and plastic forms of art—painting, drawing, sculpture, but perhaps also photography, film, and video—are only displayable in the museum as objects for our contemplation. Portrayals of figures such as monarchs, clergy, state officials, the military, or police are now made available as aesthetic experience, their symbolic link to actual power severed. Or as feminist art historian Carol Duncan explains, this space "belongs decisively to this realm of secular knowledge, not only because of the scientific and humanistic disciplines practiced in them—conservation, art history, archeology—but also because of their status as preservers of the community's official cultural memory."[8]

If we scale up this secularizing and aestheticizing process to the level of society itself, then "the current status quo," Groys argues, "is similarly immobilized."[9] The primary example Groys uses to affirm this process of reification through art is to remind us of how French revolutionaries defunctionalized symbolic representations of monarchal power under the Old Regime through their profane desacralization within the newly secularized halls of the Louvre. As the philosopher puts it, "The museum is much more of a cemetery than any real cemetery. Real cemeteries do not expose the corpses of the dead; they conceal them. . . . It is a purely materialistic death without return—the aestheticized material corpse functions as a testimony to the impossibility of resurrection."[10]

But Groys's analysis, while compelling, overlooks a crucial factor: the role of capitalist production over the decades in creating these very same disempowering conditions he assigns to art; and it does so far beyond defeated monarchies and clergy. A total capitalist aesthetic increasingly enmeshes all of society, high and low and in between, within its ever-augmenting trajectory. But it also opens, as will be examined in chapter 10, problem-spaces and problem-times involving competing versions of this same spectacularized condition. Is it not the case that contradictions are not always or consistently resolved through annexation? When capitalism subsumes resistant forms, it necessarily internalizes negations and conflicts along with their productive capacities, contradictions that reappear in translated form, generating new sites of potential dissent and rupture.

CAPITALISM AS REVOLUTIONARY AESTHETIC COMPULSION

Philosopher Gilles Lipovetsky takes an opposite approach from Groys, arguing that capitalism's total aestheticization provides society with a cornucopia of commodities, and thus offers us all the necessary tools to make our existence more pleasing and more aesthetic. It has accomplished this through distinct successive "stages of sensibility and process design, through a systematic work of styling goods and commercial spaces, of generalized integration of art, look and effects of the consumerist universe."[11] For Lipovetsky, the notion that it was vanguard art that radically secularized the world is simply fatuous. Instead he stresses that "capitalism has done a lot more than any of the major reformers in this respect! It's capitalism that makes it possible to change the way we live! The avant-garde didn't change anything. . . . Artistic capitalism is the system that systematically integrates the aesthetic dimension into every aspect of consumerism, including products, images, services. . . . I can't think of anything that escapes that system."

While Lipovetsky's prescriptions for creative industries remain politically passive and painfully celebratory, his core insight—that capital, not art and certainly not the artistic avant-garde, has rendered our lives fully aestheticized—is far more convincing than Groys's account, at least regarding recent decades when "artistic capitalism" has decisively eclipsed the avant-garde. Let us also recall the work of the seldom-remembered and highly idiosyncratic Italian Marxist Manfredo Tafuri, who asserted that the entire avant-garde was merely an expression of capitalist aesthetics.[12] This insight points again toward the pivotal historical irony mentioned above: the ambitions of the artistic avant-garde to disrupt bourgeois normalcy by merging its experimental aesthetics with everyday life have found their realization in the micro- and macro-extractive quarrying of that same everyday life along with the depoliticized spectacular consumerism of the capitalist marketplace. We can even characterize this as capitalism's socioeconomic masterpiece, a digitally networked capitalist repurposing of the avant-garde's most radical aspirations; a total capitalist aesthetic like some massively scaled-up and perverse Beuysian "Social Sculpture."[13]

COMMODIFICATION OF VANGUARDISM AND DOUBLE-EDGED "LIBERATION" OF AESTHETIC FORMS

The triumph of the avant-garde within total capitalist aesthetics reduces the very concept of vanguardism to consumer slogans and marketing copy, from Apple's famous "Think Different" campaign aimed at Microsoft's market dominance in personal computers to the hip marketing of fragrances, automobiles, wristwatches, and eyeglasses that promise to make you cutting-edge, trailblazing, forward-looking, or even revolutionary.[14] This commodification of vanguardism reveals how thoroughly capitalism has absorbed and neutralized the disruptive potential of self-avowed radical aesthetics, transforming them into lifestyle choices and brand differentiators. Still, in fairness, some will reasonably object that this travesty is not an *authentic* avant-garde. That, in fact, an authentic avant-garde still exists elsewhere in practices such as institutional critique, or within the educational undercommons, as theorized by Harney and Moten and discussed in chapter 7; or perhaps in emerging decolonial practices, especially in the Global South; or even in marginalized dark matter, although this was never my assertion but rather an interpretation proposed by others.[15] Curiously, this inscrutable location where the avant-garde is still alive and kicking is, much like the nowhere space we call utopia, difficult to visualize and harder to arrive at. We only get a glimpse of it when a preserved dispatch randomly floats ashore.

Grant Kester wittily comments, regarding Adorno and critical theory, that it is as if the theorist just sat back and contemplated "the disaster of the current moment from the relative privilege of the academy and the art world, dispatching encrypted messages to an imaginary revolutionary future, like so many bottles cast into an indifferent sea."[16] The occasional message in bottles aside, the true avant-garde must always remain incommunicado. Therefore, while I won't rule out that an uncharted avant-garde island is out there somewhere, or perhaps some-*when* (as I will consider in my conclusion), intangibility does not mean these same conditions of total capitalist aesthetics eliminate all possibilities of artistic resistance in the Unpresent, as the book's parts III and IV propose. Indeed, let us not neglect Martha Rosler's aspirational comment that "the artistic imagination continues to dream of historical agency. Artists, like other participants, wish to lend themselves to social transformation and utopian dreaming, but not necessarily within institutionalized frames."[17]

However, what is perversely obvious today is that forms, tactics, and ideas linked with the historical avant-garde have become accessible within a far broader sphere thanks to neoliberalism's total aesthetic. This process accelerates as neoliberalism itself wanes, generating the disturbing broken time we now experience, and as the institutional art world's historical claims to autonomy continue to atrophy, a condition I address through the concept of a bare art world in the next chapter. In short, the usefulness of disruptive artistic practices, including protest aesthetics, is no longer limited to the political left, if it ever was, or confined to commercial marketers; such practices are also accessible to MAGA and the nationalist right in their bid to become the new cultural hegemon. For, even as this total capitalist aesthetic inadvertently opened up possibilities for protest culture more broadly, as witnessed by the overlapping spheres of artistic activism and the activism of art, this same opportunity does not necessarily lead to a critique of authoritarianism, white supremacy, or capitalism.

That is to say, the aesthetic toolkit frequently associated with progressive politics (although not infrequently used by and occasionally expanded by the counterhegemonic right)—from nineteenth-century trade union banners made for parades and demonstrations, to street stencils, posters, and pamphlets, on up to laser messaging projected on building facades—has become all the more accessible to all political or commercial forces operating within the ultraspectacularized twenty-first-century public environment. The point is that it is not the new nationalist right that has weaponized left culture, as some decry; it is far more the result of an endless melting down and repurposing by capital of all established forms and institutions, including vanguard aesthetics, which paradoxically frees it for expanded use while alienating it from its origins.

This is the critical context for understanding how ultranationalist movements like MAGA have been able to mobilize a wide range of aesthetic strategies so effectively. These strategies include making use of the same networks and platforms that allowed other types of dark matter expressivity to brighten by enabling previously marginalized groups to establish their own visibility and develop a broader social presence, including reactionary political interests. The new nationalist right is not looting progressive cultural forms and tactics; rather, it is learning to operate within the same conditions of total aestheticization that enable all contemporary political expression. This raises a crucial question about the avant-garde's fate under these conditions. Rather than simply disappearing or being wholly absorbed, the very notion of the avant-garde may have split into three different temporal modes: (1) the ongoing total aesthetic of advanced capital; (2) the rearward momentum of the ultranationalist right, including MAGA; and (3) the "phantom archive," with which artists conspicuously experiment using time itself as a form of resistance, taken up in the third and fourth parts of this book. If this three-way split has in fact occurred, this fracturing is itself a significant consequence of the Unpresent. After all, when time is at war with itself all temporal directions represent possible front lines, and therefore are, theoretically, either cutting edges or avenues of escape.

SETTING THE STAGE FOR MAGA VANGUARDISM

This total aestheticization of social life provides the essential backdrop for understanding the cultural phenomenon examined in the next chapter: how MAGA has emerged as a genuinely contemporary vanguard movement, albeit one whose "revolutionary" energies are directed not toward an emancipated future but toward the restoration of a mythical past.[18] It also possibly explains why the very term *avant-garde* is so seldom invoked these days, since it seems as if a serious coding error in reality has simply become an everyday matter and a primary constituent of the marketplace for commodities focused on lifestyle branding. The same conditions that enabled the brightening of progressive dark matter have also illuminated such reactionary equivalents, creating a cultural battlefield where aesthetic strategies have become a primary weapon of political engagement.

The emergence of the Unpresent further problematizes this confrontation. To wit, what happens when the state of capitalist realism that we have somehow learned to survive within has itself been disrupted—not by a radical, revolutionary break as hoped for by Groys, but rather by becoming inverted and uncanny, like a looking-glass reality with a decimated temporality throwing everything, time as well as space, out of joint? It is to these questions that we now turn.

5

THE UNPRESENT AS CAPITALIST UNREALISM

The Unpresent is a condition in which time and space appear simultaneously the same as before and yet completely transformed. It lacks both an affirmative past and future, offering only a doubly estranged experience of now time. While Mark Fisher's concept of capitalist realism cited in chapter 2 helps trace part of the genealogy of this phenomenon, the Unpresent represents a distinct cultural and political mutation of the already skewed sense of time that preceded it—a temporal inversion in which time itself is flipped inside-out. We have vaulted from capitalist realism to capitalist unrealism. This condition first developed (or first became apparent) during the momentum leading up to Brexit and the first Trump presidency, was dramatically quickened during the Covid quarantine of 2020, and reached its full manifestation with Trump's return to power in 2025. Like the perplexed MAGA insurrectionists transfixed by the irreality of their actions, liberals and leftists now find themselves suspended in a temporal glitch that renders everything familiar while utterly strange.

As a concept, the Unpresent also emerges from a specific lineage of analysis with roots that go back as far as the late nineteenth century. Here I will mention more recent theorists, including Fredric Jameson's landmark analysis of postmodernism in the early 1980s as late capitalism's cultural logic: a surrealist pastiche of empty historical signifiers juxtaposed randomly and without depth or even a notion of the Freudian unconscious.[1] Slavoj Žižek captured this same temporal foreclosure when he observed that we now live in "the end times," where apocalyptic

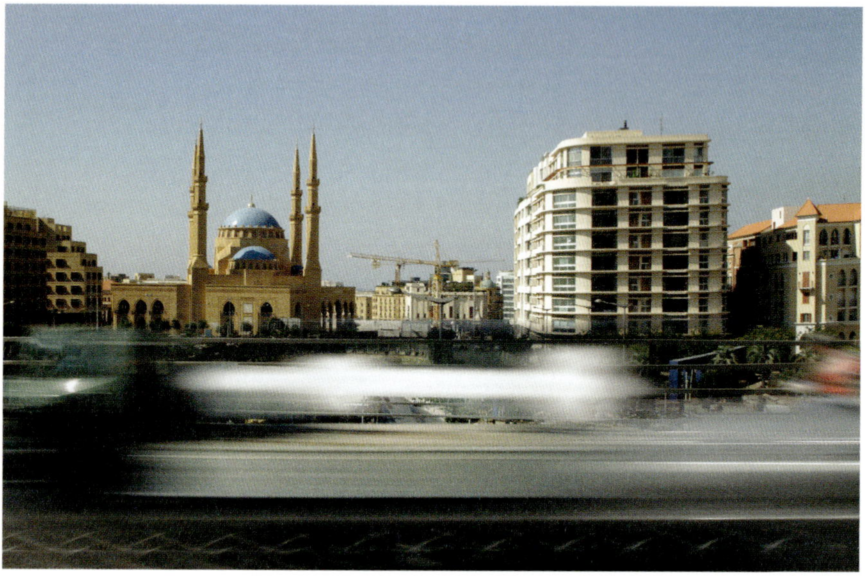

FIGURE 9

Joana Hadjithomas and Khalil Joreige's *Rocket Society* (restaged series, 2012) recreates Lebanon's forgotten 1960s space program through real-scale photographs of the Cedar 4 rocket transported through Beirut. Originally designed by Armenian researchers as a peaceful effort toward scientific progress, these rockets now evoke warfare and suspicion. The artists' reenactment questions Lebanon's suppressed technological aspirations and reveals how historical amnesia erases utopian dreams, transforming symbols of hope into objects of fear. Image courtesy of the artists.

imagination has become more accessible than visions of systemic transformation.[2] Fisher's capitalist realism built upon both of these tenets, and the Unpresent follows logically as our inability to imagine any alternative is weaponized by authoritarian movements.

THREE INDICATORS OF THE UNPRESENT

A trio of early indicators foreshadowed this spatiotemporal glitching, each representing different facets of the Unpresent's manifestation within art and culture. First came the brightening of cultural dark matter, discussed in chapter 1, but especially of a socially resentful and reactionary strain of this missing mass. This process brought previously marginalized creative practices into mainstream visibility, including not only progressive elements but also right-wing forces that had long been rendered invisible by cultural gatekeepers. Second, the superimposition of artistic forms of public activism on top of activism as art, as analyzed in chapter 2, helped free up a large repertoire of aesthetic forms, both "high" and "low" (along with artistic aestheticism itself), for use by social movements, including MAGA and the ultranationalist right. When everything becomes aestheticized, activism necessarily adopts artistic forms as art meanwhile functions as a mode of political intervention. This reciprocal relationship creates a disorienting feedback loop where distinctions between representation and reality flatten out. The third sign emerged within contemporary art itself: what Claire Bishop identifies as a spectral, déjà vu logic operating under conditions she labels "OS XXI," or Operating System 21, referring to the disordered attention spans of the twenty-first century.[3] Unlike the modernist artwork that concerned Theodor Adorno, art has passed from modernism through postmodernism to arrive at a new form of viewer receptivity.

THE SPECTRAL LOGIC OF CONTEMPORARY ART

Bishop explains that this new form of reception is "predicated on quantity and speed rather than narrowness and depth. Modern spectatorship, premised on fully focused presence and deep attention, no longer seems appropriate or necessary."[4] Much like Walter Benjamin's notion that mass culture and early cinema were assimilated through tactility and distraction rather than reflection, Bishop informs us that "the depth model of culture has been rocked by the rise of digital technology. Memes and the viral have put a new model of engaged looking into circulation."[5] This leads to a hybrid form of attention that was "compounded and intensified by the COVID-19 pandemic."[6] To this observation, I will add two queries. First, has not our sensorial, aesthetic perception today been altered in this same manner, regardless of whether we are encountering *art* or taking a selfie with friends or sending a WhatsApp image of our trip abroad? And second, as I have already proposed, if the avant-garde's long-stated objective of merging art with life has now been realized not through artistic action but through neoliberalism's ubiquitous communications networks and all-pervasive value-mining operations, then Bishop's disruptive OS XXI ethos is less a break with the past than the fulfillment of that merger by other, far less emancipatory means.

Furthermore, how can art claim detachment from society when everything—including art—circulates within the same spectacular networks of commodities and digital expressions of commodities? Is it that such aloofness functions today as an empty convention, a proxy for the exceptional status that high culture once claims to have possessed? The assertion is understandable, even expected, but no longer credible. Still, the ghost of artistic autonomy past continues to haunt the domain of contemporary art despite high culture being reduced to a nakedly commercial mise-en-scène.

Bishop acknowledges just such a consequential haunting within contemporary visual art by ascribing to it a sense of cultural déjà vu experienced by artists and viewers alike. Through a meticulous and granular survey of installations, video works, and research-based artworks, she explains that "the Déjà vu effect results from a common approach to the modernist heritage: an invocation that both cements the significance of that referent and legitimates the younger artist while simultaneously emptying the referent of ideological content."[7] And yet, is this not another facet of the consequential hollowing-out of time and space described earlier? And if so, is it the vacuous echo of modernism producing delusions of artistic legitimacy decades after its famous demise, or the relentless assimilation of the networked capitalist aesthetics reanimating this or that archive, overwhelming us with digital visual overload?

In truth, don't these same déjà vu specters also haunt contemporary curators, collectors, and scholars of art, furnishing them with those ever-so-brief moments in which attention deficit disorder as much as bare art's naked monetization feels temporarily postponed? Like the lifting of mental depression, we know this welcome pause is going to be short-lived, even as we continue to hope it will return for keeps. Perhaps this is what separates a manageable depression from all-out despondency? Notably, Fisher, who suffered from this illness, understood it as at least a partly rational response to the social and political claustrophobia of capitalist realism. In this regard, the restoration of American greatness by MAGA may be one more example of a disordered déjà vu attention span in search of relief. Bishop even suggests as much when she flatly states that "disruption and transgression can no longer be automatically aligned with left or right, good or bad, however we construe them."[8]

These three indicators—the brightening of reactionary dark matter, the aesthetic-political feedback loop where activism and art become indistinguishable, and what Bishop identifies as contemporary art's spectral déjà vu logic under OS XXI—converge in a fourth condition that both encompasses and exceeds them: what I call a bare art world within capitalism's total aesthetic. It is to this concept of a nakedly nonautonomous art world that I now turn.

BARE ART WORLD

Taking my cue from Giorgio Agamben's notion of "bare life," we find ourselves confronting bare art: the condition that emerges when art's protective claims to independence and high-cultural authority are peeled away layer by layer.[9] Left behind is something vulnerable and exposed, where the financial and political contradictions that fuel the art world become as impossible to ignore as the economic forces that now openly govern daily existence. Just as financialization has made the power structures of everyday life brutally visible, the art world now exists in a condition of enforced transparency, stripped of the romantic illusions that once provided cover.

Gone is the mystique (even if many refuse to admit the king's clothes are missing). What once passed for high culture's refined aesthetic qualities now reads as straightforward data—measurable, trackable, utterly mundane attributes. The 1960s dream of artists becoming cultural workers has come true with a vengeance: today's artists are simply workers, period. They blend seamlessly into the broader landscape of NFT hustlers, viral content creators, and TikTok stars, just another branch of the creative labor force. Ben Davis captures this condition succinctly when he writes that the "aestheticization of capitalism is complete," referring to the way culture has migrated to virtual platforms.[10] This observation—echoing earlier arguments by Groys and my own analysis in *Delirium and Resistance*—names the endpoint of a process where artistic production becomes indistinguishable from content creation.[11] The only distinction that remains is the art world's laughably antiquated caste system, complete with gatekeepers desperately manning barriers that were overrun long ago by every conceivable type of cultural insurgent.

The institutional art elite now operates in full view, openly consorting with their true constituency: mega-developers, oligarchs, and petro-criminals. This nakedness also leaves art institutions peculiarly vulnerable to political capture. When autonomy is stripped away, there's little defense against ideological colonization. Meanwhile, in what Jacques Rancière might recognize as a brazen redistribution of "the sensible," the cultural underground that once challenged high art gets systematically harvested for its emotional capital, sometimes packaged under banners that include socially engaged art practice.[12] In truth, this appropriation is to be expected. It might also be the reason decades-old methods of institutional critique no longer retain any serious critical impact. These blatantly transactional expectations make perfect strategic sense: when traditional markers like technical skill, artistic lineage, and professional credibility no longer carry weight, you need new methods for creating cultural hierarchy and differential value. Monetization becomes the default. Nonetheless, the condition of bare art should not dissuade artists committed to finding and leveraging the gaps in the system. In point of fact, finding and leveraging the gaps in the system has never been more necessary.

THE RUSSIAN EXAMPLE

In the absence of autonomy—real or imagined—the contemporary art world is more likely to become a prime target for politically right ideologists who will coopt its institutional authority without necessarily spoiling its appeal to financial capital. This is all the more probable under conditions of the Unpresent. To get a sense of how this can work, we can scrutinize what has happened to contemporary art in Russia following Putin's full-on 2022 invasion of Ukraine. For a time, Russian artists and art institutions imagined they still belonged to an autonomous and specialized global contemporary art world. But this was illusory, and had been so for quite some time. Vladimir Putin and his circle of ultrawealthy capitalists consolidated political power starting in the late 1990s as support for high culture shifted from the state to private capital over the 2000s. This was the period of such initially independent institutions as VAC Foundation, founded by Leonid Mikhelson, CEO of Russia's largest natural gas producer, Novatek, and The Garage, founded in 2008 and supported by Roman Abramovich whose enormous postsocialist wealth derived from trading in formerly public assets of oil, steel, and aluminum. The first speedbump in the apparent independence of this cosmopolitan art scene came in 2012, following the arrest and trial of the performance art group Pussy Riot for their anti-Putin "Punk Prayer" in the Cathedral of Christ the Saviour in Moscow.[13] Then, in the wake of Russia's invasion of Ukraine, the already falling hammer came down hard as countless Russian artists either fled the country or faced arrest.

The Garage Museum of Contemporary Art was subsequently searched and shut down by FSB security forces, reprogrammed, and then opened again as a simulacrum of its former cosmopolitan-oriented, risk-taking self. This process of institutional excavation, housebreaking, and ultimately self-estrangement is uncannily similar to descriptions of Orbán's Hungary. While, certainly, local social and political conditions in Russia must be factored in, the fate of contemporary art in post-Cold War and now postneoliberal Russia is a warning sign to other nations sliding into ethnonationalist autocracy. Not that the Russian situation went completely unanswered. In St. Petersburg, the art collective Chto Delat (What Is to Be Done?), on the cusp of fleeing Russia, produced a

PART II

GENEALOGY

time. But with Freud and psychoanalysis, it is interior spaces that appear strangely familiar.

In addition, this weird experience of the *unheimlich* does not affect groups or entire societies in Freud, but impacts only individuals struggling with suppressed memories of childhood trauma reoccurring in the present. The shift from uncanny space to uncanny time, and from one person's experience to that of society, becomes theoretically accessible with intellectuals of the German Frankfurt School in the 1930s who sought to ground psychoanalysis in historical materialism in an effort to analyze not neurotic mechanisms affecting individuals but those of historically constituted social groups.

THE FRANKFURT SCHOOL'S COLLECTIVE UNCANNY

In Theodor Adorno and Max Horkheimer's prominent 1944 study *Dialectic of Enlightenment*, Freud's psychoanalytic concepts are applied to interpret the rise of fascism in Europe.[7] There is just one distinct reference in the book to the Freudian concept of the uncanny, and it links anti-Semitism to feelings of repulsion toward the strangely familiar. And yet this application of the *unheimlich* is expanded to buttress Adorno and Horkheimer's broader hypothesis about collectivized forms of xenophobia. In this respect, individualized psychological unease becomes a symptom of fascistic social associations that operate under the name of "leagues, factions, rackets."[8] Underlying this unhealthy group consciousness is also a decline in other potentially mitigating social experiences; above all, that of education. They observed at the time that "today, when education itself is withering for economic reasons, unprecedented conditions are created for the paranoia of the masses."[9] Adorno and Horkheimer's words resound with their own *unheimlich* effect today in the age of the Unpresent, for example in the twenty-first-century nationalist right's attack on established institutions of learning (addressed in the next chapter).

Adorno and Horkheimer draw on Freud's analysis of group psychology to understand fascism, noting that Freud described certain pathological groups as forming an "asocial formation" that endeavors to "achieve by private means what is affected in society by collective effort."[10]

Though Freud himself did not term such formations fascist, Adorno and Horkheimer recognize in his description of the structure of fascist collectivity a morbid expression of social cooperation, perhaps even a strangely inverted version of social collectivism. This may be why they acknowledge that even these pathological group formations still "retain something of the collectivity which preserves individuals from pathological symptoms."[11] We can counterpose this type of obsessively defensive collectivism to what Jean-Paul Sartre described as the group-in-fusion (*groupe en fusion*), in which the act of working in consort for the broader good transcends, rather than further amplifies, personal and social alienation. Sartre wrote: "The essential characteristic of the fused group is the sudden resurrection of Freedom."[12] Ultimately, however, being afraid to believe in their own madness, asocial group formations come to see acts of proselytizing and conspiracy everywhere. Thus, the same desire to disavow and counteract paranoia transforms into projecting suspicion onto others. Adorno and Horkheimer describe the Hitler Youth organization as not simply "a relapse into the old barbarism but the triumph of repressive égalité, the degeneration of the equality of rights into the wrong inflicted by equals. The fake myth of fascism reveals itself as the genuine myth of prehistory, in that the genuine myth beheld retribution while the false one wreaks it blindly on its victims."[13] Against these fabricated nationalist identities, the cosmopolitanism of the "stateless" Jew, so Joseph Goebbels ranted, but also the internationalism of the communist, as Adolf Hitler fulminated, came to form two frequently conjoined targets of the German Reich's campaign of eradication.[14]

MAGA'S NOSTALGIC VANGUARDISM AND THE MYTHIC PAST

The invocation of a speculative past—the alleged primordial horde of brothers who eradicate their tyrannical father in Freud's 1913 treatise *Totem and Taboo*—is woven into a modern fable for the fascists' own dubious brotherhood, justifying resentment-fueled revenge.[15] Yet this mythic past does not resolve group neurosis but magnifies and redirects it toward external targets who become the horde's victims. Crucially, these "repulsive" others are integral to the group's very formation: Jews, Romani people,

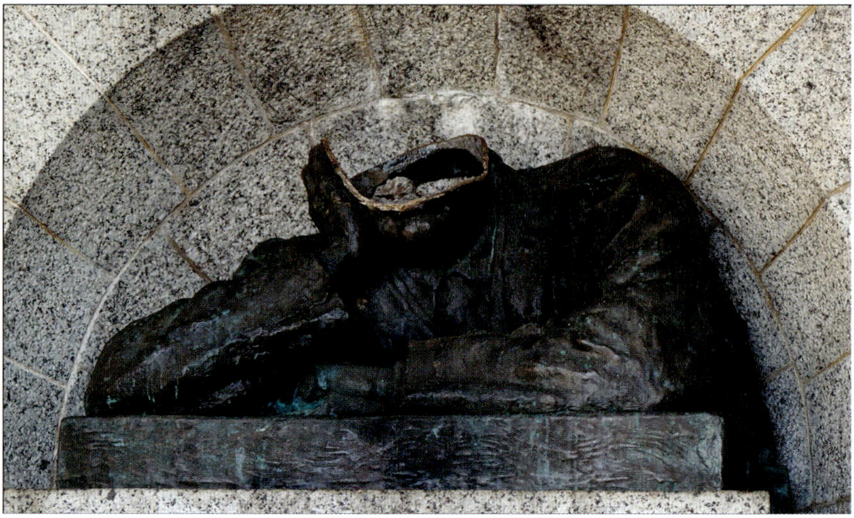

FIGURE 12

The decapitated bust of Cecil Rhodes at the Rhodes Memorial in Cape Town, South Africa, July 2020. The statue was beheaded during South Africa's #RhodesMustFall movement, which began in 2015 as student protests against colonial symbols and transformed into a broader decolonization campaign across South African universities. Rhodes's legacy of white supremacist colonialism found its fullest expression in South Africa's apartheid regime, another asocial formation built on fabricated ethnic hierarchies and the systematic exclusion of those deemed racially inferior. Creative Commons, Zaian, https://commons.wikimedia.org/wiki/File:Rhodes_bust_decapitated.jpg.

other non-Aryans, LGBTQ individuals and people with disabilities, as well as communists, socialists, anarchists, and even democratic socialists (and of course today we must add the trans community). Again, if we cross-reference these observations from the 1940s with the events of the 2017 Unite the Right rally and its chants of "Jews will not replace us," we can see how the two threads of Adorno and Horkheimer's argument, the paranoia of the brotherly horde and the fear of substitution, reflect the uncanniness of the MAGA phenomenon. It is not just any enemy of the group that must be defended against, but specifically those who are effectively the group's own doppelgänger. In August 2025, one MAGA member stated this rather bluntly: "eight years ago you were an extremist if you protested being replaced by immigrants . . . your life was over if you talked about stopping or reversing it. Now it is official @WhiteHouse policy."[16]

Viewed differently, MAGA's collective desire is to restore a past even if it never actually existed, while administering comeuppance to those who deform MAGA's sense of time and space operating within an ethnically structured patriotic idealism. Inevitably, their wrath falls on those who they assert have brought about this uncanny condition in the first place: alien intruders, liberal elites, globalists, educated professionals most vociferously, with non-cis-gendered individuals, Muslims, and people of color close behind. Yet the deepest anxiety lies not in superficial differences but in uncanny resemblances, and the fear that these others could *replace* the horde precisely because they are its distorted double, capable of occupying the same social position. We sense that time has been mobilized by MAGA for its own ends, and consequently it will be a different mobilization of time that marshals resistance to MAGA. It is as if time is at war with itself.

REBECCA BRYANT AND THE "UNCANNY PRESENT"

Coining the phrase "uncanny present," anthropologist Rebecca Bryant scales up the notion of the *unheimlich* while applying it to both the time and space of a particular place, the island of Cyprus in the eastern Mediterranean. Decades ago, in 1974, Cyprus was forcibly separated into two geographic factions, one ethnically Greek, the other Turkish. But according to Bryant, it was circumstances that arose thirty years later that brought about the sense of temporal uncanniness. For years, the United Nations had sought a way to reunite the island into a single nation, and the 2004 Annan Plan referendum, named after UN Secretary-General Kofi Annan, would be the last of many attempts. In the lead-up to the vote, Bryant perceived that for Cypriots on both sides, the very sense of the present had become "unfamiliar in its *present-ness*."[17]

Think of this as an experience of the present so hyperaccentuated, so laden with a sense of critical immediacy, that it brings about both an individual and social blocking-off of future possibilities. Significantly, it also obstructs access to the past. "The uncanny present," she writes, "refers to moments when the present that I usually do not perceive as such becomes anxiously visceral to us as a moment caught between past and future."[18] The anthropologist's invented terminology helps us bridge the conceptual distance between Freud's sense of a haunted space experienced by an individual and that of time transformed into something strangely familiar at a social level. It is, in other words, one step closer to my proposed term, the Unpresent. Bryant notes that during the lead-up to the referendum, "time itself had become weightier, . . . it bore a particular burden of the future."[19] Yet the past's traumatic return haunted any possibility of success. The referendum failed, and Cyprus remains territorially divided, manifesting a present unable to move forward, perpetually burdened by what cannot be left behind.

Regarding this haunting return, Bryant adds that it is lacking any "teleological ordering."[20] And if time no longer possesses any sense of sequential movement toward or from the future or past, a temporal claustrophobia takes hold, including despair over the deprivation of historical time. One is left only with the present, much as Fisher's description of capitalist realism is that of time doubling and redoubling without a future horizon.[21] Consequently, the uncanny present just keeps returning to the uncanny present. Notably, Bryant suggests that a different result might have been possible had there been a mobilization of "forgotten pasts to develop a new intentional stance towards the future."[22] If one can manage the *unheimlich* effect upon time via intentional social organizing, one might also treat the enervating symptoms of the uncanny present itself, much as Freudian analysis employs the talking cure to address individual neurosis. Perhaps the mobilization of the phantom archive via conspicuous acts of repair, repurposing, and reenactment as discussed ahead functions somewhat akin to the talking cure.

FROM SPATIAL TO TEMPORAL HAUNTING

Bryant's ethnographic attention to Cyprus reveals how the uncanny present operates in postconflict zones where past and future have collapsed into uncertain stasis. We have already encountered versions of this rupture: Jameson's postmodern condition with its depthless historical pastiche, Žižek's end times where apocalypse seems more imaginable than transformation, Fisher's capitalist realism with its foreclosed futures, Rushkoff's present shock. To these I add Lauren Berlant's cruel optimism, where subjects remain attached to fantasies that block their own flourishing, David Scott's problem-space/problem-time, and the contemporary successors to Marx's historical materialism, with Scott and Marx both discussed ahead. Despite important differences, what these parallel diagnoses confirm is that temporal disruption has become a defining feature of our moment, one demanding analysis at multiple scales, from the intimacy of Cypriot memory work to the global reach of digital media to the structural violence of postneoliberal capitalism.

As I have interpreted Bryant, the proposed cure of the uncanny present is the mirror opposite of the MAGA horde's drive to free itself from the eerie state of the Unpresent by rejecting the future in favor of the restoration of a nonexistent past. It is also worth speculating that while many within MAGA sincerely wish for an end to the disquieting effects of a time out of joint, any possible cure would effectively disempower the movement itself. Whether this is consciously grasped by the faithful or only intuited is difficult to know. Decisively, the stagnant temporality of the Unpresent manifests differently at different scales. At the structural level, futures (and pasts) remain foreclosed. The uncanny present returns endlessly to itself. Yet at the phenomenological surface, this stasis generates a paradoxical delirium: the dizzying daily churn of crises, spectacles, and reversals that characterize the Trump era. The vertigo is real, but it's circular motion within a fundamentally static condition, like a hamster on a wheel spinning furiously while going nowhere.

WHY THE APOCALYPSE LOOKS SO YESTERDAY

In contrast to the tense trauma of Bryant's uncanny present, but also different from Adorno and Horkheimer's invocation of a lingering paranoiac mythos, the phenomenology of the Unpresent appears remarkably identical to what was just here a moment earlier, except that we cannot escape the sensation that it is also completely divergent, inverted, and dissimilar. This state of repetitive crisis is distinct from the type of total catastrophe that levels a city, burns a town, or drowns a village beneath mud and water. The Unpresent is a sense of catastrophe in which things by and large look outwardly the same. And yet they are identical yet not identical, having changed everything in the blink of an eye. The wheel keeps spinning. Still, no amount of blinking can refocus our vision on what has changed, except that there is no denying the sensation that everything is no longer as it was. If the catastrophic end times have arrived, we are by now far too addicted to the spectacle of unreality to pay it much mind—or at least no more than we pay to countless other day-to-day crises, real or not. It's as if the continuous state of emergency around the globe is just another multimillion-dollar streaming studio product to eyeball on our glow screens.

Culture, as always, reflects the mood of the population. I do not need to list the plethora of dystopian and apocalyptic movies, online series, video games, novels, and songs that eerily parallel the delirium and crises of both the world capitalist economy and global events since the start of this century. Armageddon appears to have already happened, or it is well under way in the age of the Unpresent. And once that possibility becomes feasible, once it takes hold, the sameness of a disaster taking place in all directions and all at once simply finds its place alongside all our other cravings for novel consumer products, ever-renewed brands, seemingly fresh cultural experiences. Our dependency on total capitalist aesthetics incorporates everything into its panorama, from the latest wars,

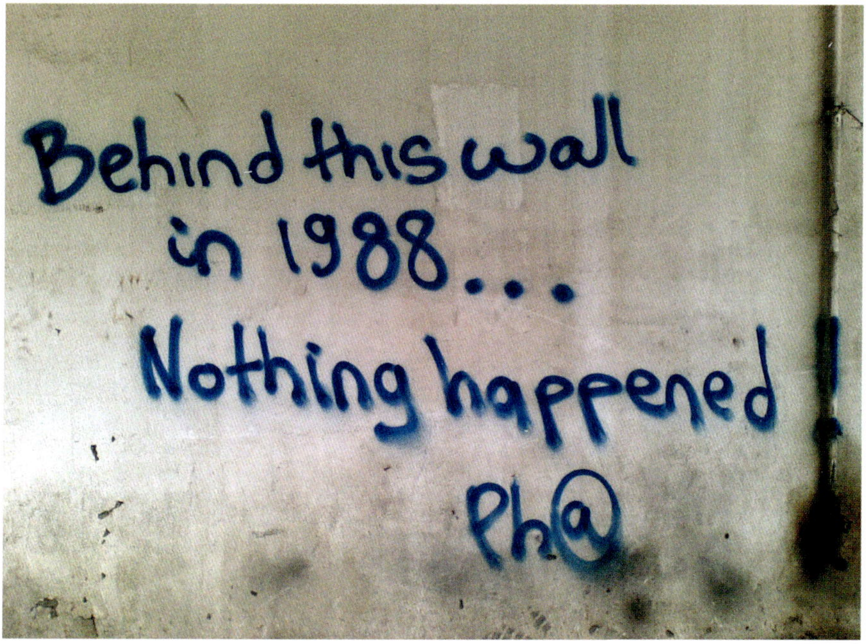

FIGURE 13

Tony Chakar, *Behind This Wall in 1988 . . . Nothing Happened!*, 2008. This photograph of graffiti scrawled on a weathered Beirut wall has become central to Chakar's ongoing investigation of collective memory and historical erasure in post-civil war Lebanon. The ironic text asserts absence where traumatic presence persists, and exemplifies what Chakar calls "spectral iconic appearances," moments when catastrophic events create disruptions in our spatial-temporal perception of normality that endures as a specter "not haunting, but hovering, lingering, distractedly waiting to be redeemed" (Ellen Mara De Wachter, "Spectral Iconic Appearances: An Interview with Tony Chakar on De-sanctified Icons, the Space of Catastrophe and the Aftermath of the Lebanese Civil Wars," *springerin*, no. 4 [2008]). The artist has deployed this image across multiple contexts—lectures, publications, and installations—sometimes with additional textual interventions, treating the urban surface as a palimpsest of unresolved histories. Image courtesy of the artist.

traumatic events, and minor political strife to everyday-life situations. All become equal.

An entire Palestinian city is leveled by US bombs with children trapped under rubble; more grisly details follow the commercial break. Unhoused people gather in an urban tent are tear-gassed, their flimsy shelters slashed and flattened. A product reduces suffering from a condition we have never heard of and that we did not even know afflicted us. Grainy police-vest cameras document verbal abuse, beatings, and murder of Black men, women, and children, meted out by those sworn to keep the peace. Our smartphone alarm signals it is time for yet another Zoom meeting. Students voicing opposition to state-sponsored ethnic cleansing are arrested, some expelled, others threatened with deportation. The Zoom alarm reminder goes off once more. A Ukrainian grocery market and a day care center are both demolished by drones from a neighboring nation determined to rejuvenate its former imperium. People waste away from intentional famine as the world watches genocide unfold. And interspersed throughout is a cascade of promotions for pharmaceuticals, automobiles, luggage, accessories, vacation spots, and recently fashionable vegan cuisine.

Theorist Susan Buck-Morss advanced a useful interpretation for how the spectacle of mass consumption was already well at work before the twentieth century, decades earlier than the era of postwar mass media and advertising, and long before Guy Debord designated it the society of the spectacle in 1967.[23] Discussing the Great Exhibition in London (1851), the Crystal Palace of Paris (1855), and subsequent world's fairs of the nineteenth century, Buck-Morss follows Walter Benjamin's lead by describing these phantasmagorias as vertiginous spectacles of mass consumption, adding that they so amazed working-class audiences as to deny "the very existence of class antagonism" while promising "social progress for the masses without revolution."[24] The digitally animated phantasmagoria of our day certainly retains this same function; however, there is one major adjustment to this pledge of endless merchandise as social advancement without revolution. The very concept of history as progress from a less equitable, less educated social past toward a brighter, more enlightened future has been withdrawn with nothing to replace it.

Sure, we might be promised new technologies to allegedly make our lives easier, more pleasant, and increasingly aesthetic, just as Gilles Lipovetsky proposes. And we can debate whether mobile phones have done that, or whether they have transformed our entire waking lives into nomadic offices exposed to constant oversight. We can also question whether AI and robotics represent a rosy tomorrow for humans where drudgery is replaced with creative quality time or a dystopia of unemployment, surveillance, and exacerbated social inequalities. But what is absent from the capitalist realism of the postmodern world as compared with that of the nineteenth century is the idea that history travels like time's arrow and human emancipation is its destination. For roughly two centuries—from the Enlightenment through the Cold War—this notion of inevitable progress dominated Western social thought, culminating in Fukuyama's brief "end of history" triumphalism after 1989. Which is why, other than the dubious digitized future proposed by tech bros (and they certainly are a male cohort), including Mark Zuckerberg, Elon Musk, Marc Andreessen, and Peter Thiel among others, the future appears to be one of armed conflict over diminishing resources. Or, alternatively, a gradual human fadeout due to environmental deterioration of our planetary biosphere. Fisher also got this right. He proposed that "there is no punctual moment of disaster; the world doesn't end with a bang, it winks out, unravels, gradually falls apart."[25] Perhaps that last twinkle will be captured on TikTok, or more grimly by the Department of Homeland Security's Office of Intelligence and Analysis.

Indeed, when an elite group within society anticipates future survival in luxury doomsday bunkers or glass-domed villas on Mars, essentially planning emancipation for themselves exclusive of that same society, "we" do not have a future but a feudal endgame. "Capitalism continues to mine the remains of the dead," Tao Leigh Goffe states before reminding us gloomily about the system's necropolitical logic: "what, after all, are fossil fuels but the accumulated bio matter of the ancestors, organic material transformed?," adding with a glimmer of hope that "our fate is sealed as the fossils of the future."[26] Yet this grim formulation contains a temporal paradox: if we are already fossils of a future that mines us, then that future is haunting us backward into the present. Like Fisher's "future relics" demanding our attentive listening today, or Oliver Ressler's visualization of actively blocking today a catastrophic tomorrow (see figure 54), Goffe's fossilized fate travels back through time to reach us, converting, at least in theory, what is fate into contingency.

And yet, what makes listening to our future fate so difficult is the calculated delirium of the Unpresent. To cite only a few examples, consider the subversion of the post-World War II political order by the second Trump administration, including humiliating former allies and undermining NATO, the latter, ironically, a long-standing demand of the left, even as the president sidles up to dictators while burnishing his own autocratic credentials. The Unpresent dissonance is perhaps best summarized by his eyeing the bombed-out remains of oppressed people's homes in Gaza as the site of new real estate development, perhaps dreaming of creating Mar-a-Lago Middle East.[27] It is not that the unexpected, inconceivable, or simply faked reality is becoming a new and therefore a seemingly authentic truth all its own, but that the very classification of reality itself is vanishing as though it had never existed. Hannah Arendt asserted something similar in the late 1960s: "The result of a consistent and total substitution of lies for factual truth is not that the lie will now be accepted as truth and truth be defamed as a lie, but that the sense by which we take our bearings in the real world—the category of truth versus falsehood is among the mental means to this end—is being destroyed."[28] If the very category of truth is being destroyed, as Arendt warned, then the institutions tasked with preserving and transmitting it, including universities, museums, schools, news media, become both problematic refuge and a primary target of the Unpresent.

All said and done, if this is indeed the apocalypse, then where are the four horsemen, the scorpions, and boils, and why have the heavens not "rolled up like a scroll," or the tombs split open to release the dead?[29] Or wait, has all of this happened already, and I was too busy watching the latest season of *Squid Games* to take notice? Hello, Unpresent.

7

LEARNING AFTER NEOLIBERALISM

THE SPECTACLE OF ENDLESS EMERGENCIES

The modern university system has long been the target of critique from both the political left and right, but it is the critique from the left that is the focus of this chapter. Exemplary of this tendency are Stefano Harney and Fred Moten, who inform us that "a professional education has become a critical education. But one should not applaud this fact."[1] What becomes of this left critical tradition at a time when liberal education is under assault and when US Vice President JD Vance has stated that "universities in our country are fundamentally corrupt and dedicated to deceit and lies, not to the truth"?[2] How can we parse the different yet consistently critical takes on higher education in a time and space so profoundly out of joint? What options remain today for what Irit Rogoff, Kristina Lee Podesva, and Claire Bishop among others dubbed "the pedagogical turn" by artists, activists, and critical educators toward experimental, alternative, and counterinstitutional forms of learning, a para-institutional trend that arose in the late 1990s and early 2000s?[3]

THE LOST PROMISE OF PROGRESSIVE EDUCATION

Wait. How can things be so relentlessly bleak? What happened to the covenant in which advancing knowledge through progressive education

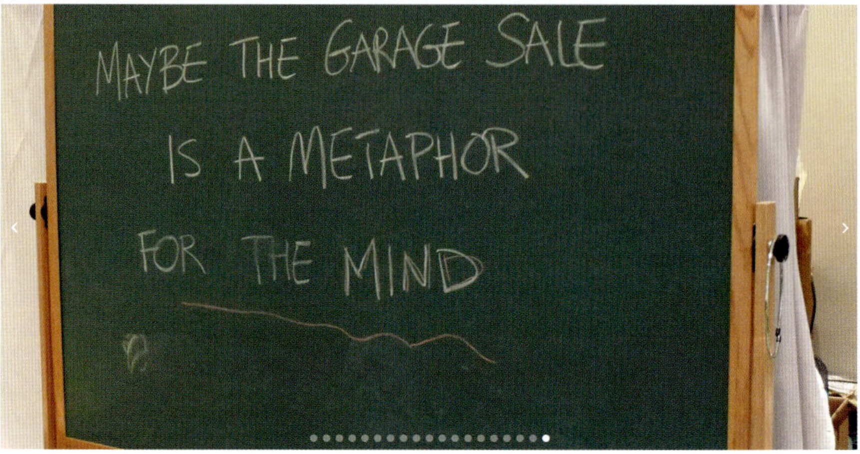

FIGURE 14

"Maybe the garage sale is a metaphor for the mind": A chalkboard declaration from Martha Rosler's pioneering *Meta-Monumental Garage Sale*, a performance art installation first created in 1973 and recreated at various venues, including MoMA in 2012. The blackboard format frames these questions as a kind of public pedagogy, turning commercial space into a classroom for critical thinking, and its provocative statement was part of the original *Monumental Garage Sale* at the University of California San Diego, where Rosler simultaneously advertised the event as both an art exhibition and an actual garage sale in local newspapers. Rosler's work transforms everyday commercial exchanges into artistic interventions, inviting visitors to browse and buy secondhand goods organized, displayed, and sold by the artist while questioning consumerism, value systems, and social economies. Image courtesy of the artist.

pushes back against the dark? Isn't this the very narrative of historical enlightenment as a forward-moving arrow of time? And did not Adorno and Horkheimer attribute the withering of education to the rise of fascism in the 1930s as a kind of historical regression? Even though Fisher has mixed feelings about the role formal schooling plays in generating capitalist realism, he nevertheless states that "education, far from being in some ivory tower safely inured from the 'real world,' is the engine room of the reproduction of social reality, directly confronting the inconsistencies of the capitalist social field."[4]

Allow me to temporarily rewind by acknowledging that had this book been completed years earlier, as originally planned, I would likely have begun this chapter as follows:

> Have we not already won the battle, if not the war? We artists, radicals, dreamers, dissenters, critical thinkers, haters of unfreedom, and lovers of all that is challenging and curious and liberatory? Have we not infiltrated—virtually out of necessity—the highs and lows and ins and outs of the knowledge-producing system like a legion of rhizomatic tendrils, spreading from grammar and high schools to higher educational institutions and into every corner of the social mind? Yes, assuredly, the teaching of art and literature in educational institutions is frequently marginalized, defunded, and has been at times demonized, and yet, incrementally, unhurriedly, accumulatively, it has infiltrated the collective societal mind.

My reasoning was straightforward at the time. Just imagine how many countless thousands of students of all types and grades have been introduced to critical thinking and inquiry-based learning thanks to a culture of enlightened thinking unafraid of its own deconstruction. This includes exposure to culture and the arts in all their modernist, avant-garde, postmodern, and contemporary manifestations. And, of course, who was teaching this critical cultural curriculum? Chronically underemployed poets, novelists, musicians, painters, sculptors, film and video makers, critics, curators, and art historians fill this role. What's more, once this cultural portal is opened, other vistas of knowledge appear, including Marxism, feminism, anarchism, queer theory, Black art, and anticolonial struggles. Indisputably, no one can teach the history of high culture over the past century, and especially over the previous few decades, without raising these topics, these left-subversive topics, that facilitate the development of intellectual spaces involving resistance and dissent.

Perhaps it is even fair to state that the true extent of the victory I had hoped to celebrate involved the near-normalization of an enlightened culture of dissent. If this was my thinking in 2022, it now comes off as fanciful, as though written in some far-distant time and place. Since the start of 2025, every day brings another attempt by the MAGA government to dismantle this very same culture of critical inquiry and experimental learning. Still, it is also worth adding that this widespread, hypothetical mind-opening did not prevent the reelection of Trump, nor did it stop his party from gaining control of both House and Senate. And yet, is this outcome not evidence that charges made by MAGA followers about the systematic indoctrination of students by "leftist" professors, feminists, Marxists, and so forth are purposely exaggerated, and therefore aimed at deception?

COLD WAR FUNDING AND THE EDUCATIONAL US RENAISSANCE

Despite what many on the nationalist right insist, fostering a critical outlook was never a leftist educational conspiracy. Challenging norms and stereotypes, as well as the social, political, and economic assumptions shaping everyday thought and action, belongs to the very zeitgeist of formal learning in the Enlightenment tradition. It also presupposes a process of questioning existing laws, ideas, theories, and institutions, including the university itself. When it is successful, studying art and culture is a similarly transformative process, although critical reflection gained through the arts takes place differently, through the intensity of seeing rather than merely looking. As long as these methodologies were aligned with a belief in the gradual expansion of rights and resources for all, the imagined arrow of time continued its journey forward from one generation to the next, propelled in part by the university's emancipatory mission. This is why opening higher education to working-class people was crucial for liberal and left democracies. Funding for World War II veterans kick-started this process, but it took a Cold War-era crisis for these class-based barriers to really begin to fall in the US.

Immediately following the surprising success of Soviet rocketry science in 1957, including the launch of Sputniks 1 and 2, the world's first artificial satellites, the US National Defense Education Act of 1958 committed billions of dollars to education-related spending. The era of low-cost student loans had begun. With cosmonaut Yuri Gagarin's unprecedented orbit around the Earth just three years later, getting a college degree began to seem like a prerequisite for a successful adult life in the US. With the establishment of the community college system in the 1960s, accessible, low-cost education became increasingly affordable and commonplace. With this explosion in access to higher education also came exposure to the arts and humanities. An emphasis on analytical thought was further inevitable given the context of the civil rights and anti-Vietnam War movements and the emergence of a youth-oriented counterculture at the time.

Consider, therefore, the myriad of young people encountering the arts as a required elective to fulfill academic requirements aimed in other career directions, including law, medicine, corporate management, public policy, and so forth. One other significant experience that the arts provide, along with a break from the intensity required to study case law, human biology, mathematics, or marketing statistics, is exposure to an essentially noncapitalist and often socially dissident sphere of production and experience. However naked and commercial the mainstream art world has become, art in the school setting has been and still is generally taught in its ideal form, illustrating for students what *not* working for a wage might be like and why finding one's creative self is necessary for a full and rounded education. With the rise of the so-called creative industries, such training even moved from the humanities to the field of business management, as when the *Harvard Business Review* proposed in 2008 that the MFA is the new MBA.[5] Briefly stated, some degree of understanding, if not also an actual appetite, for a form of learning that challenges conventions has long been woven into mainstream educational curriculum, right alongside the notion that social good should surpass individual desire.

Again, if this form of critical thinking is a leftist conspiracy, then its intrigue is both part and parcel of the establishment and has spectacularly failed at bringing down the system. Instead, agnostic analysis and skeptical interpretation but also dissident, avant-garde ideas are routinely taught by schools in precisely those nations most dedicated to capitalism. This fact should make business leaders, and especially tech bros, eager to decry Vice President Vance when he declares that professors are "the enemy" and universities are "dedicated to deceit and lies."[6] The vociferous silence from such university-trained corporate figures as Jeff Bezos (Amazon; Princeton), Alex Karp (Palantir; Goethe/Frankfurt), Elon Musk (Tesla/X; Stanford dropout), Sundar Pichai (Google; IIT/Stanford), and Mark Zuckerberg (Meta; Harvard dropout) is one more symptom of the inverted "Upside Down" of the Unpresent. Yet is it not possible that their collective hush evading any defense of higher education also reflects something more ideologically coherent than mere opportunism? Consider academic Nick Land's *The Dark Enlightenment* (2012), a foundational text of the neoreactionary movement, which explicitly rejects liberal democracy and Enlightenment values in favor of technocapitalist acceleration beyond democratic constraints.[7] In truth, these individuals are already living in a version of what they consider an exemplary "future" reality, one that is set far apart from most of us but has consequences for all of us.

My own schooling in the mid to late 1970s not only benefited from the surge of Cold War educational spending; it led me to discover such nonconformist cultural figures and collective formations as Jackson Pollock, John Cage, Carlos Castaneda, Sun Ra, and Ursula K. Le Guin as well as Dada, surrealism, and the Soviet avant-garde. This exposure to dissident culture happened not at an elite institution but at a suburban community college outside Philadelphia—the same swing district that delivered Pennsylvania to Trump's MAGA ticket in 2024, the same location where Trump staged his media-saturated "shift" at a McDonald's drive-through. My own employment in those years meant slinging pizzas at a neighboring parlor and mopping floors as a late-night janitor at an industrial plant to cover tuition. That is to say, arts and culture education once reached working-class students in run-of-the-mill locales, without prep school pedigrees or private school resources.

MAGA'S WAR ON CRITICAL THINKING

Returning to the opening question: if it did appear that *we* progressives were about to win the battle of social convictions, hearts, and minds, then why is all of this critical pedagogical accomplishment suddenly under attack? Is it perhaps a neon sign pointing to our success? Or the logical site of exhaustion for commencing the attack itself? Let me recap the situation thus far: a resurgent Trump directorate has withdrawn billions of dollars in funding from noted Ivy League universities using as his justification mostly peaceful pro-Palestinian demonstrations by students and faculty, even though many of these same schools forcefully, even violently, allowed security and police to dispel and arrest protesters. And this has included terminating between $3.3 and $3.7 billion in federal research funding to universities, while seeking to completely dismantle the Education Department founded in 1979 by Democratic President Jimmy Carter, a process that has already reduced the department's staff by nearly half.[8] On February 6, 2026, Defense Secretary Pete Hegseth announced that the Pentagon would sever all military education ties with Harvard, ending graduate-level professional military education, fellowships, and certificate programs beginning in the 2026–2027 academic year. Calling Harvard a "factory for woke ideology" and one of the "red-hot centers of Hate America activism," Hegseth declared, "We train warriors, not wokesters."[9] Hegseth holds a master's degree from Harvard.

Trump has also stated ominously that the aim of these and other related actions is to end teaching that was being provided by "radicals, zealots and Marxists."[10] Such a purge would not only include the study of anticapitalist theories, but also such unorthodox cultural phenomena as avant-garde art and contemporary socially engaged activist practices, the primary focus of my practice and research for several decades. It would effectively condemn any field or discipline MAGA perceives as averse to its conservative political and cultural ambitions. While this agenda has generated limited pushback from some larger universities, it has already crippled curriculum and hiring related to DEI (diversity, equity, and inclusion) and suppressed the teaching of select subject matter, including Plato's *Symposium* at Texas A&M University because is discusses homosexuality and suggests there are more than two genders.[11] More recently, the Trump administration has moved to revoke accreditation from institutions deemed insufficiently compliant, weaponizing the accreditation process itself as a tool of ideological enforcement. I suspect that in addition, the embargo of certain areas of study will, if unchecked, spread to such fields as labor studies and labor history. Regardless of any claims to the contrary by the new nationalist right, it will sooner or later become necessary to nullify all support structures for labor union organizing while endorsing open-shop manufacturing policies if the US wishes to remain globally competitive with an uneducated workforce. And given the exceptionally heterogeneous makeup of the American working class, the knock-on effect of this suppression will be all the more disastrous for diversity and inclusion, even as artificial intelligence and robotics threaten to radically reduce human labor in general, but especially that type of employment working-class students once aspired to reach via higher education: the professional sector, the paragon of upward mobility a college degree in the West has promised since the end of World War II.

Still, the current vulnerability of the university has another dimension to it that is fully part of a much older tradition dating back to its medieval origins, advancing through the Renaissance, and flourishing in the modern era of the Enlightenment and after. A certain openness to self-critique is intrinsic to the very nature of higher education, including from people like me, a member of a dissident academy within the academy. But in truth, at this moment of MAGA aggression toward the university and all that it represents, has this intellectual openness not also played a role in fostering the university's current institutional distress? The balance of this chapter will take up these questions by way of perhaps the most vanguardist thinking about the university in the work of Stefano Harney and Fred Moten, who offer at best guarded support for the university as a sanctuary for dissidents, coupled, however, with a biting critique of its role as a primary manufacturer of capitalism's liberal managerial class.

Harney and Moten's concept of fugitivity pivots on an elusive and semiclandestine spatial concept that goes by the name *undercommons*. I will attempt to decipher this below. This collaborating duo of management theorist and scholarly poet has combined lyrical critique with institutional dissent to challenge the baked-in contradictions of the American university system, as heightened by decades of neoliberalism where everything, including learning, is monetizable. The question now is what happens when the neoliberal university system and its concept of enlightenment, however flawed, are confronted with abolition from the decolonial left and outright replacement by the right in the form of a pro-MAGA simulacrum of their former selves?

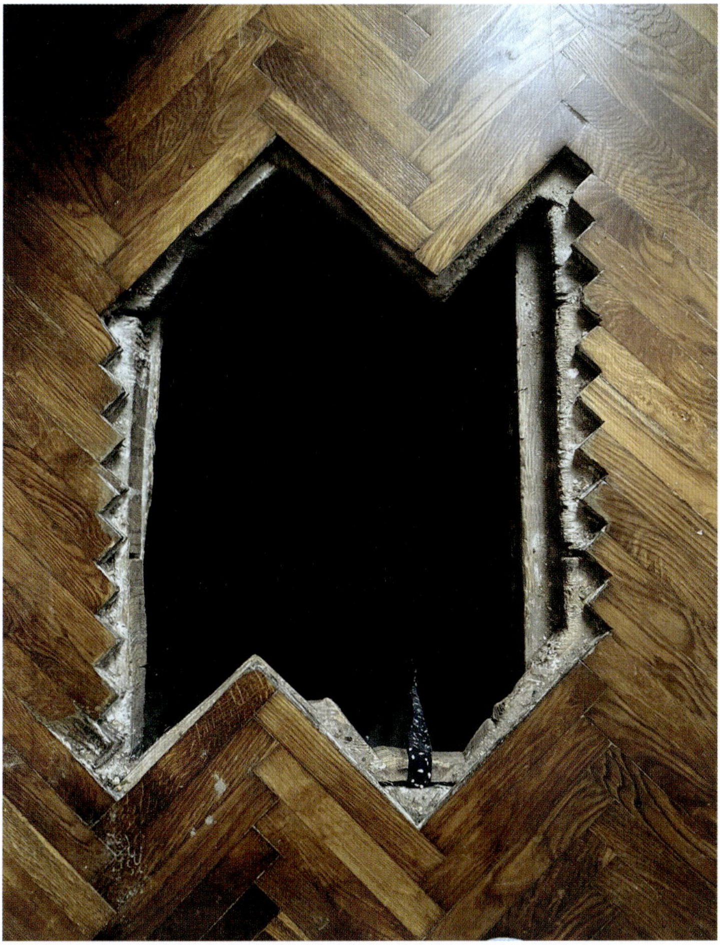

FIGURE 15

A jagged opening cut through herringbone parquet flooring reveals the dark void beneath, part of Natalia Romik's *Hideouts: The Architecture of Survival* at Zachęta Gallery. This reference to a Holocaust-era hiding place for Jews transforms invisible survival architecture into visible testimony, honoring the architectural creativity and resilience of those who carved out spaces of refuge within ordinary environments during an existential threat. Natalia Romik, *Hideouts: The Architecture of Survival*, Zachęta—National Gallery of Art, Warsaw, Poland, 2022. Image courtesy of the artist.

FUGITIVE UNDERCOMMONS: A REFUGE FOR DISSENTERS

Published over a decade before the start of Trump's efforts to dismantle higher education in his second term, Harney and Moten's 2013 book *The Undercommons: Fugitive Planning and Black Study* sets up a complex argument about the American university system:

> The university works for the day when it will be able to rid itself, like capital in general, of the trouble of labor. It will then be able to reproduce a labor force that understands itself as not only unnecessary but dangerous to the development of capitalism. . . . The university still needs this clandestine labor to prepare this undifferentiated labor force, whose increasing specialization and managerialist tendencies, again contra the restorationists, represent precisely the successful integration of the division of labor with the universe of exchange that commands restorationist loyalty.[12]

Significantly, they argue, the university is also a place of refuge for maverick scholars and educators such as themselves, and yet it both is and is not also a place of learned enlightenment. This is because it is first and foremost a neoliberal educational factory turning out products in the form of system-compliant graduates, who in turn go on to reproduce the university all over again. For this reason, Harney and Moten reject the proposed restoration of the university that would return it to some previous *pure* state. Such a virtuous place of learning has never actually existed, but a restorationist agenda, if successful, would only serve as a pretense for safe, acceptable forms of institutional critique, while shunning truly subversive learning. It is, in a word, the system's "undercommons," with its own rules of entry: "To abuse its [the university's] hospitality, to spite its mission, to join its refugee colony, its gypsy encampment, to be in but not of—this is the path of the subversive intellectual in the modern university."[13] Modern? Perhaps. Yet a version of this critique is already present in the Enlightenment with Immanuel Kant's insistence that the university must remain a site of conflict, right versus left, about which I will return to below.

Harney and Moten's undercommons exists in an intermediary zone or intellectual bivouac that is not an actual place but is instead a subversively supplementary semispatial concept. It is both internal and external to the university, functioning much in the way philosopher Jacques Derrida's concept of a supplement does: an accessory that simultaneously completes a primary idea, belief, text, or institution while revealing that it is actually incomplete without the added supplement.[14] Undoubtedly, this critique also has a much longer lineage that extends from Kant's *The Conflict of the Faculties* (1798) through Herbert Marcuse, Paulo Freire, Ivan Illich, Pierre Bourdieu, Gayatri Chakravorty Spivak, bell hooks, Bill Readings, and ultimately through Derrida to Harney and Moten, thus forming a left philosophical tradition that analyzes the university as both the site of enlightenment promises via rigorous debate, as well as the location for the institutional reproduction of hierarchical power relations inside and outside the pedagogical citadel.[15]

Harney and Moten's fugitivity of the undercommons serves this genealogy as a necessary auxiliary that through the act of naming opens a space for both dissent and defense in relation to the university. However, because their undercommons is populated by a piebald troop of educational laborers and academic mavericks whom the university marginalizes or attempts to outright suppress, it is at once secondary and essential, fugitive and abiding. The university's undercommons is populated by variegated lower-ranked literati including "composition teachers, mentorless graduate students, adjunct Marxist historians, out or queer management professors, state college ethnic studies departments, closed-down film programs, visa-expired Yemeni student newspaper editors, historically black college sociologists, and feminist engineers."[16] In many ways, it is equivalent to the missing mass or dark matter of the high art world.

MAGA'S WAR ON HIGHER EDUCATION

I hardly need to point out that the captains of MAGA, and the nationalist right in general, see the rich diversity of the university quite differently. They see no internal conflicts or contradictions, or consider them irrelevant. Trump, Vance, Orbán, together with Stephen Miller, Trump's policy architect whose leaked emails revealed promotion of white nationalist content, along with Ron DeSantis, the "anti-woke" governor of Florida, do not draw any distinctions between the official "above-ground" university and its motley undercommons of dissidents, misfits, self-identified radicals, and foreign infiltrators. Their view is reflected in the very title of a book by Christopher Rufo, another ultraconservative and DeSantis appointee: *America's Cultural Revolution: How the Radical Left Conquered Everything*. The book captures the essence of MAGA's conspiratorial worldview. It lumps together all liberal and left-of-center politics into one clandestine deep-state cabal. This worldview recalls Adorno and Horkheimer's analysis of fascist hordes and their paranoia, eagerly seeking to reveal hidden enemies responsible for their own alleged misfortune. The next chapter will examine a virtually identical far-reaching subclinical paranoid outlook, though focused on the world of contemporary art rather than universities. Still, from the perspective of critical and reflexive pedagogy, Rufo and company are correct. The liberal enlightenment-oriented university might turn out armies of professional managers, but it is not presently equipped to arm them with lockstep ethnonationalist values, and certainly not with fiercely conservative White Christian principles characteristic of MAGA. On the contrary.

ORBÁN'S BLUEPRINT: WHEN THE SHELL BECOMES THE SYSTEM

Rufo's apparent reward for (ironically enough) making it onto the "liberal" *New York Times* bestseller list is disconcerting: Governor DeSantis appointed the conspiracist to the board of his state's New College of Florida. The intellectually open and experimental public school was subsequently transformed into a laboratory for incubating right-wing education. While New College of Florida was described by pro-MAGA tacticians as creating a blueprint for broader university capture by MAGA, in truth Orbán had already provided the right-wing takeover gameplan when he gutted from within the Soros-funded Central European University (CEU) in Budapest. But instead of the institution's overt replacement with a completely different educational entity, CEU was internally modified, as journalist Andrew Marantz describes after his own unsettling visit to

CEU in 2025. Like a gumshoe detective arriving at a puzzling crime scene, he writes:

> The more I poked around, though, the more I saw indications that the institution had, in fact, been hollowed out—a Potemkin university with a sleek façade. . . . Inside, though there were still department markers on the walls (Gender Studies, Historical Studies, International Relations), many of the offices were either empty or littered with debris. I passed an office with a light on, and a young man at a computer looked up, clearly startled to see anyone. He politely explained that he worked for a video-editing startup, which was renting the office by the month.[17]

Even as the name, physical institution, and alleged function all remain visibly intact, the once internationally renowned university is today not unlike the alien pod-infested town of Mill Valley, California, in the 1956 film *Invasion of the Body Snatchers*. CEU has become a nugatory doppelgänger of itself, fully in keeping with the uncanniness of the Unpresent.

THE UNIVERSITY AS NEOLIBERAL EDUFACTORY

Uncannily anticipating MAGA's gutting of liberal educational institutions, Harney and Moten described the university in 2013 as embodying a "kind of empty shell of what used to be called education."[18] It is this hollow vessel that then serves as a means for "exporting the apparatus of policy all throughout the social world."[19] As a result, a primary goal of their investigation is understanding "how it is that the essential conditions of our own situation are being exported everywhere."[20] Their pre-MAGA analysis equated the university's dissemination of its highly monetized policies not only with "extreme neoliberalism" but with the systemic transformation of surveillance into oppressive juridical procedures. "One moment there are vicious kind of drones against the poor, these night riders making policy from anywhere said to be fixed against anyone said to need fixing, and then the next minute, governance is deployed against the poor."[21] The description has parallels with the vertiginous disorienting spectacularity of what I and other theorists call the total capitalist aesthetic, which, as I have argued, is the breeding ground of the Unpresent.

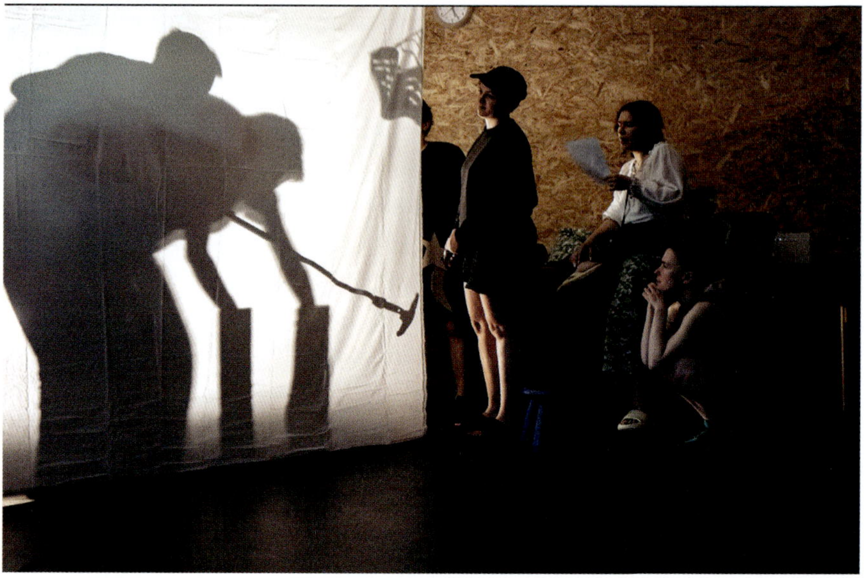

FIGURE 16

During Marina Naprushkina's transformative WHW (the curatorial collective What, How, and for Whom?) seminar at the Akademija Summer School in Zagreb, Croatia, fourteen international artists explored socially engaged practice through collaborative shadow theater. This experimental workshop wove together personal memories, individual narratives, and collective demands into powerful artistic activism, demonstrating how imagination and community organizing can address social marginalization through nonhierarchical feminist approaches to political art-making. "Out of the Needs" workshop with Marina Naprushkina, May 2023, Zagreb. Photo by Sanja Bistričić Srića.

Harney and Moten, however, situate this ideological hothouse squarely within the provinces of liberal higher education rather than in the ubiquitous marketplace for products and lifestyles.

Specifically, their example of "drones against the poor" points to the way invasive biometric monitoring technology has been developed in tandem with US universities thanks to funds from such government programs as DARPA (the Defense Advanced Research Projects Agency). Notably, in fiscal year 2024, DARPA's budget was $4.122 billion, with a significant portion of this money allocated to university-based research projects. This is consistent with federally funded research and development (R&D) across US universities, which totaled nearly $60 billion in fiscal year 2023 and accounted for 55 percent of total R&D expenditures at these institutions.[22] Crucially, the data generated by such studies ultimately feeds back into the university system itself, where it is used to fine-tune technological strategies for more efficient social management as well as teaching curriculum. It is this cycling feedback loop that Harney and Moten draw critical attention to, and against which they insist university faculty must choose sides, either for or against. The choice is clear: step onto the treadmill or escape into the undercommons. Simultaneously, the military-university learning loop energetically draws one in, offering access to a vanguard of knowledge creation while promising front-row access to new technologies. It is all very seductive. Furthermore, having a regular salary, an office, and additional research funding is unlikely to stoke one's institutional antipathy. But there is something else at work here as well.

System disruption and the surmounting of previous norms and standards, long desired by the artistic avant-garde, is also a product of the edufactory. It too forms a feedback loop continuously amplifying in scale and intensity. This expanding recursiveness is fully in accord with capitalism's own vanguard project, which, as Marx stated, "constantly reproduces the capital relation itself," with progressively "more capitalists or larger capitalists at this pole, more wage workers at that."[23] If, for example, we substitute this or that supposedly novel consumer accessory for the military drone—such as a product promising the buyer enhanced sexual allure or personal freedom—and nicely package it up by way of a university art student trained in avant-garde graphic design, we can see how iterations of creative-industry circuitry also repeat and repeat and repeat. But what seems radically cutting-edge when we are inside the coiling turbine of alleged innovation remains squarely within the predictable realm of manufactured tastes and expectations. Such seemingly liberatory consumer choices are methodically tracked, quantified, and programmed back into the system's algorithms. And increasingly, it is AI operatives who sort, classify, and modify this eternal return of the same, which goes by such monikers as *new*, *original*, *cutting-edge*, and of course, *avant-garde*.

WHITHER THE UNDERCOMMONS NOW?

These are the battle lines emerging today. They have everything to do with our fading perception of history as a movement toward an all-inclusive and just future. Neither is this some leftist conspiracy. Rather, defense of civil society and inclusive emancipation are fundamental precepts of civil society. The transparent weakening and ultimate inversion of this principle of democratic self-defense as defense of authoritarianism is one of the most dangerous characteristics of the Unpresent.

Furthermore, such upended logic forms the basis of the "great replacement theory" being promoted by MAGA figures such as Tucker Carlson and Christopher Rufo. Variations also appear with Italy's Matteo Salvini and Hungary's Viktor Orbán. If this is the case, threatened democracies must act to aggressively substitute their own core principles for such detrimental cultural outgrowths wherever they appear. Harney and Moten's escape route via the fugitive undercommons offers one possible semi-egress out of this timeless circularity. It provides a means of tunneling beneath the neoliberal university's ideological superstructure. But what will happen now, when the entire institutional edifice is itself under explicit ideological attack?

Do we begin to relocate Harney and Moten's undercommons to other, more sympathetic jurisdictions? And where are these, exactly? In theory, one refuge surely exists within para-institutional educational projects, of which there have been dozens, if not hundreds, founded over the course of this century thus far.[24] But these too are fugitive, and generally only sustainable when parasitically connected with larger, better-financed

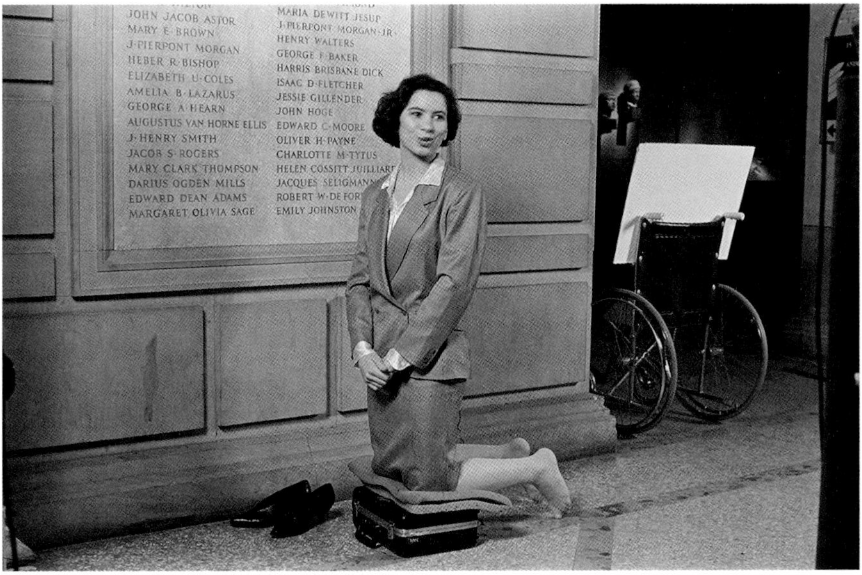

FIGURE 17

Andrea Fraser, *The Public Life of Art: The Museum*, at the Metropolitan Museum of Art, New York, 1988. In this photograph by artist Louise Lawler, we see Fraser in professional attire kneeling before an institutional wall displaying donor names, shoes carefully removed, in a definitive performance of institutional critique. Fraser's work exemplifies how critical education in the arts taught generations to see and question the structural relationships between wealth, power, and cultural institutions, the very pedagogical tradition now under attack. Photo: Louise Lawler.

academic facilities. Essentially, they are already a type of undercommons in themselves, or a temporary autonomous DIY (do-it-yourself) undercommons, if you like. Alternatively, we might propose striking up alliances with pedagogical programs operated by left political organizations, or perhaps progressive labor unions, a "united front" for higher learning. But the heyday of such liberal-left coalition building was back in the 1920s to 1950s, and much work lies ahead if it is to be reimagined today.[25]

FUGITIVITY AND STRATEGIC REDARKENING

In any event, there is yet another problem. All these options inevitably transform Harney and Moten's transient alter-enlightenment zone into a no-longer-fugitive, no-longer-subsurface entity. After all, doesn't the very concept of the undercommons require at least the shell of a liberal education system as its *overcommons*? Otherwise, where would the university's barely tolerated maroons and gypsies, old Marxist moles, and precarious art teachers find shelter, let alone establish their makeshift underoffices and alter-communications networks? Certainly, all evacuation strategies must be considered. Still, even more challenging and tragic is the likelihood that if the nationalist right succeeds in Orbánizing higher education in the US, then most working-class people, MAGA elements included, will find their current precarious economic circumstances increasingly compromised as they lose not so much the urge to fight the system's extractionism as the critical tools necessary to analyze how it functions and why. This is a conundrum fully in keeping with the disorienting conditions of the Unpresent, which also possibly furnishes its own means of egress.

Consider this scenario instead: MAGA's assault on higher education might just accomplish what decades of left critique could not: making ultratransparent higher education's role in capitalist accumulation and the shoring-up of state security and military power. As enrollment drops and students increasingly choose working-class employment over credentialing, might not the undercommons model, or something similar to it in which education is fugitive study rather than capital investment, become not a utopian alternative but a practical necessity? The "dark matter" of precarious teachers, radical pedagogy, and alter-institutional networks will not be hiding anymore; they will become the only game in town for acquiring knowledge, even as they operate tactically, and almost certainly fugitively, in order to resist institutional capture by the wrong players. Under such conditions, the larger question isn't whether liberals and leftists, labor unions and progressive movements, can form an alliance; this is after all a proposition that seems both doable and imperative. The question is how such an oppositional front can also acknowledge that any pedagogical undercommons cannot become a permanent instrument of resistance: only a provisional space of rehearsal and experimentation for possibilities not yet realized, knowledge not yet confiscated, futures still to be assembled.

Here we can even cite Kant as much as Derrida on the university as its own parliament of debate and discord, with the former insisting that intellectual conflict within the university is a search for truth, and therefore can never end and must never be regulated by the state (or the church). Derrida effectively agrees, except he seeks to do so without any recourse to foundational truths or laws. Instead, the poststructuralist philosopher embraces the critical performativity of disputation itself as a kind of lever that one leans on to displace something binary and fixed. If indeed prospects for the post-neoliberal university as a counterinstitutional space of learning hinge upon methodologies of displacement and cunning as much as repurposing and repair, or even perhaps on a tactical redarkening—not a retreat into invisibility but a more sophisticated relationship to visibility that I will return to in the book's conclusion—then one assignment stands out first and foremost for any undercommons in the age of MAGA: to ensure that the future of public knowledge is inseparable from knowledge about the future, including, above all else, the very possibility of a future. It might even be found in the most unlikely of places.

8

THE CULTURAL ASPIRATIONS OF THE NATIONALIST RIGHT

Having explored Moten and Harney's radical critique of liberal education, we now turn to its conservative mirror image. British commentator and painter Alexander Adams alleges that the art world is dominated by an opportunistic left feminist ideology often operating stealthily through weak or hoodwinked liberal administrators and institutions. By contrast, Adams asserts that "true art" should deliver "the inspiration to live up to ideals. True art gives the encouragement to think and feel deeply. True art causes a yearning to harmonize with truth and beauty."[1] Armed with these premises, he challenges contemporary museums to abandon "artivism" (the merging of art with activism) and return to aesthetics as transcendence. Yet Adams's treatise soon reveals an inevitable impasse as he professes a passionate faith in both the preeminence of true art and its place within the capitalist marketplace. As we will see, Adams often demonstrates significant insights, yet his inability to resolve this basic contradiction demonstrates how deep the impasse runs. Whether attacking progressive art and education from the left or the right, all known exits appear blocked as the Unpresent transforms cultural conflict into an upside-down theater where time and historical redemption have lost their coordinates.

ALEXANDER ADAMS AND THE BATTLE AGAINST "ARTIVISM"

In his book *Artivism: The Battle for Museums in the Era of Postmodernism*, Adams strives to explain not so much what artivism is (for him, it is always

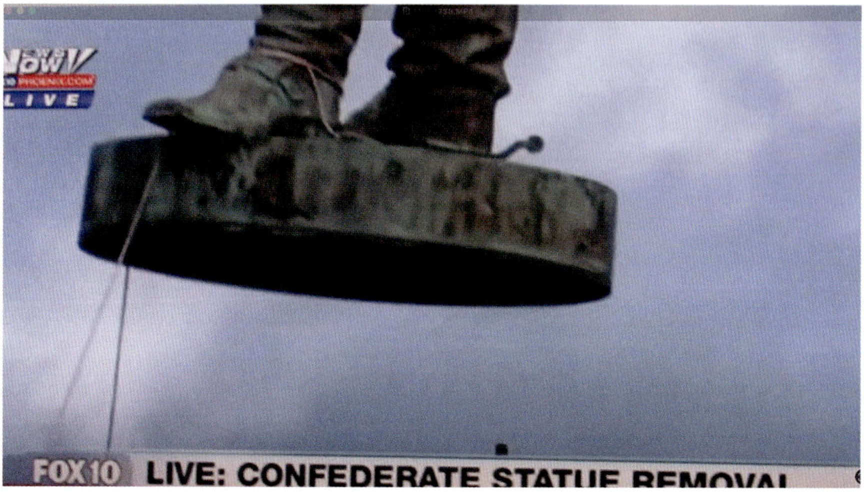

opportunistic if motived by leftist ideas) or where it came from (a product of the radical, eco-feminized avant-gardists) or who he believes it benefits (those unmarketable and mostly non-Anglo-European artists, along with the mediocre ranks of cultural managers and liberal elites), but why it is that artivism is always aligned with a leftist critique of traditional cultural values. Perhaps what bothers Adams most is artivism's alleged dominance within the mainstream art world over the past few decades. "Artivism," he argues, "is an important income source for artists who have difficulty producing art that appeals to consumers. . . . Artivism is a way in which unskilled artists in search of resources exploit utilitarianism in arts bureaucracy, framing it as high-status avant-garde art and claiming political kudos by adopting the elite's preferred causes. In crude terms, it

FIGURE 18

The statue of Confederate General Robert E. Lee was removed to cheers in New Orleans on May 17, 2017. Erected in 1884 during the violent reassertion of white supremacy, the monument served not to preserve authentic local memory but to enforce racial hierarchy through public space.

is unemployed artists pretending to be social workers for the satisfaction of bourgeois art administrators and consumers."[2]

It is useful to spend a bit of time now with these ideas for several reasons. Even though Adams does not belong to the American MAGA movement and he distances himself from the overt zealotry of the alt-right, his polemics do resonate at times, but also clash with, these tendencies in ways both anticipated and unexpected. Curiously, he is himself the graduate of a very liberal if not leftist-oriented institution, Goldsmiths, which advertises its art program as dynamic, cosmopolitan, and internationally respected.[3] In addition, in his endeavor to clarify all that is wrong with artivism, Adams offers a glimpse into the internal fractures that will likely grow more caustic inside the cultural hegemony of the new nationalist right, including MAGA, but also in general within postneoliberal autocratic capitalism.

Notably, Adams's book appeared in 2022, two years before Trump's return to power, an event that may have seemed unlikely when he penned his study. Still, in his extensive polemic we find a list of grievances and denunciations that are frequently in line with MAGA, while at other times they veer toward an older, traditionally conservative view of high culture in which art is elevated above an otherwise mundane or unrefined society. At other times, Adams contemplates the tactical possibilities of artivism becoming a tool for the political right. This is when his own internal conceptual tensions become most apparent. We find the painter and critic genuinely torn between his desire to topple left culture from its alleged institutional pedestal and the dodgy attractiveness of repurposing artivism as the means of carrying out that sabotage. Ultimately, Adams's internally discordant musings fail to bring these conflicts into conceptual alignment.

In point of fact, Adams sincerely struggles with the experiential breakdown of time and space so characteristic of total capitalist aesthetics and its inside-out mutation, the Unpresent. This is why his diatribe veers between ideological expediency on one hand and full-on conservative restoration on the other, causing him to sometimes align with and other times collide against such alt-right strategists as Steve Bannon, Andrew Breitbart, or Hungary's Viktor Orbán. Adams's incoherence becomes clear when contrasted with the deliberate temporal calculus of figures like Hungarian far-right theorist Márton Békés. Where Adams flails between nostalgia and pragmatism, Békés articulates a patient strategy stating that "the lengthy and dynamic process of establishing a cultural majority often begins with the début of an intellectual avant-garde, which then begins the accumulation of original intellectual capital."[4] Consider also the way Békés, who holds a PhD in history, repurposes Marxist Antonio Gramsci's notion of counterhegemony as a mission involving "nothing less than piecing time and space together; the political system shall be embedded into an adequate cultural era. Although the dominance of liberalism appears to be nearing its end in a political and economic sense . . . the construction of a counter-hegemony is a laborious and enduring mission."[5]

I suspect Adams would wince at the notion that an "*adequate* cultural era" might be constructed in support of a conservative viewpoint, given that he believes that true art is inherently timeless. Furthermore, it is exactly this type of expediency with regard to great culture that he denounces as leftist opportunism. Nonetheless, Adams's and Békés's objectives are ultimately the same. Whether right-leaning cultural dominance is to be constructed anew (Békés), or restored from the past (Adams), both strategies amount to the same defensive formation: circling the wagons against liberal and leftist adversaries. Békés makes this siege mentality explicit by invoking, of all people, Malcolm X: "only a fool would let their enemy teach their children," his spin on the revolutionary Black leader being that "a right-wing regime is homeless in a liberal era."[6] Less outwardly sectarian, Adams's approach is rooted in place-based identity politics, which is perhaps the most blatant and apolitical consequence of total capitalist aestheticization.

ANYWHERES VERSUS SOMEWHERES

For his part, Adams casts aspersions on "anywheres," a term he borrows from British New Labour academic David Goodhart's book *The Road to Somewhere: The Populist Revolt and the Future of Politics*.[7] Anywheres are individuals who, as Adams interprets Goodhart, have "no strong attachment to place, people or national history and view themselves as internationalists and world citizens."[8] Accordingly, *anywheres* are the perpetrators and beneficiaries of artivism. They stand opposite *somewheres*, who have "a firm attachment to regional community and locale."[9] A far more rigorous approach to the problem of location and belonging is made by urban scholar Cindi Katz, who asserts that it is global capital that produces a condition of vagabondage that unsettles and makes destitute—socially but also materially—large segments of the world's population.[10] If so, then we could say that anywheres are far more somewhere in an ultracapitalist world than somewheres are with their fanciful notion of locality. Of course, things are seldom so elementary.

TANIA BRUGUERA AND THE CUBAN ART-STATE CONFLICT

With this framing in mind, let's take another look at artivism itself to get a clearer sense of what Adams objects to before returning to these conceptual inconsistencies regarding tactics and convictions. Many readers will likely associate the term *artivism* with Cuban artist Tania Bruguera, who did not invent the expression that combines the words *art* and *activism* but has used it to describe her own practice of performative protest aesthetics. Bruguera even named her para-institutional educational entity in Havana the Instituto de Artivismo Hannah Arendt, or INSTAR, describing its mission in 2016 as "a place where people's ideas can become civic actions."[11] In a Gramscian spirit, she adds that "the Institute proposes the need to think about civic education on the rights that every person possesses."[12]

The project operated openly in Cuba, although without official state recognition or permission, and was therefore subject to government surveillance and not-infrequent police intervention. In October 2021, following years of conflict, including intervals of house arrest for the artist and her circle, Bruguera negotiated with the Cuban government to leave the country for the US in exchange for the release of imprisoned artists and intellectuals.[13] She is now on the faculty at Harvard University. Writing about Bruguera's exit, Adams describes this incident as an anywhere being ejected by somewhere: "It is difficult not to interpret this episode as a socially conservative government identifying

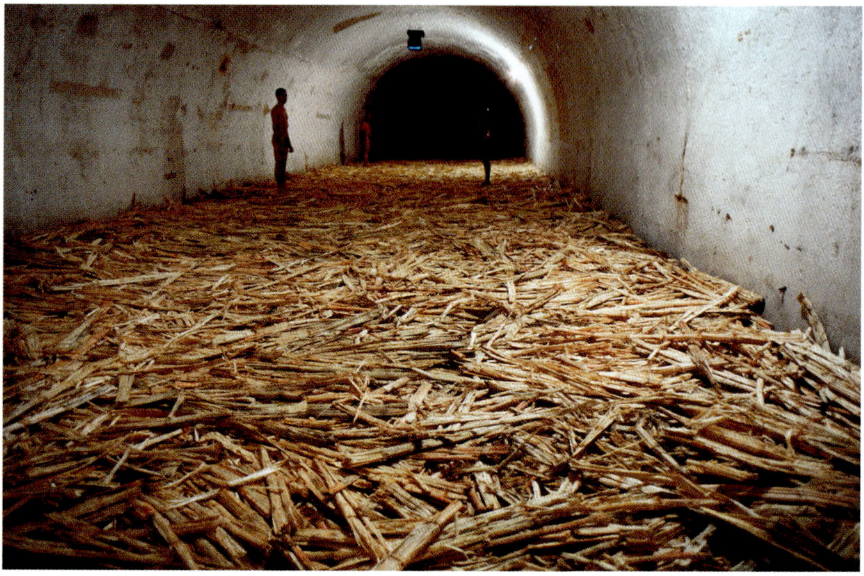

FIGURE 19

In Tania Bruguera's *Untitled* (Havana, 2000), visitors navigate a dark tunnel carpeted with sugarcane husks while Fidel Castro's image loops overhead from a vintage television, and four naked figures emerge from shadows. Cuban authorities shut down this claustrophobic installation within minutes of its debut at the 2000 Havana Biennial, marking the first of many confrontations Bruguera would have with the government before her final departure for the United States in 2021. Image courtesy of the artist.

subversion of an artivist promoter of globalist values and removing her from the country."[14]

If a country that defines itself as socialist and therefore is linked with the tradition of international working-class solidarity across lines of nationalism, race, and gender is also conservative and antiglobalist, then what exactly are the "globalist values" that Adams rejects? His inventory lists the "taming [of] free-market capitalism, curbing the unpredictability of democracy (however limited), governance by experts and reducing personal freedom in a system of surveillance, nudge and control—all in the name of environmental sustainability."[15] Adams adds that these are goals of "super-wealthy globalists, international firms, NGOs and civil servants."[16] We will see that there is a fine line, or perhaps none whatsoever, separating these neoliberal capitalist shortcomings from capitalism per se.

Such reasoning raises a set of provocative questions about the ideological standpoint of the new right in general. First, in terms of cultural outlook, can one truthfully conjoin free-market capitalism to romanticism in the way Adams circuitously is attempting through his critique of contemporary art museums? Second, politically speaking, is it possible to fuse an untamed free-market libertarianism with the strictures required by patriotic national identity, presumably possessed by somewheres? And finally, does such territorial exclusivity tip at some point into ethnonativism?

THE PARADOX OF FREE-MARKET ULTRANATIONALISM

The answer in the era of the Unpresent is yes to all three. Certainly, Trump's tariff wars, for example, might appear retrograde in light of the global economic interconnectedness that neoliberalism forged over the decades. However, one could say he is attempting to bolster capitalism in one nation, perhaps akin to Stalin's goal of establishing socialism in one country (the Soviet Union), which some have argued transformed the USSR's economy into a form of state capitalism. Comparably, the mythos of the eccentric, anticonventional artistic genius championed by romanticism serves the right today as a legitimating reason for conserving "timeless" masterpieces while militating against those who demote such everlasting value by claiming "therapy, community work, social outreach, education and advocacy" as legitimate forms of artistic practices.[17] And though I doubt it is Adams's intention, we can see how animosity toward globalists and anywheres slides swiftly into xenophobic rhetoric or worse.

But the real culprit, Adams tells us, is the arrogant support by the postwar UK's Arts Council for avant-garde art that defied, if not mocked, the taste of taxpayers. It was this "promotion of globalism, with palpable contempt for the general population," that finally led to museums' patronizing "minorities-as-minorities" in recent years.[18] Adams's primary critical focus, therefore, is to denounce the way the liberal administrative class (as he terms it) has come to dominate museums and other art institutions. But while he finds liberalism objectionable, it is the way that it has allowed itself to deviate toward progressive, leftist ends that above all stokes his indignation. However, considering the left's ardent critique of the same liberal establishment, as we explored in the previous chapter, Adams is forced to devise a collusive mechanism of a *party within a party*, or entryism, to explain the left's scheming connivance. It is a hallucinatory confabulation worthy of the faultiest AI systems insofar as it offers him a far too convenient affirmation for his own accusatory polemics and further proof that artivism is ultimately not art but anti-art. As a consequence, Adams is pulled ever further toward the conspiratorial world of the alt-right, even though he distances his own conservatism from it without a hint of irony, let alone the type of reactionary satire found on platforms such as BitChute, Rumble, or 4chan/8chan. In her book about conspiracy culture, art historian and theorist Larne Abse Gogarty seemingly peers wryly over Adams's shoulder when she writes: "the mobilization of irony by the contemporary far right has two primary functions . . . it allows for a disavowal of responsibility, and secondly, it enables entryism."[19]

ENTRYISM AND THE LEFTIST CULTURAL TAKEOVER CONSPIRACY

Drawing on the somewhat archaic concept of *entryism* in which an organized political movement or party infiltrates its opponents, Adams traces what he sees as the gradual takeover of the tolerant and pluralistic liberal high art world by sectarian Marxist-feminist-environmentalist elites. But in a twist, the ousted professional museum managers decide to embrace their own usurpers because it entitles them to "bask in artivist environments, attend the private views, donate and congratulate themselves at these leftist-led excoriations."[20] Entryism was first proposed by Leon Trotsky in the mid-1930s at a time when establishing a united front between liberals and Marxists against fascism was of prime concern. In another twist, what is perhaps the most recent use of entryism was not carried out by leftists but by UK Conservative leaders. In 2015, the Tories called for their members to vote for Labour Party candidate Jeremy Corbyn on the assumption that should the left-wing contender be elected leader, Labour would then fail in the general election.[21]

Adams's entryist scenario is so much larger and more clandestine that it seems almost like a plot in *Game of Thrones* or John Carpenter's cult movie *They Live*. Things only get more fanciful as Adams unmasks a virtual cult of leftist secularism in which the museum is transformed into a space for paganistic, orgiastic, and decidedly matriarchal artivist rituals that "may include shedding of blood; the feminist performance may involve nudity. Attendees are moved to tears or reduced to silence. The tribal bond is reaffirmed through observance, acts of charity and communal activity under the guidance of the artivist-shaman-priestess."[22] It is as though a coven of succubi have furtively drained art not only of its innocent delight in truth and beauty, but also of its manly detachment from emotion.

At other times, it is the legacy of the Russian avant-garde that Adams blames for the corruption of artivism, describing essentially the early Soviet Proletkult or Proletarian Cultural movement (1917 to circa 1921/1923) in the most withering terms. According to Adams, postrevolutionary artists were compelled to produce not real art but a plethora of pro-socialist utilitarian products including "pictures, murals, sculpture, theatre sets, posters, fabrics, clothing, furniture, crockery, buildings and every material component of a new world."[23] This period has had an effect on contemporary artists, Adams argues accurately: " blurring boundaries between fields and without recognition of any such being as a private person, early Soviet art set the template for the political zealotry of artivism in later periods."[24]

surrendering our historical museums. . . . It is the revival of this approach which is at the core of an alternative artivism, one that generates great lasting art."[28] Two synopsizing remarks are in order regarding this statement as well as Adams's broader take on activist art, or artivism. The first is that his proposal for building an alternative institutional framework closely resembles proposals by the left that he clearly detests, including my own "artivist" engagement in the 1980s with the New York City collective Political Art Documentation/Distribution (PAD/D). In a spirit similar to that of Adams, the group declared that it "cannot serve as a means of advancement within the art world structure of museums and galleries. Rather, we have to develop new forms of distribution economy as well as art."[29]

Nothing is terribly surprising here. Whenever self-organized social groups are excluded from visibility or are denied financial resources within the mainstream, they typically develop independent networks of mutual support for circulating ideas, exchanging labor, and sharing opportunities for exhibiting or performing work. Perhaps more than anyone else, theorist Marco Baravalle has developed ways of analyzing the formation and politics of "alter-institutions" generated by artists and activists. Conspicuously acknowledging their own speculative existence, he notes that they operate "in juxtaposition to the 'real,'" while taking clear advantage of this gap space in between reality and world-building invention (which also might be thought of as a gap in time).[30] What is different between Adams's approach and that of the left is his assertion that established "historical" cultural institutions are the right's ancestral patrimony; they belong, in other words, to *somewheres*, not to internationalist *anywheres*. In this case, they also belong to a certain nativist, ethnonationalist British demographic.

Second, he is certainly right to insist that museums are resources for the populace. The problem lies in what part of the population has access to such institutions. And in fairness, until quite recently the left has chiefly viewed high art, much as has the mainstream art world, as an Anglo-European affair, criticizing its historical alignment with the elite, anti-plebeian values of ruling monarchs, aristocrats, and clergy. At the same time, other facets of the left have approached this same legacy in a conflicted, even schizoid manner. Let me unpack this.

Recall that it was the radical bourgeois French revolutionaries who appropriated the Louvre as a secular treasure for all citizens. More ironic for Adams's position is that over 120 years later Lenin reclaimed tsarist Russia's artistic property for the newly emancipated proletariat (even if he also sought to sell the Hermitage museum's holdings to support early Soviet industrialization, with most actual deaccessioning taking place later under Stalin). Similar to Adams, Lenin also criticized the Proletkult and other Russian avant-garde art movements as both opportunistic and intellectually elitist. Unlike Adams, however, Lenin considered such experimentalism a distraction from the immediate task of building socialism after 1917. Ever since the early twenty-first century, leftists have been split over what constitutes a genuine *people's* art of the working classes. Is it the inheritance of centuries-old high art, which must be preserved and exhibited in secular museums for all of the liberated masses, or is it more expedient and ephemeral forms of protest culture generated by radical social movements and typically displayed at rallies, on the streets, or in alternative cultural centers maintained by dissidents, labor unions, universities, and so forth?

The high art tradition that Adams defends is still revered by many on the left and for a variety of reasons, including the ambition to make "great" art accessible to the proletariat while affirming a secular vision of society. Art is also valued for its historical significance and the way it represents the past, even if distorted by class prejudices and other ideological filters. And finally, for many on the left, some works of art manage to portray humanity's higher, nonmonetary aspirations. Notably, politically progressive detractors of socially engaged artivism, such as Claire Bishop, place social value on the aesthetic judgment of artistic form, without ever defaulting to the restorative and conservative cultural position as Adams does. This may explain why many on the political left perceive artivism, protest culture, activist art, and so forth as primarily necessary for carrying out the grinding labor of directly supporting social change, but not as a true artistic pursuit. Artivism's material output can easily be discarded after use, or at best gathered into an archive. Needless to point out, it is just this type of bifurcated thinking, veering back and forth between artistic activism and a "higher" artistic calling, that this book and most of my own writing on art has sought to challenge and to complicate.

THE IMPROBABILITY OF RIGHT-WING ARTIVISM

Would it not be more accurate to contend, as Adams himself does at times, that, however art is defined or distinguished, its legacy embodies a sphere of ideological dispute that is continually being fought over under ever-changing circumstances? And is not Adams's own ontologizing of high art in virtually Neoplatonic terms, therefore, fundamentally flawed? After all, anything that has the power to fulfill our yearning for harmonious truth and beauty is, by definition, immune to actual, material historical conditions and therefore incapable of being weaponized, to use the popular argot, in a bid to overpower one's political or cultural adversaries. And yet that is exactly what has emerged on both the left and right today. As I proposed in chapter 1, if the growing visibility of MAGA and the nationalist right is, as it seems, an inevitable consequence of dark matter's illumination, then this emergence is itself a product of neoliberalism's voracious enclosure of life. Even practices claiming avant-garde transgression cannot escape this dynamic.

This is why when Adams pensively ponders, "would right-wing artivism be feasible,"[31] he inadvertently acknowledges that any winning anti-leftist strategy demands recognizing the unrestrained and immoderate eruption of visual production by the populist right that is anything but enduring, beautiful, or truthful. Instead, MAGA culture, in its profuse populist mode, manifests as Pepe the Frog gifs, bored-ape NFTs, Proud Boy logos sporting Trump's "stand back, stand by" orders to his Freikorps-like street gangs, and let's not forget the unending and unctuous AI-generated deep-fake animations in which the American president transforms into a golden-hued, liberal-slaying superhero. There is also the love-hate relationship with celebrity culture, such as the right denouncing Hollywood liberals as elites while elevating other celebrity figures who support the MAGA cause. Similarly, Trump's critique of mainstream media as "fake news" merely accompanies his sensationalist disinformation campaigns dispensed via an alternative-right media ecosystem that is moving ever closer to mainstream legitimation. These contradictions are not incidental to Adams's critique; they are constitutive of it, just as they constitute MAGA and its ilk as the contemporary, retro-vanguard movement of the Unpresent.

WHEN HIGH CULTURE BECOMES BARE CULTURE

The conundrum continues as Adams writes that "video-sharing, crypto-currency and peer-to-peer decentralized networks—plus crowdfunding—could all be used to grow counter-establishment artivist networks" to do battle with "a progressive elite in control of state resources and mass media."[32] This obvious 180-degree turn from art as truth and beauty forces Adams to qualify his overall position by assuring readers that "the conservative and reactionary would use artivism purely instrumentally because they would not consider [such] actions to be art."[33] Even if Adams was himself capable of actualizing such a paradoxical position, it is unlikely that other forces of the new nationalist right would be capable of doing so. Thus, the entire critical edifice of *Artivism* becomes compromised as the author's primary argument against left artivism is rendered negotiable.

And yet beneath it all, do we not also sense that Adams, perhaps sub rosa, wishes to see the restoration of high art conservatism as the next avant-garde? Even if that means looking the other way when confronted with the flood of aesthetically dubious right-wing memes, merch, gifs, and animations? He cannot overtly admit this because his theory of cultural causality is boxed in to such a degree that for him all avant-gardism is at best "a masterful elite action."[34] By contrast, the Hungarian theorist Békés understands far more clearly what is required to achieve cultural domination, and states it in more blatant, Machiavellian terms. Békés has no problem lecturing fellow nationalist-right actors, traditionalists and populists alike, about the need to establish an ultraconservative culture "by any means necessary."[35]

What Adams refuses to confront is the role of the marketplace and its assault on his own ideals of artistic authenticity. He does not entertain that the culprit here is not leftist artivism but capital's relentless reduction of creative labor to exchangeable commodity, its colonization of every aspect of life that once stood outside the production of exchange value. Even when he stumbles into a confrontation with this predicament, he uses it only to confirm his own enmity toward left opportunism by pointing out that "maintaining an anti-capitalist stance requires the support of an advanced capitalist economy with surplus money reallocated through taxation to social goods in a generous and self-critical public-arts system."[36] Rather than interrogating the significant paradoxes his exposition has disclosed, we find a stern rebuke against artivists who don't understand that "without capitalism, artivism would not exist."[37] Seldom have truer words been expressed, but not only for or even primarily for the reasons he thinks. Most probably, all the tensions outlined above will eventually reveal themselves as larger expanding ruptures within the new right's ideological power structure, some of which have emerged already in late 2025 over the release of the Epstein files and extending subsidies for the Affordable Care Act (though, notably, no major news outlet has addressed these fracturing issues in the same piece).[38] Therefore, while we await the ultimate MAGA breakdown as just one more casualty of the Unpresent, let us not forget Andrew Breitbart's tin-pot doctrine: all politics is downstream from culture.[39]

INTERLUDE

A POST-AVANT-GARDE MONTAGE

Key:

- **Bold text: excerpts from avant-garde art manifestos.**
- [Bracketed and roman text: dialogue from January 6, 2021, taken from Parler's video archive.]
- *Italicized text: notes on "decolonizing" the narrative of the artistic avant-garde.*

"Let's be off! See there the Earth's very first dawn!" (Futurism, 1909)[1]

[Early in the day:] "Hold the line."

"You're going to lose your country; it's your last chance."

"Stop the Steal, 1776!"[2]

The very term avant-garde *was first used by a French military newspaper to defend the postrevolutionary Jacobin Reign of Terror in 1794, before it was repurposed by socialist philosopher Count Henri de Saint-Simon some thirty years later, the same year as his death in 1825. According to David Cottington, Saint-Simon believed that artists, along with industrialists and scientists, were tasked with realizing a new socialist society in which the unleashed engine of capitalism worked for humankind, rather than exploiting the majority of its population for the private accumulation of a few. Saint-Simon's follower Benjamin Olinde Rodrigues put it this way: "It is we artists who will serve as your vanguard; the power of the arts is indeed most immediate . . . we address ourselves to man's imagination and to his sentiments. We therefore ought always to exert the most lively and decisive action. . . . This is the duty of artists, this their mission."*[3]

New York 2044

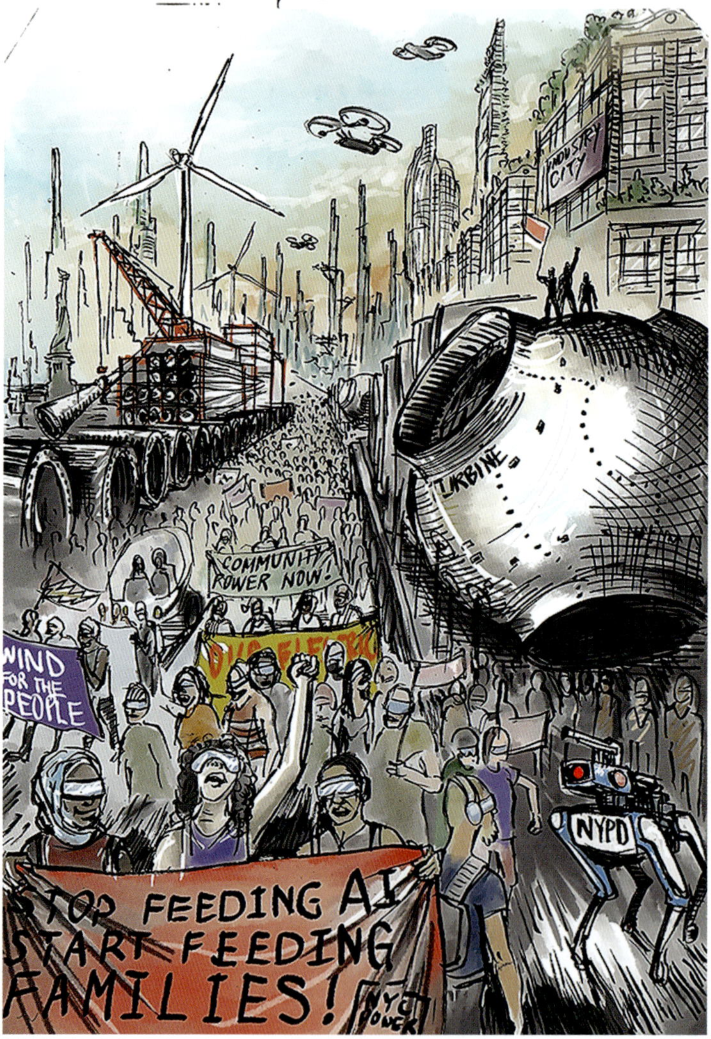

"With our Vortex the Present is the only active thing." (Vorticism, 1914)[4]

[Early in the day:] "Let us in, let us in."

"USA USA USA USA."

"I want my fucking flag back."[5]

These ideas about the artist as "the man of imagination" were stimulated, so writes Donald Drew Egbert, by such Enlightenment thinkers as Jean Jacques Rousseau and the early German romantics.[6] *However, after his demise, Saint-Simon's followers sought to realize this marriage of art and science in the newly purloined French colony of Algeria. And it is here, argues Osama Abi-Mershed, that the "Occident and the Orient" were supposed to meet and give birth to an artist-driven, vanguardist "modern society: technological and industrial in its economic enterprises; peaceful and spiritual in its sociopolitical relations."*[7]

"The future is behind us." (Rayonism, 1913)[8]

[Around 2:15, a young man and young woman have a break-up while storming the Capitol.] He says to her: "[I] tried to take care of you." She replies, "You said you cared about me and would protect me." Him: "I will, I'll give you the tools." Her: "There is only so much you I can do when you say no." Him: "I still love you." Her: "I don't love you?" Him: "You don't love me!" [A breakthrough

FIGURE 21

A page from Noah Fischer's graphic novel *New York 2044* reimagines the city through speculative graphic journalism, presenting a utopian future where affordable green housing flourishes and inequality has dramatically narrowed. Created through interviews with activists and community organizers, Fischer's retro-futuristic newspaper series transforms present-day struggles into joyful visions of possibility, distributing hope through public spaces while acknowledging familiar urban challenges and paradoxes that persist even in this optimistic tomorrow. Offset and digital, 2024. Courtesy of the artist and MORE ART Inc.

takes place at the front line and is followed by excited shouting as the crowd steps into the Capitol].[9]

Needless to say, the outcome was less than utopian. Early, idealistic policies proposed by followers of Saint-Simon involving modernization and ethnic absorption, whereby Arab customs would naturally be abandoned for "superior" European values, gave way in 1865 to the French proposing that Africa's Muslims could apply for citizenship on the condition "they admit the inferiority of their customs and institutions."[10]

"Let each man proclaim: there is a great negative work of destruction to be accomplished." (Dada, 1918)[11]

[Throughout the day:] "Drag 'em out."

"Where are the fucking traitors?"

"Do not hurt the cops."[12]

We could say that this facet of the avant-garde's promise to the future failed even before it started, though defeat did not prevent artists from repeatedly attempting to realize art's utopian aspirations or desire to liberate social agency from unfreedom. Perhaps the seemingly unattainable character of this quest is also precisely its attraction. Regardless, the dream of historical agency that Martha Rosler attributes to the artistic imagination also possibly provides a means of navigating the bends, twists, and cul-de-sacs of the surplus archive and its overlooked provinces of nonreflective dark matter.[13]

"[The highest art] has been visibly shattered by the explosions of last week, which is forever trying to collect its limbs after yesterday's crash." (Dada, 1918)[14]

[Before breaking in to the Capitol, first man, possibly John Sullivan, shouting:] "There's so many people, let's GO, this shit's ours." [A different man? (unclear):] "This shit's ours." [First man:] "Fuck yeah!" [Second man:] "I can't believe this is reality—we accomplished this shit . . . we accomplished this shit together." [First man:] "Fuck yeah—" [voice breaking with emotion] "this is fucking history . . . we're all part of this fucking history." [Loud whooping and yelling].[15]

Apart from the 1886 "Symbolist Manifesto," all of the most highly recognized proclamations about new and radical artistic movements surfaced in the first two decades of the twentieth century. This includes cubism (1912), vorticism

(1914), Dadaism (1916, Hugo Ball; and 1918, Tristan Tzara and, separately, Richard Huelsenbeck), De Stijl (1918), constructivism ("Realist Manifesto," 1920), and surrealism (1924), though first and perhaps most significantly of all came futurism (1909). Nonetheless, thanks to a wave of new decolonial scholars, it is becoming increasingly clear that not only did the influence of these early European avant-garde movements spread quickly to non-European (and sometimes nonmasculinist) movements, but influence also flowed the other way around.

"We are already outstripping one another." (Suprematism, 1919)[16]
[Afternoon:] "Mike Pence in the ditch!"
"Whose house? Our House!"
"Let's go, let's go, let's go, let's go."[17]

Jill Richards states that "in the early decades of the twentieth century, avant-garde and women's rights movements were in much closer contact [with the] . . . socialist international that financed the distribution of radical newspapers, journals, and pamphlets across the Atlantic."[18] *Earlier still, the first use of the term* modernism *was not in Europe; it was coined by Nicaraguan poet Rubén Darío in the late 1880s.* Modernismo *was a Spanish-language literary phenomenon throughout late nineteenth- and early twentieth-century Latin America, including El Salvador, Mexico, and Cuba in particular. Strikingly, we also find here an early connection between artistic innovation and political activism and rebellion. Darío's autobiography briefly recalls an incident from the cusp of the Mexican Revolution in which stones were thrown at the house of the Spanish authorities. Later the poet comments that this was "the first thunder of the revolution that brought the dethronement [of Mexican dictator Porfirio Díaz]."*[19]

"We are radical. We revolutionize/make revolution." ("Mavo Manifesto," 1923)[20]
[Mid-afternoon, man watching action:]
"They're climbing up the wall!"
"Let's go you, you guys are savage!"
"Let's fucking go!"
"Holy shit, they're bad as fuck."[21]

"Thunder" is certainly one way to describe Filippo Tommaso Marinetti's startling 1909 "Manifesto of Futurism," simultaneously published in France, Italy, and

Romania and allegedly dropped as leaflets from airplanes over Milan as if in anticipation of the imminent aerial warfare Germany, Italy, and Spain would use against urban populations.[22] *Marinetti vowed to "demolish museums and libraries, fight morality, feminism and all opportunist and utilitarian cowardice," while declaring that racing cars and "machine-gun fire [are] more beautiful than the [Hellenistic sculpture] Victory of Samothrace."*[23] *Notable too, is that excerpts from Marinetti's manifesto and news of futurism already appeared in the 1909 St. Petersburg newspaper* Evening *(*Вечер*), and its influence quickly spread to the Arabic world via Egypt, the author's place of birth. Nevertheless, as recent scholarship demonstrates, the manifesto's demand to completely and violently sweep away the past was strangely tangled up in a fascination with "nonmodernist" cultures and bodies, including those of Arabs, Africans, African Americans, and Native Americans, not to forget Silicon Valley tech bro Marc Andreessen's invocation of Marinetti's proto-fascist manifesto in his own Techo-Optimist Manifesto from 2023.*[24]

"MECHANIZATION has revolutionized the world . . . has established the most profound change humanity has known." ("Yellow Manifesto," 1928)[25]

[Mid-afternoon, inside Capitol building:] "I never thought I would live to see this shit."

[Woman staring in awe:] "Amazing."

[Man filming her:] "Put your mask on. I don't want them to see you."

[Other trespassers:] "We are in the halls of Congress." "We don't want war but we're prepared to fight for our liberty." "Hold the Line." "They're gassing us all right now." "We're in, We're in."

[2:37: Man grabs telephone receiver and miming for the camera demands to speak with Pelosi:] "We are coming for her and also for Pence the traitor."[26] [He then carefully hangs up.]

Warsaw-based theorist Przemysław Strożek describes how avant-garde movements including constructivism, Dadaism, and Italian futurism embraced African-American jazz as well as the cakewalk, a dance originating among US plantation slaves featured at the club Nouveau Cirque in 1902 Paris and soon to become a sensation in Europe.[27] *But above all, it is futurism that most clearly exhibits a complex reciprocity between Eurocentric beliefs and all those other populations whom White culture sought to colonize, eradicate, or, curiously, at other times emulate. "It is this passionate love of Reality that makes us prefer the American cake-walk to hearing the Valkyrie," the futurist painter and sculptor Umberto Boccioni insisted in 1914.*[28] *Meanwhile, the 1924 "Manifesto of Futurist Music" cited African American jazz as a primary model, while the 1912 "Manifesto of a Futurist Woman" proposed to skeptics that "if you don't like this, you should have your weakly sentimental head split open by an Apache-dancing tramp with a pistol."*[29]

"The abolition of pasta will liberate Italy from the costly burden of foreign grain and will work in favor of the Italian rice industry." ("Manifesto of Futurist Cuisine," 1930)[30]

[Around 2:42 inside Capitol Chamber:] "They're kicking the door in—they're going in."

[Inside the Chamber:] "Where'd she go?—Treason, treason, treason, treason!"

[A woman behind a man in helmet and military gear:] "We're in the fucking Capitol, bro."

[Man on bullhorn:] "Our tax money paid their salaries, freaking 40K dollars of furniture in their offices, and we have families starving in the street!"

[After being pepper-sprayed inside Capitol, a man shouts:] "This is insane . . . this is insane!"

"If this makes me lose my reputation, I don't care—talk is cheap—I don't see any teachers here—I am doing this for my daughter." [All the while, "Stop the Steal" and "USA, USA, USA" are repeatedly being chanted in background].[31]

Marinetti was himself born in northern Africa in the French colony of Alexandria, Egypt. Whatever ambivalence the futurists expressed toward Africa, Africans, and African American culture, the futurists roundly denounced Blacks and Jews following Mussolini's 1938 enactment of anti-Semitic pro-Aryan laws in alignment with his Nazi German allies. Much more than hints of bigotry, however, were present from the movement's beginning, including the "Futurist Manifesto," in which the poet compares a muddy ditch to the breast of his African wetnurse. His novel Mafarka le futuriste, *which was completed the same year, was similarly misogynist, as well as pro-colonialist and explicitly racist. Thus, for the Italian futurists, a certain allure in non-white culture always kept company with a virulent racism regarding "skin color" and prejudices about "African roots," which involved concepts of "deformation" and "otherness," reflecting the politics of Italian colonization at the time.*[32]

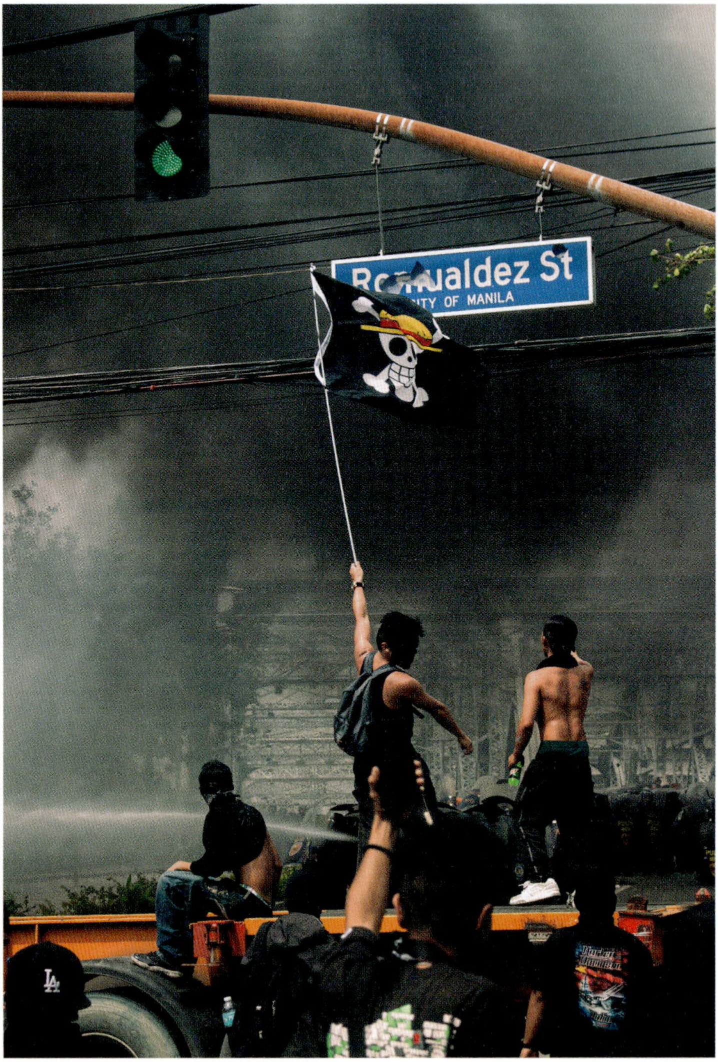

FIGURE 22

Gen Z protesters wave the One Piece flag during demonstrations at Ayala Bridge, Manila, Philippines, September 21, 2025. Photo: Cyberneticboylol, CC BY-SA 4.0, via Wikimedia Commons.

"Architecture and war are not incompatible. Architecture is war. War is architecture." (Lebbeus Woods, "Manifesto," 1993)[33]

[Around 2:53: Man in blue Trump hat and sunglasses:] "We have taken the Capitol . . . it is ours now . . . we will see which side the military are on!"

[A giant flag is unfolded and crowd is singing "The Star-Spangled Banner" while pledging allegiance with hands over their hearts.]

[The intruders are videotaping the inside of the rotunda while milling about. Many hold out cell phone cameras, narrating and uploading documentation to the Parler website. They now appear as merely a group of tourists who are startled to be inside the prize they violently acquired, gawking at the building's architecture and art.]

[A man talking into his phone:] "Hi, I'm live at the Capitol, where we have overtaken the building and I am wondering if the media hears us now. I don't see any media . . . the Proud Boys are here . . . There is no Antifa . . . Do you hear us now?"[34]

Italian futurism's involvement with Mussolini's Fascism did not go unnoticed or unopposed by other vanguard art movements. This included André Breton's procommunist and antifascist surrealist movement from the early 1920s, and Mayakovsky's anti-imperialist poetry reading during his 1925 trip to the US, Mexico, and Cuba. Later, Harlem Renaissance poet Langston Hughes translates Vladimir Mayakovsky's writings into English during his own journey to Moscow in 1932.[35] *In the late 1930s, the group Art et Liberté was founded in Marinetti's birth country of Egypt. The largely but not exclusively surrealist-inspired faction's Nazi-mocking manifesto "Long Live Degenerate Art" denounces religious, racist, and nationalist prejudices that "make up the tyranny of certain individuals who, drunk on their own temporary omniscience, seek to subjugate the destiny of the work of art," which is undoubtedly a reference to Marinetti himself.*[36]

"The movie was dead and called for resurrection." (Dogme 95, 1995)[37]

[Around 3:07: Rioters exit the building to cheers of "way to go," "way to go."]

[Minutes later: A woman holding a flagpole over the crowd below smiles with her tongue thrust out at a nearby cameraperson.]

[Emergency alert alarms go off on several phones as a man explains:] "it's a Mexican stand-off and the National Guard are being called in. [His shaky camera sweeps the crowd. A woman speaks in Spanish then in English:] "The Mayor just gave us a curfew." [The man responds:] "They also told us not to storm the Capitol." [Both he and the woman chuckle, "hehehe."][38]

All in all, many lesser-known, non- or openly anti-European cultural movements flourished alongside those of the better-known vanguard, including the Bengal School of Indian artists, who curiously sought to combine avant-garde and nationalist elements in order to forge a non-British cultural identity within the 1905 Swadeshi Movement. Likewise, Brazilian poet Oswald de Andrade's 1928 "Manifesto Antropófago" encouraged artists "to devour European culture, digest it, and transform it into something Brazilian."[39] Some seven years later, the Martinique-born poet and intellectual Aimé Césaire co-founded the African Diasporic movement known as Négritude, calling on Black youth in 1935 to "[turn] its back on the tribe of the Old. The tribe of the Old says, 'assimilation.' We respond, resurrection!"[40]

"Stuckism embraces all that it denounces. We only denounce that which stops at the starting point—Stuckism starts at the stopping point!" ("The Stuckist Manifesto," 1999)[41]

[About 3:09: The Capitol police try to turn intruders back from going further upstairs by reasoning with them, while many insurgents walk about as if trying to find something to do, with chants of "Pelosi, come out" as the phone camera pans back and forth on a dense crowd.]

[We see cosplay as a large man dressed in a Nero outfit holds a flag while taking a selfie.]

[A man:] "Going in . . . well, I always wanted a tour of the Capitol—I didn't think it would be like this." [Different voice:] "We're in the motherfucking Capitol." [Police are seen walking around and not interacting with rioters.]

[Crowd:] "It's our fucking house." [A door is rushed and a woman exclaims:] "Hold the line!"

[Around 3:16: A woman proclaims:] "We have the Capitol . . . all the cops have gone home."[42]

Interdisciplinary scholar Mike Sell relates that right from the start, surrealism "took a collective stand against French colonialism," supporting Morocco's anticolonial movement, while simultaneously helping foment the antifascist surrealism elsewhere.[43] Sell provides a rich chronicle of the less well-known non-European avant-garde, including Black surrealist factions that explicitly, often militantly rejected fascism, as well as also frequently denouncing capitalism. With roots in late nineteenth-century Black Marxist radicalism, but also in surrealism and the Harlem Renaissance, Césaire's contribution to the Négritude movement included co-founding the influential Caribbean-based journal Tropiques *(1941–1945), a short-lived Afro-surrealist publication co-edited with Suzanne Césaire and René Ménil with support from French surrealist founder André Breton, then living in Martinique along with anthropologist Claude Lévi-Strauss and Afro-Cuban painter Wilfredo Lam. Before the island was liberated by the Free French Resistance, the local pro-Nazi Vichy government sought to shut down* Tropiques *over its antifascist politics.*[44]

"The Futurist is dead. Of what? Of DADA. A Young girl commits suicide. Because of What? DADA. The spirits are telephoned. Who invented it? DADA. Someone walks on your feet. It's DADA." (Dadaism, 1921)[45]

[Around 3:21:] "They shot a girl (Ashli Babbitt) . . . the fucking Capitol police. [A raspy-voiced man on Capitol steps, camera swinging from him to crowd and back again:] "Then they say, 'Do you want to be next?'"

[Gesturing toward police:] "Take their shields, take their shields." [A group of insurgents yank plastic shields away from two police on the steps outside of the Capitol. While some cheer, others make an effort to protect cops.]

[A young man reviews video of his own day at the Capitol with another insurrectionist:] "Dude, you gotta check this out." "Look at the woman." [Someone passing by then tells him despairingly that a "girl" was shot in the neck.]

[3:25: Man dressed as "QAnon Shaman" (Jacob Chansley) slowly descends the Capitol steps with US flag in hand before stopping to howl "Freedom!" as others then join in.][46]

Both Aimé and Suzanne Césaire were influenced by an even earlier, 1932 Martinique-based student journal Légitime Défense *co-founded by "Black surrealist" Étienne Léro and immediately banned on the island after just one impassioned issue.*[47] *Léro's editorial "Légitime Défense Manifesto" references the notorious trial of the Scottsboro Boys, nine Black teens falsely accused of raping two white women in Alabama, with their defense supported by the international communist movement.* Légitime Défense *merged surrealist bliss with anticapitalist militancy, a combination often encountered in post-World War II activist art, including that of the Situationist International. As Léro wrote at the time, his publication was aimed "especially at young blacks, this is because we believe that they especially have had to suffer from capitalism (outside Africa, witness Scottsboro) and that they seem to offer, in that they have a materially higher potential for revolt and for joy."*[48]

"I have destroyed the ring of the horizon and got out of the circle of objects, the horizon ring that has imprisoned the artist and the forms of nature." ("Suprematist Manifesto," 1915)[49]

[Around 3:27: A woman who left before the occupation began is speaking into her phone as she walks:] "We are almost at our hotel." "We have no idea what happened at the Capitol, but I am going to tell you my impression based on what I saw today." [She gestures emphatically:] "There were several infiltrations by Antifa dressed-up as MAGA. That is who stormed the Capitol . . . this was all set up to make us look bad, it was not patriots."

[Minutes later: Someone in large crowd holds up a bust of Trump in front of a phalanx of police standing between protesters and the Capitol:] "Make a hole, the cops are leaving."[50]

Césaire also influenced many other artists, activists, and thinkers to come, including such understudied factions as the Chicago Surrealist Group, cofounded by Penelope and Franklin Rosemont, Robert Green, and others in the mid-1960s. The Chicago group developed links with Students for a Democratic Society (SDS) and the International Workers of the World (IWW or Wobblies). Their avowed leftist, pro-Black cultural focus linked up with the Situationists as much as with Afro-surrealism, Frantz Fanon, W. E. B. Du Bois, and C. L. R. James. A 1998 issue of the group's ironically titled Race Traitor *journal was dedicated to "Surrealism: Revolution Against Whiteness."*[51]

"Time and Space died yesterday." "Divert the canals so they can flood the museums!" (Futurism, 1909)[52]

[Around 3:53: A man with black bandana spotted with yellow stars sniffs:] "Uugha, the tear gas was real, and that ain't no shit." [Eyes bulging, his phone camera swings around to show the Capitol building behind him.]

[4:04: A man (possibly off-duty police?) speaks instructionally into his phone:] "Alright guys, we are at the Capitol right now; we're going to go back in. I'm the only one with a shield so I don't know why anyone did not bring a shield, but I brought one just in case they start shooting. Make sure if you ever take over the Capitol or any big place, ah, make sure to bring a shield. You can't get one except at the cop's hands. Alright guys, thanks for watching."[53]

"These artists are destroyers, materialists, and sensualists dealing with process directly. These artists are destructivists." (Rafael Montañez Ortiz, *Destructivism: A Manifesto*, 1962)[54]

[During the initial push into the Capitol:] "Has anybody got some water? Get me some water . . ."

"This is a revolution, motherfuckers, let's go."

[A different man's voice now:] "We're taking this shit."

"I need more water, I need more water." [All throughout this exchange, chants continue:] "USA, USA, USA, USA, USA, USA."

"I need more water."

"This is a revolution, let's take this shit . . . this shit's ours."

"Water, man . . . hey, gimme some water."

"I have no water, fuck."[55]

PART III

RESISTANCE

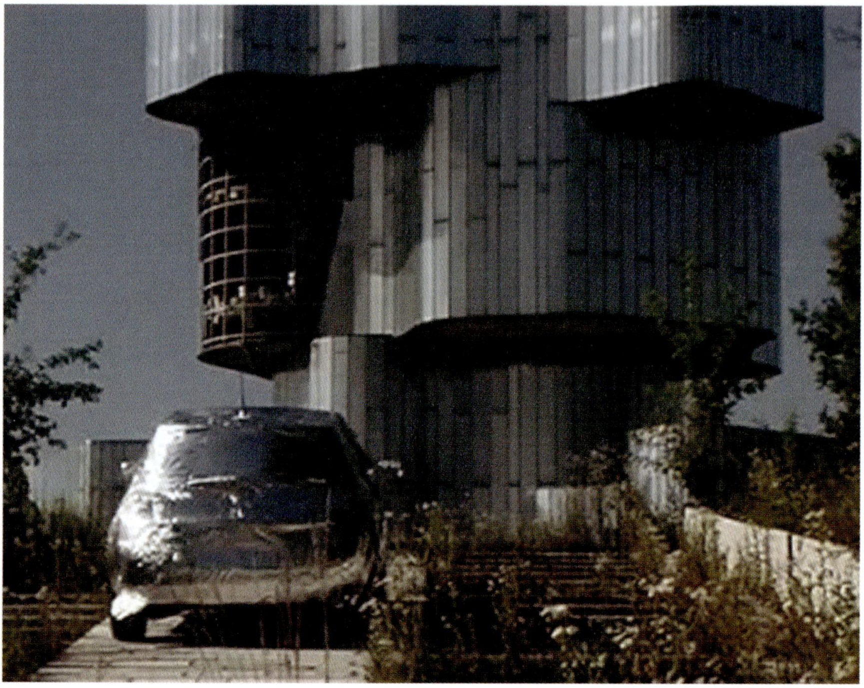

FIGURE 23

David Maljković, *Scene for a New Heritage*, 2004, still from a color video, Mini DV on DVD (4:33 min.). *Scene for a New Heritage* captures the Petrova Gora monument in Croatia, a decaying modernist memorial from Yugoslavia's socialist era. In this video still, a futuristic silver vehicle approaches the monument, suggesting a temporal collision between socialist utopian aspirations and postcommunist abandonment. The wild vegetation surrounding the structure emphasizes how this once-ideological landmark has been reclaimed by nature and recontextualized as a ruin. © David Maljković, courtesy of the artist and Sprüth Magers.

9

THE PHANTOM ARCHIVE

Raucous public pageants, banner drops, giant puppets, politicized street performances, protest art made for demonstrations, occupations, interventions, and picket lines, graphics or projections pasted to or lighting up urban walls, buildings, plazas, and spray-painted slogans, poems, warnings covering the broken plinths of toppled historical monuments: these festive yet serious engaged and activist art practices draw promiscuously upon an expansive range of previously enacted and imaginative cultural forms, tropes, deeds, and resources, often doing so unknowingly, as if receiving dispatches from some off-screen archive, and all the while doing so without regard for established notions of aesthetic autonomy, artistic reflexivity, or "advanced" artistic, avant-garde ideals. The possibilities of these dense and often tumultuous practices appear overwhelming for anyone in search of a clear and satisfactory means for interpreting or historicizing them, as we already encountered in chapter 6. But what if we focus less on specific outcomes, and instead turn our attention to *where* and *when* this exuberant repertoire of aesthetic possibilities springs forth? This is the overarching theme of this chapter, as well as more broadly of part III of this book. This question becomes especially urgent in our current moment when, as we've seen, the nationalist right has proven equally adept at drawing on aesthetic repertoires, such as the cosplay revolutionaries at the Capitol, folk-inflected bus shelters in Hungary, nostalgic invocations of 1776. If MAGA operates as our retro-vanguard, parasitically

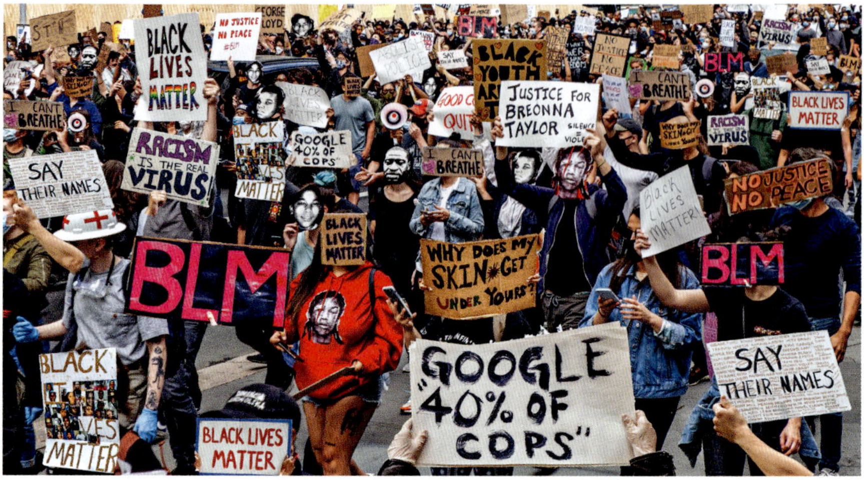

FIGURE 24

A Black Lives Matter protest in June 2020 captured by photographer Russ Rowland shows demonstrators holding handmade signs demanding justice for George Floyd and Breonna Taylor. Created for the Museum of the City of New York's participatory #ActivistNY campaign, Rowland's digitally altered image *Day 85: obfuscation experiment #3* addresses the ethical challenges of documenting protesters. Rather than blurring faces, and muting the power and emotion of the protest, Rowland mixed and replaced protesters' faces to protect their identities while preserving visual impact. The effect is as unsettling as it is conspicuous. Image courtesy of the artist.

feeding on the total aesthetic of neoliberal capitalism, then what distinguishes progressive engagement with the phantom archive from reactionary plundering of the past? The answer lies not in exclusive ownership of forms or tactics, but in their temporal orientation and reparative intent, raising one of the first questions that must be addressed at this point: Given the fragmented ephemerality of such activist art practices, can they also have any meaningful backstory?

DEFINING THE PHANTOM ARCHIVE: MATERIAL TRACES AND SPECTRAL TRANSMISSIONS

Surely anyone attempting to historicize these diverse activist art forms will quickly come to recognize that they constitute a phenomenon with no singular manifesto or specified aesthetic protocols, emerge from no official school, and have no generally accepted canon of great works or principal artists. Instead, these practices constitute a discontinuous overflowing archive, a fragmented and boisterous reservoir of past interventions, experiments, repetitions, and compromises, as well as minor victories and outright failures. For the sake of convenience, I will refer to it simply as a *phantom archive* that operates not as a static collection of things or information, but as a dark temporality or adjacent shadow time. Its access requires speculative processes of recovery, rearrangement, repair, and reactivation. We want to consider, therefore, the reparative practices of borrowing and repurposing as forming not only a haunted, overlapping space between contemporary activist and early avant-garde art practices, but a productive gap, one in which both materials and grand ideals are assembled through the processes of reuse and repair.

Furthermore, as a laundry list of forms involving the aesthetics of protest, such evident creative reworking does not belong solely to the world of credentialed, university-trained artists but is now—thanks to the total aesthetic of neoliberal capitalism—accessible for use by politically minded individuals on the left and the right. That is not to suggest that the contours of this archive remain invisible or intangible. On the contrary, its material traces abound. One need only attend a mass demonstration almost anywhere in the world to experience a cacophony of "slogans, art, symbols, slang, humor, graffiti, gestures, bodies, color, clothes, and objects," as described in books such as *The Aesthetics of Global Protest*.[1] The images, sounds, movements are derived from sources high and low, from iconic artworks such as Pablo Picasso's *Guernica*, to the amateur graphics of social movements. But as a formal collection, this largely ephemeral and performative material culture is limited to a few specialized physically maintained archives. It is also visible today online, because over the past few decades such content has appeared in numerous internet blogs, newsletters, shareable platforms, websites and other modes of DIY social media publishing. And yet, given the accelerating commercial, legal, and security-oriented circumscription of online content, it is the seemingly archaic material archives that are becoming the real backstop for accessing and reanimating protest aesthetics. This is perhaps why the keepers of Interference Archive in Brooklyn welcome physical contact with their shelves, boxes, and flat files teeming with posters, documents, newsletters, flyers, pamphlets, books, and so forth, never requiring visitors to slip on white cotton gloves or to replace their ink pens with small stubby pencils, as are the rules with other institutional collections.

THE HAUNTOLOGICAL NATURE OF ARCHIVES

But it is a different mode of contact with the phantom archive that interests us here. This apprehension is what makes its nature both material as well as spectral or phantasmagoric. For what is tangible is only partial. It serves more as the shadow practice or residuum of something dynamic and disruptive. It is the carcass of the archive, or the archive of the archive, if you will. And when artists draw upon this double repository, they sometimes encounter its visible and physical provinces including the materials, documents, images, recordings, and objects that make it up, as with Interference Archive, for example (see figure 25). But they might also encounter it more elusively while passing a wheat-pasted flyer in the street, or through an idea or cursory comment shared by another artist, as well as, of course, in the multitude of results from an online Google image search. In sum, the phantom archive is a doubled entity, existing simultaneously as tangible material collections and as intangible,

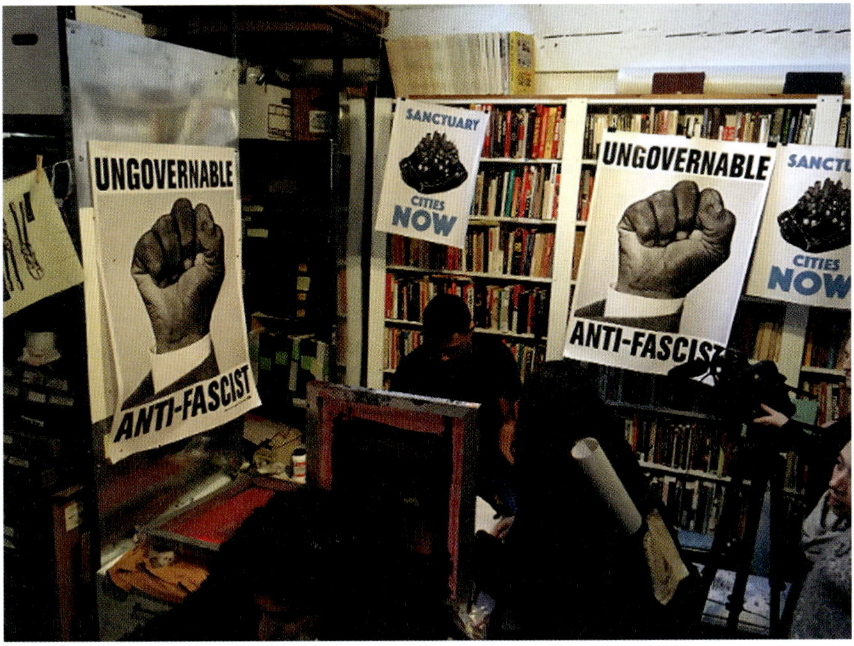

FIGURE 25

Founded in Brooklyn in 2011, Interference Archive preserves and activates the cultural artifacts of social movements. This volunteer-run organization houses over 10,000 items including posters, zines, and ephemera that document grassroots activism. Through exhibitions, workshops, and public programs, the archive illuminates how creative expression emerges directly from collective action rather than individual artistic virtuosity. Visitors are encouraged to discover unfamiliar materials and social movements purely through happenstance. Image courtesy of Interference Archive.

offstage, spectral presences, with all of its variegated and surplus possibilities spanning both the physical and the imaginary. It is, in a word, hauntological: Jacques Derrida's neologism for an unsettled obligation that may originate from the past, or the future, or both, but returns as an uncanny haunting of our now time.[2] Think of Marx and Engels's "specter" from the *Communist Manifesto*, or the way traditional notions of artistic autonomy continue to trouble our concept of high culture despite its relentless commercialization (recall the discussion of bare art in chapter 5). And while these hauntological obligations that shadow us from elsewhere are shaped by their origins in another time and place, they can only truly manifest in our present circumstances, for this is the only possible domain it can frequent. The hauntology of the Unpresent is, therefore, that of the phantom archive.

This is why to engage with the phantom archive of activist art is also to fundamentally disrupt established frameworks and expectations about art and aesthetics, as well as potentially politics and temporality itself as these typically appear in historical narratives. Building on Kim Charnley's characterization of activist art as a "glitch," the phantom archive operates as a coding error in the normative way art and art history function.[3] It also finds echoes in theorist Kuba Szreder's notion of artistic time machines, which focuses on the extreme multitasking required of artists in the contemporary context. Szreder describes the artistic time machine as organizing artistic labor circulation "into patterns of what we can call the speculative time complex, which remixes future, present and past," adding that "for precarious art workers, every passage from one project to another, every passing opportunity, every deadline and every application is a time machine that eradicates the present."[4] My emphasis on the conspicuous repair, reuse, and repurposing of time via the surplus possibilities of the archive might be thought of as the positive, dialectical corollary of Szreder's concept insofar as the socially engaged artist with similar intensity seeks to alter their own as well as our perception of historical events and their potential meaning. In this sense, it is a repurposing of artistic labor's ultrarapid circulation but for other purposes that are critical, even perhaps political. If recognizing this makes one both untimely and also contemporary, as Agamben tells us, following Nietzsche, then perhaps an entirely new definition of being present is the sense of being unpresent.[5]

By way of illustration, let me return to the experiential policies of Brooklyn's Interference Archive. These evoke the conviction that as we examine their collection of unguarded primary materials, we are not merely admiring the bones of the past but are tangibly and intellectually opening up the possibility of collaborating with the past. That is to say, we are collaborating with other, now already-gone seekers, pilgrims, and investigators who have left something undone for us to complete in our own time, or perhaps merely to work over and then to transfer again into the next time.

TEMPORAL COLLABORATION AND BENJAMIN'S COMMISSION

Theorist and filmmaker Jalal Toufic argues that no artist or intellectual is simply avant-garde or "ahead" of their time, but when a catastrophic crisis occurs, their work can undergo a temporal transformation, giving it a particular allure in the future. This crisis, or what Toufic calls a "surpassing disaster," acts to withdraw artistic works from the present, leaving it to future collaborators to reinsert them meaningfully into their present (our future).[6] But what if these temporal withdrawals also work in reverse, including acting upon the collective labor of their producers? We want to consider this practice of borrowing and repurposing as forming a haunted, overlapping space not only between contemporary activists and previous socially engaged practices, but also between artists. We want to look at this temporal space as a productive gap, one in which materials, forms, narratives, and ideals are assembled through the processes of reanimation, repurposing, and repair.

This is more than an act of faith or nostalgia; instead, it is a politically charged and inescapably social-collective method of temporal dislocation and interpretation. It takes seriously Walter Benjamin's commission that the work of historians must recognize what will be lost if they fail previous generations by disregarding their hopes for future redemption: "There is a secret agreement between past generations and the present one. Our coming was expected on earth. Like every generation that preceded us, we have been endowed with a weak Messianic power, a power to which the past has a claim. That claim cannot be settled cheaply. Historical materialists are aware of that."[7]

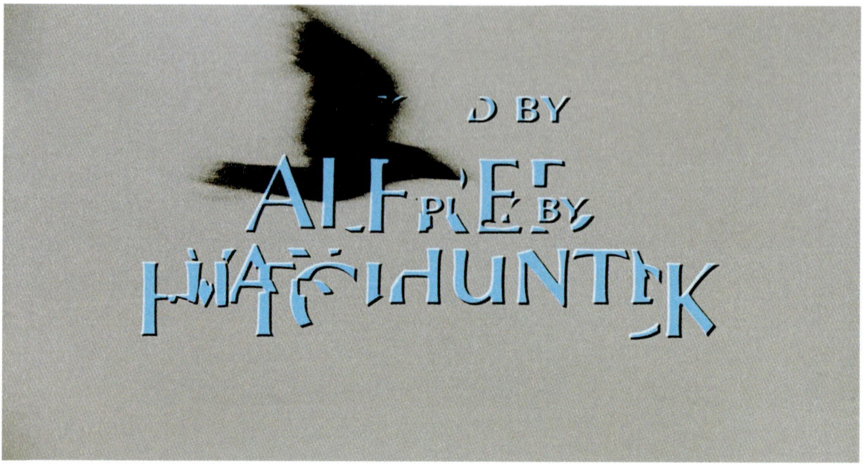

FIGURE 26

Jalal Toufic's *a line of flight from one radical closed space to another version 2* (conceptual film, 4 minutes, 1997) shows a black silhouette of a bird in motion, captured as a blurred shape against a pale background. The work connects to Toufic's analysis of how birds haunt art and cinema—from Van Gogh's *Wheatfield with Crows* through Hitchcock's *The Birds* to Kurosawa's *Dreams*—as visual motifs accumulate meaning while traversing different artistic contexts across time, each iteration carrying traces of what came before. Image courtesy of the artist.

Our encounter with what I call the phantom archive is also a confrontation with the temporal agency of social collectivity. This anticipatory praxis, in turn, generates a critical epistemology within the nonlinear backstory of activist art practices, as much as it may also offer one solution to the problem of causality found in conventional Marxian methodologies of historical research. For, if what I describe as activist art lacks a properly sequential history, and if it is a glitch or coding error that taps into a phantasmagoric panoply of tropes, figures, images, and patterns forming a chaotic archival reservoir rather than a linear chronology, or proper art history, then any attempt to assemble a genealogy for it requires equally uncommon investigative and representational techniques. Such methods could include dispatching a researcher into the past for a close-up look at all things merely departed, as well as currently missing. Nonetheless, as we know from so many books and movies, time travel is hazardous both for the journeying chrononaut herself and for us in the present. Furthermore, where in time would we send this unstuck investigator of the phantom archive?

THE HAZARDS (AND EXUBERANCE) OF TIME TRAVEL

Virtually every time travel yarn involves the unforeseen consequences of temporal meddling that then ripple (gravely) into the future, which is our present. Ray Bradbury's hypermacho tyrannosaurus hunter is summarily executed because of a crushed butterfly stuck to his boot; Chris Marker's nameless time traveler witnesses his own future assassination, the memory of which had haunted him since his childhood; Octavia Butler's African-American protagonist Dana is compelled to repeatedly travel back to the antebellum South in order to save her racist white ancestor from dying, or she risks vanishing in the present; and the accidental creation of a time travel machine by two brothers in the film *Primer* inadvertently generates their own multiple duplicates who—in a bid for temporal dominance—become increasingly paranoid and brutal, like a pair of endlessly replicating Cains and Abels.[8] In brief, meddling with the past is fraught with undesirable repercussions in the present, even if the lesson never seems to stick. And let's not forget poor Vic from Philip

K. Dick's *Time Out of Joint*, who, along with the main character Ragle, his brother-in-law, discovers that the charming world of their 1950s American suburbia is actually a fabrication built in the future to imprison them for a set of reasons too complex to detail here, except to add that as Ragle plans his escape, Vic and his wife Margo decide to remain behind with their atemporal if illusive comforts intact.[9]

In one way or another, each of these time travel narratives inevitably depends upon the protagonist's awareness of a preexisting and recognizable past (as well as the assurance that the future, some future, will arrive). The protagonists also need to realize that the perceived past is also existentially enmeshed with their own present. This is why the causality of time's arrow is supposed to remain sealed off from access or tampering. For this reason, the plot device of time travel is first and foremost about the violation of arrangements, in this case the laws of chronological time. It is also why the typically negative outcome of these stories stems from infringing on these temporal conventions, as much as it is perhaps due to the breaking of agreed-upon literary narratives. Not surprisingly, severe penalties apply, just as they do in real time, past, present, and future.

COURBET AND THE VENDÔME COLUMN

In 1871 Paris, after the Communards toppled the Vendôme Column and the revolution was crushed, the French state went after one prominent survivor of the insurrection, painter Gustave Courbet, and charged him with the column's reconstruction. (Since Courbet had seen the column as a symbol of war and conquest and wished to see it disassembled, this commission was a punishment.) Let me advance that the real aim of the state's retribution was to publicly retaliate against someone who dared to tamper with the temporal order itself, an order that had been objectified in the monument's officially sanctioned visage. Above all else, any antagonist agency bent on interrupting the visible arrangement of history must be proven reckless. And the Communards' monumenticide against the Vendôme Column was very much an act of collective antagonistic social agency, as we shall see in chapter 15.

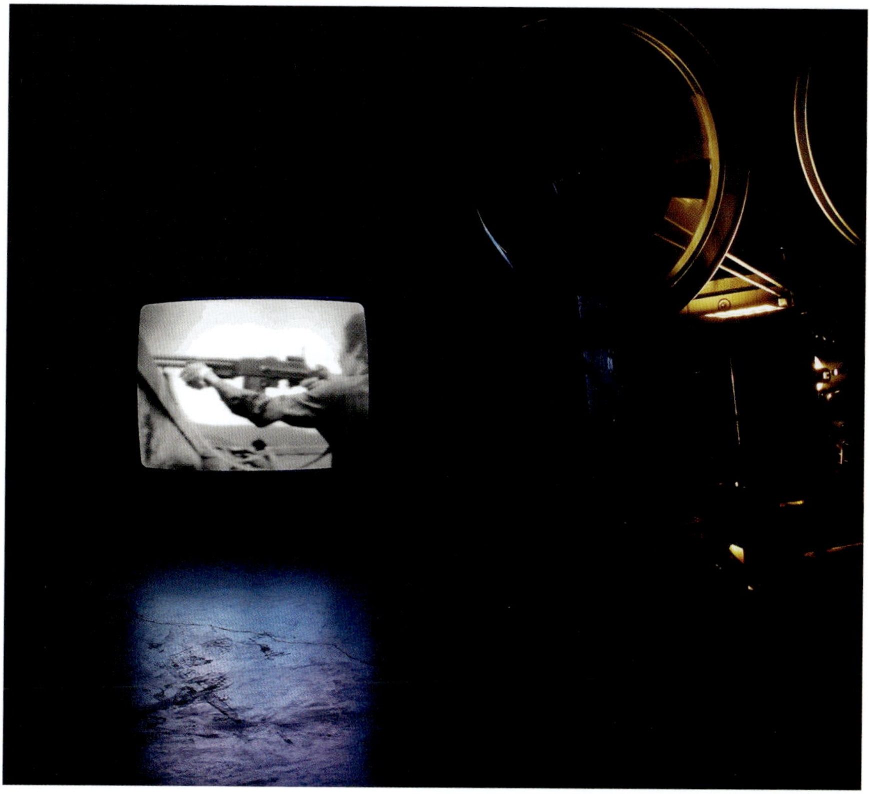

FIGURE 27

Jeffrey Skoller, *The Promise of Happiness: Stranded Images from the Age of Revolution*, 2016, four-screen installation, 16mm/analog/digital video. Jeffrey Skoller cannibalizes images from his own films of Soviet, Cuban, Vietnamese, and Nicaraguan revolutions, creating an "afterimage" of twentieth-century revolutionary struggle. As these idealist movements passed from the present moment, their film images remain, asking what meanings we make of such imagery as history shifts around them. Image courtesy of the artist.

REVOLUTIONARY DESTINATIONS

One immediately tempting landing-point to send our temporal pathfinder is the Paris Commune. This was a time and place when artists and artisans (and by no means only Courbet) worked with a newly forged, revolutionary socialist government to establish remarkably forward-looking policies about arts and culture. However, just a few weeks after it was birthed, the revolution was brutally suppressed. We could instead send our time traveler to New Caledonia later that same year, which became a place of banishment for many Communards not slaughtered in the Paris streets. Who would not be tempted to meet the anarchist feminist Communards Nathalie Lemel and poet Louise Michel (the latter apparently continuing her revolutionary activism while in exile by siding with the island's indigenous Kanak people in their failed anticolonial struggle against France)? Or for that matter, why not travel still further back to the stirrings of revolutionary insurrection in Saint-Domingue (later Haiti) and its heroic leader Toussaint Louverture? Anthropologist David Scott describes Louverture in the pages ahead somewhat ironically as a "conscript of modernity," while eulogizing Louverture's political and moral gift to future generations as an "awareness that our own struggle for alternative futures, beginning as they do with the inheritance of what has gone before, has always to be tempered by our remembrance of his example."[10] Carlos Garrido Castellano has argued that, when we focus on the little-known history of anticolonialism and artistic activism, what is highlighted is the "heterogeneous, productive ways in which these creative currents help us to make sense of our own experience and future expectations."[11]

THE LOGIC OF NONLINEAR TEMPORALITY

And yet every time I run this thought experiment again in my head, the same (non)monumental drawback reappears: if the genealogy of activist art is nonlinear and everyday in tempo, then isn't any singular point in time and space equally infused with a multiplicity of worthy and distinct possibilities for our investigation? Put another way, it is necessary to build up a sense of temporal resistance across time rather than in a particular time. We should look at a time not made up exclusively of those spectacular moments of revolution or uprising per se, but including the moments before and after, as well as in between. For it is not only the great heroic events that we must pay outstanding attention to, since after all they tend to gather and enfold historical narratives around them and need no assistance; instead it is the rhythm and cadence of that *longue durée* of resistance toward liberation which we must seek out. Therefore, pinpointing one standout terminus for our chrononaut's destination rubs against the very logic of the phantom archive's dark temporal energy and what it offers.

CONTEMPORARY THEORETICAL FRAMEWORKS

Before returning to the potential liberatory potential of the Unpresent's temporal dislocation, we need to address the way contemporary theorists perceive the role of time as it relates to interpretations of history, and for several reasons. We want to understand how other thinkers account for the possibility of social liberation if time has indeed come to a standstill, as outlined in part I of this book. Where does culture, and specifically the visual arts, with its legacy of temporal intervention via modernism and the avant-garde, fit into these concerns? In addition, if progressive political change is attainable, then what is the agency of that transformation in social and historical terms? How does it potentially relate to a phantasmagoric archive of still largely unlit dark matter of interventions, experiments, repetitions, and compromises?

First up is the work of anthropologist David Scott, who engages with a similar predicament of flattened time and the possibilities that remain for achieving historical justice. Scott's work is followed by an overview of four current Marxian-derived theories as outlined by art historian Steve Edwards, in which the well-known, but also frequently contested if not simply denounced, concept of historical determinism is challenged from within the historical materialist tradition. We will look now at Scott on the tragedy of the past within the tragedy of the present, and consider his proposition in relation to the broken time of the Unpresent, while bearing in mind philosopher Giorgio Agamben's comment that "only he who perceives the indices and signatures of the archaic in the most modern and recent can be contemporary."[12] My argument in this book is that this temporal doubling, the archaic in the contemporary, is now all-pervasive.

10

DAVID SCOTT: PROBLEM-SPACE/TIME

PROBLEM-SPACES AND PROBLEM-TIMES

"Revolutionary romance presupposes a horizon of overcoming, of emancipation," anthropologist David Scott observed in a 2005 interview with Stuart Hall.[1] However, such aspirations have also likely evaporated today, as he admits in his celebrated study of the Black Marxist intellectual C. L. R. James, *Conscripts of Modernity*. "The present," Scott frets, "appears to have congealed into an immobile structure of implicit and unchanging determinations."[2] Published several years before Fisher's *Capitalist Realism* (2009), but also well before the Brexit referendum and US election outcomes of 2016, the events of January 6, 2021, and the US presidential election in 2024—the three most conspicuous switching points for the onset of the Unpresent—Scott addressed strikingly similar conditions that have only now become fully discernible. He also raises questions comparable to those of this book, although for somewhat different reasons and objectives. As a Black scholar from an African-diasporic background, his theoretical reflections on tragedy, justice, and time suggest that substantial segments of the larger population were already experiencing the onset of an extreme atemporality, which has now come to dominate all of us. In addition to Scott's project, the concept of Afro-futurity itself strongly suggests the likelihood of this possibility.

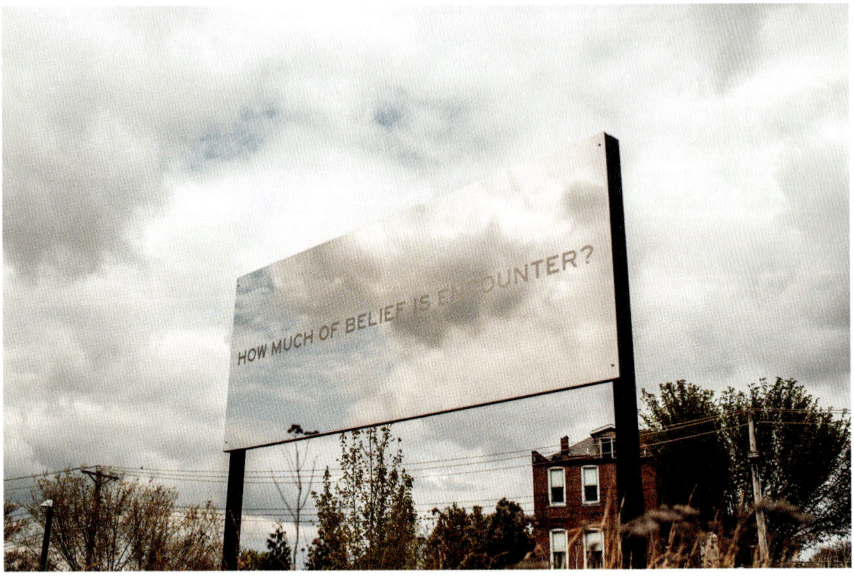

FIGURE 28

Chloë Bass, *Wayfinding*, 2019–2023: multisite installation project consisting of site-specific sculpture inspired by public signs that pose profound questions about the human experience, establishing a potential problem-space/problem-time where viewers confront their relationship to memory, place, and belonging. Bass describes her practice as highlighting the "seemingly normal as a means of questioning its stability," embracing Brecht's concept of alienation through "calling attention to structure through naming or pointing," and her wayfinding signs create what she terms "a rupture between ourselves, and what we do without thinking" (Chloë Bass, "Artist Statement," https://www.chloebass.com/welcome). This points directly to the type of problem-space/problem-time that opens up possibilities for critical intervention within everyday life. Image courtesy of the artist.

This temporal crisis within Black experience has also generated its own creative responses. The concept of Afro-futurity, for instance, emerged as one strategy for imagining Black futures when dominant culture offered none. More recently, artist Stephanie Dinkins has proposed "Afro-now-ism" as a refusal to defer liberation to some promised future: "instead of waiting to reach the proverbial promised land, also known as a time in the future that may or may not manifest in your lifetime, Afro-now-ism is taking the leap and the risks to imagine and define oneself beyond systemic oppression" (see figure 49).[3] Where Afro-futurity projects forward, Afro-now-ism insists on acting in the present, offering a temporal strategy that resonates with Scott's critique of forever deferring justice and with the phantom archive's emphasis on reactivating past (and theoretically future) forms for resisting and recoding the Unpresent.

Therefore, with (I hope) only modest liberties taken, I will discuss Scott's concept of *problem-space*, recognizing that this is also a *problem-time*, in order to help us grasp not only the Unpresent as a type of temporal coding error, but also the phantom archive as another type that contrarily opens up possibilities for critical intervention. Now let me try to weave Scott's theoretical insights into the fabric of my thesis, without erasing the contours of his own thinking about historical narratives of justice as necessary problem-spaces and problem-times.

AFRO-FUTURITY AND AFRO-NOW-ISM

> What if the present's demand on the past has altered in part because it is no longer clear what its relation to the future might be? In other words, what if the imagined futures that had given point and direction to the intervention in the present and the rehistoricization of the past suddenly evaporated as a possible horizon of hope and longing? How would this affect the kind of "effective history" histories of the present purport to be?[4]

Given such a situation as he describes above, Scott finds it nearly impossible to imagine in our now time a liberatory future, or what he describes as even the possibility of a futurity that could satisfy the longing for a progressive, perhaps revolutionary overcoming of a past burdened

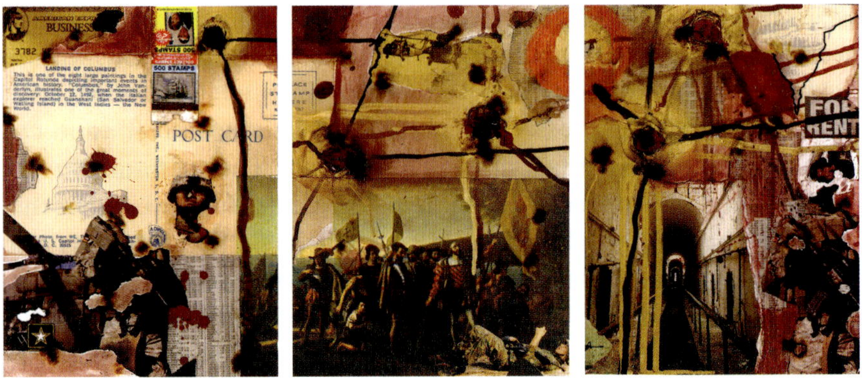

FIGURE 29

Theodore A. Harris, *Postcard from Conquest*, 2008, triptych, each board 9 in. × 11 in. The work layers together found imagery, oil stick and spray paint, and abraded surfaces to create a visceral triptych that interrogates American founding myths. The central panel appropriates romanticized Capitol rotunda paintings, while Harris adds contemporary images of soldiers sourced from military recruitment flyers, military graduation yearbooks, *Small Arms Review*, and *Soldier of Fortune* magazine, wounding the surface itself. Drawing from painter Leon Golub and the Vienna Actionists, Harris forges connections between historical conquest and ongoing violence through deliberately abraded, cinematic collage. Image courtesy of the artist.

generate expectations of inevitable outcomes, Scott raises the possibility that such interpretations inhibit or even prevent the material resolution of these past tragedies in the present day. Before proceeding, let's take a deeper look at the concept of metahistory as defined by Hayden White, whose ideas, Scott tells us, were of particular inspiration for his book *Conscripts of Modernity* (2004).

Far from providing objective descriptions of the past, White argues, historians inevitably structure their interpretive narratives of events through such linguistic rhetorical tropes as metaphor, metonymy, synecdoche, and irony. This tendency, in turn, produces a history that falls into conventional literary formats such as tragedy, romance, comedy, or satire. White tells us that Jules Michelet, for example, framed history as romance, Alexis Henri De Tocqueville as tragedy, Benedetto Croce as irony, and so forth. Scott applies a similar meta-analytical approach to European colonialism's legacy and the resistance it provoked, asking whether any projected ideal of a postcolonial future doesn't also necessitate narrating its past in a particular way. He immediately answers his own query by proposing that "anticolonial stories about past, present, and future have typically been emplotted in a distinctive narrative form, one with a distinctive story-potential: that of Romance."[12] By "romance," Scott means "narratives of overcoming, often narratives of vindication; they have tended to enact a distinctive rhythm and pacing, a distinctive direction, and to tell stories of salvation and redemption."[13] Perhaps most importantly, he adds, this romance narrative has "largely depended upon a certain (utopian) horizon toward which the emancipationist history is imagined to be moving."[14] By drawing attention to the formally plotted structure of redemptive historical narratives, Scott boldly states that his "wager in this book is that the problem about postcolonial futures—how we go about reimagining what we might become of what we have so far made—cannot be recast without recasting the problem about colonial pasts. My undertaking here is aimed at offering one approach to such an inquiry."[15]

The process of recasting involves transforming existing historical narratives into problem-spaces and problem-times in which challenging discourse and debate find enough conceptual room to develop. And in *Conscripts of Modernity*, Scott achieves this by engaging in a cross-time dialogue with *The Black Jacobins*, a storied interpretation of the 1791–1804 Haitian Revolution by the late Trinidad-born Marxist historian C. L. R. James.[16] Scott describes the metahistory James has produced as a narrative of a "revolutionary struggle in which, from a particular present, a certain past is reconstructed and deployed in the service of imagining the direction in which an alternative future might be sought."[17] Crucially, Scott adds that James revised and republished his 1938 study in 1963, just one year after Trinidad and Tobago gained independence along with Jamaica from Britain, but also the same year the US civil rights movement organized the March on Washington, and one year after Algeria became independent from its former French colonizer.

Parallels are implicit between these anticolonial campaigns and the eighteenth-century Haitian leader Toussaint Louverture, who led the first-ever victorious uprising of enslaved Black and mixed-race plantation laborers. In other words, James's heroic narration of Haiti's revolutionary past became entangled with his own militantly anticolonial present in the early 1960s, and it is this knotting together of times that generates a useful problem-space for rethinking such emancipatory narrative conventions today, over sixty years later. But there is something else going on here; something that is most important for my own argument and concerns.

THEFT OF FUTURITY

As described earlier, Scott warns us that we must not be tempted to resolve these tensions and even contradictions into a liberal fantasy about an emancipated future to come. Nor, for that matter, should we use our romantic historical narrative to construct an emancipated past, as I have suggested MAGA and other far-right nationalists seek to do. Instead, the first step when determining our current relationship with the past is to understand it as a problem-space and time. This acknowledgment precedes the possibility of any radically progressive time traveler winding their way back into the past or projecting into the future, for past and future must not be assumed; they must be grasped as a type of entangled problem. That stated, the troubling nature of this reflection about time means that time travel can only be possible as a manifestly conspicuous and nonlinear movement or drift within an archive already brimming with a surplus of possibilities. This archive includes anticipatory expectations and partially successful endeavors at liberation, but also an assortment of ghosts and demons and haunted troubles resembling time-based versions of those monstrosities feared by ancient mariners.

What at first appears to be a blank screen upon which to project either some new cultural vision or a profoundly gratifying older one can, using Scott's problem-time and space approach, better be understood as a surface so excessively etched with traces of language, history, knowledge, and material conditions that it merely appears to be an unmarked surface. These traces cannot be navigated without first recognizing how language and spatial metaphors are employed, consciously or not, in the writing of history. But it also requires understanding that historical narratives are drawn from the excesses of a spectral or phantom archive replete with a surplus of possibilities involving past, present, and future time. This is why seeking, yet never successfully managing, to fully settle our obligations with the past remains a haunted problem-space and time that can still productively become divergent from the Unpresent. Certainly this cannot be accomplished willy-nilly. As Scott has shown, past tragedies will not be swept away in the present by a vision of emancipation to come, any more than by a belief in liberty once possessed and then lost. The weight of time matters. Its carcass bears down on things, as will be discussed in the next chapter. And, surely, events played out a second time are without doubt a tragedy. But what about the third, or fourth, or umpteenth time? When time itself becomes disjointed, inverted, iterative, and out of joint as it is nowadays, even repetitions of past events take on unexpected, fortuitous potential, as I believe many of the art projects discussed and reproduced throughout this book attest.

REPETITION AND THE SPECTER OF HISTORICAL MATERIALISM

Before moving on, it is worth recalling Marx's famous gloss on Hegel in *The Eighteenth Brumaire of Louis Bonaparte*: historical events occur twice, first as tragedy, then as farce. Marx illustrates this through how "the French, so long as they were engaged in revolution, could not get rid

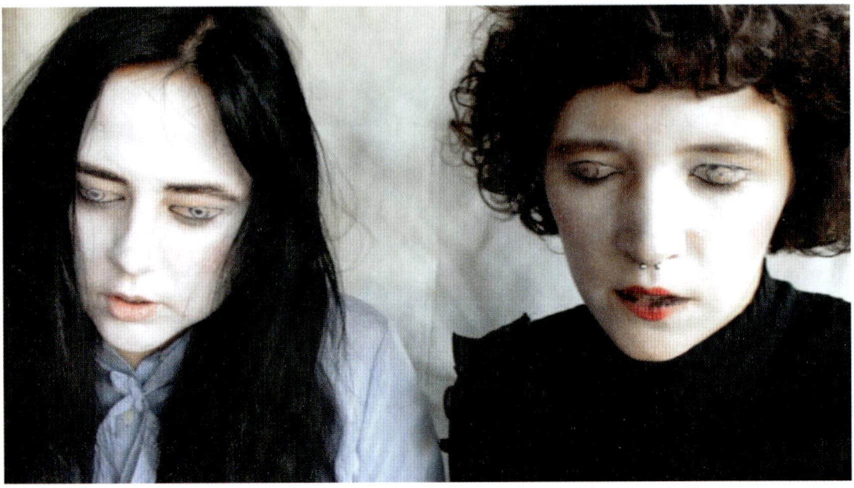

FIGURE 30

Two ethereal figures from Dana Kavelina's experimental film *Letter to a Turtledove* (2020) gaze dreamily, with theatrical makeup and striking stylization. This surreal antiwar film-poem blends archival footage from World War II with amateur film captured in 2014–2015 during Russia's proxy war in Donbas, Ukraine, complemented by the artist's original animations and staged scenes. Image courtesy of the artist.

of the memory of Napoleon," ultimately returning Napoleon III to the throne and thus producing not only "the caricature of the old Napoleon" but caricaturing "the old Napoleon himself as he must have looked in the middle of the nineteenth century."[18] Again and again, our ghosts simply refuse to leave the stage quietly.

This is, without question, a certain type of episodic repetition, with its own grotesque theatricality but also with a sense of earnestness on the part of history's main characters, in this case a threatened midcentury bourgeoisie confronting their own radicalizing working classes. And in this desperate search for a political restoration at any cost they perform an act of ludicrous time travel which is still reverberating today. We have already encountered its echo in the J6 MAGA insurrection in Washington, DC. It will repeat again, but quite differently, as we rediscover in chapter 15 temporal reverberations in the Unpresent generated as far back as 1871 by the Parisian Communards. And these time tremors don't end. As we will see, there are echoes of still earlier events, including the largest attempted slave uprising in the New World, the so-called German Coast Uprising of 1811, as it was reimagined by artist Dread Scott in 2019.

Situating temporal problems as central to the age of the Unpresent simultaneously sets up an exploration of the phantom archive as a counterpoint. To that end, we turn next to the current state of Marxian-derived theorizing about time, history, and causality. For any proper time travel yarn always has a specter haunting its narrative. The one that frequents this book is the Marxian-influenced interpretation of the past as materialist history. More than any other Enlightenment narrative, it is that of Marx, Engels and their progeny that shadows these pages.[19]

The question with which I confront these apparitions is this: If historically materialist notions of temporality have become foreclosed within the *mise-en-scène* of the Unpresent, then what becomes of the past's expectations of achieving a just and emancipatory future still to come? My own concept of a phantom archive is no exception. Let us drag out this ghost to perform now a tragedy, or a farce, or perhaps a hodgepodge of the two.

11

STEVE EDWARDS: TIME'S CARCASS

The nameless, time-traveling protagonist of Chris Marker's 1962 film *La Jetée* broodingly comments that "nothing sorts out ordinary memories from ordinary moments. . . . Later on they do claim remembrance when they show up as scars."[1] And perhaps it is indicative of the tortured atemporal condition of the Unpresent, but also of a phantom archive teeming with closeted cultural possibilities, that even some relatively canonical Marxian theorists are compelled to rethink historical materialism's characteristically unidirectional concept of universal time. One recent and especially insightful text is offered by British art historian Steve Edwards. It is appropriately entitled "'Time's Carcass': Art History, Capitalism, and Temporality."[2] The wording comes from what Edwards describes as a fascinating comment by Marx: "time is everything, man is nothing; he is at most time's carcass."[3] To be sure, for Edwards, following Stuart Hall's call for "a Marxism without guarantees," class struggle remains the central contradiction shaping political and social realities over time, but precisely without any assurance of particular outcomes.[4] This stands in marked contrast to the explicit historical stagism—as in fixed stages of historical change—advanced by such figures as Georgi Plekhanov and Joseph Stalin, both of whom promoted inflexible laws of historical development so that the writing of history, as Jairus Banaji sorrowfully tells us, "became as opaque and dream-like, and hardly as exciting, as the fantasies of surrealism.[5]

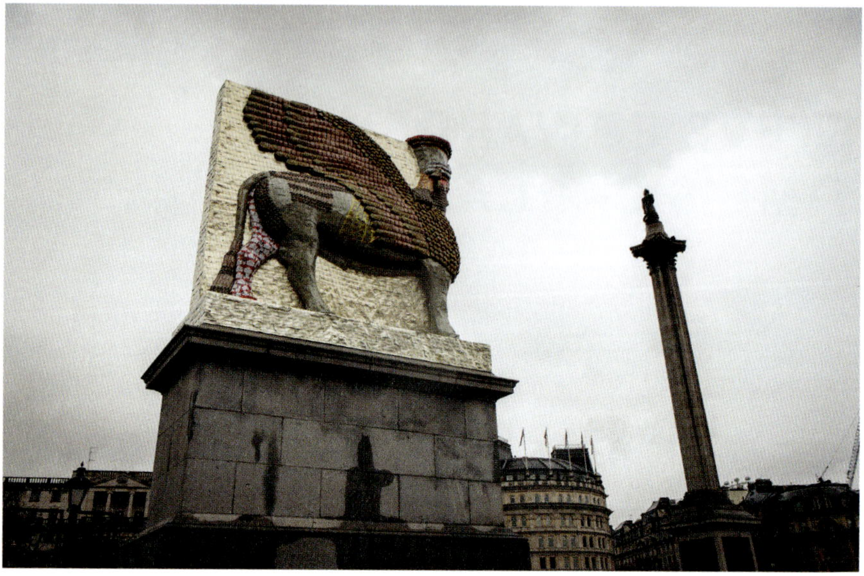

FIGURE 31

Michael Rakowitz, *The Invisible Enemy Should Not Exist (Lamassu of Nineveh)*, 2018. From 2018 through 2020, London's Fourth Plinth in Trafalgar Square displayed an ancient Assyrian lamassu that was conspicuously not a reconstruction but a seriously mischievous re-creation built from 10,500 Iraqi date syrup cans attached to a steel frame. The original winged bull deity had stood at Nineveh's Nergal Gate from 700 BCE until ISIS destroyed it in 2015. Rakowitz's version was, in his own words, "a ghost of the original and a placeholder for lives that cannot be reconstructed" ("Latest Trafalgar Square Fourth Plinth Artwork Unveiled," BBC News, March 28, 2018). By linking Iraq's devastated date industry with its endangered cultural heritage, the artist interrupted the interrupted: conspicuously refusing both the finality of destruction and the fiction of historical recovery typical of Western museums. Image courtesy of the artist.

Edwards provides a compact synopsis of the growing number of Marxian-inspired historians who are seeking to articulate alternative, more elastic theories of historical materialist temporality. In addition to Banaji, we find Stavros Tombazos, Harry Harootunian, Peter Osborne, and Dipesh Chakrabarty, as well as Marxian forebears such as Paul Ricoeur, Perry Anderson, Henri Lefebvre, Louis Althusser, and Antonio Negri, not to overlook Walter Benjamin, Ernst Bloch, Leon Trotsky, and Marx himself. Their collective dispute with what Edwards describes disdainfully as "stagism" (the belief that there are fixed sequential stages of history) has in turn inspired any number of art historians who employ notions of nonlinear time for their interpretation of high culture. Some of these varied ideas are more pertinent to my own arguments than others, although all of them have some bearing on the political interpretation of time and are therefore worth exploring in some detail. The Unpresent, after all, is the condition of Marxian theory after telos—history's linear temporal structure collapsing when both capitalism's and actually existing socialism's promises of progress have failed, yet material relations, class conflict, and the need for equality and justice persist.

FOUR ALTERNATIVES TO LINEAR HISTORICAL MATERIALISM

Edwards effectively assembles his subject matter into four thematic groupings. Each in its own way seeks alternatives to the stagist notions of historical determination rooted in a rigid and sequential concept of temporal linearity, with its dogmatic faith in the ineluctable appearance of a communist society at history's end. One of the central critiques raised therefore involves what determines social change in a Marxian framework, if not, as was previously proposed, such mechanisms as class struggle between workers and capitalists, and/or the mutating forces of capitalist production itself. It is no coincidence that this broad critique finds increased traction in art historical circles, for a few reasons.

First is the rise and then fall of both modernism and the artistic avant-garde, concepts that gradually lost most of their previously vehement force in the postwar years, and especially after the collapse of the USSR and socialist Eastern Europe. In addition, the very notion of art as a practice represents a time-based problem for historical linearity insofar as it persists unchanged as a social category, but also as a form of (relatively) noncommodified labor, from generation to generation. And finally, to again cite Adorno, the work of art is simultaneously a social fact with all the influences of its particular time embedded within it, including commodification, as well as something autonomous from and resistant to the rationalized needs and monetized time of a capitalist society.[6] And even despite what I and a few others have described as art's hollowing-out as bare art, it still exists as, at minimum, a signifier of self-determined labor, as Dave Beech and Marina Vishmidt maintain; and thus art represents something of a conundrum for generating surplus value, total capitalist subsumption, and commodification.[7]

While Edwards banks on the fact that this cultural enigma lies at the heart of high culture's historical record—for surely he is not addressing what I consider informal modes of artistic dark matter's productivity—his text explores a quartet of theoretical methods that, to one degree or another, dissociate themselves from dogmatic notions of "teleological progress and decay."[8] Taking readers on a whirlwind tour of alternative Marxian temporalities, Edwards first discusses, not surprisingly, Walter Benjamin's anachronistic and messianic interpretation of the past in which memory, as opposed to history proper, must be "grasped as it flashes up in a moment of danger."[9] It is in this same vein that Benjamin also memorably commented, "Marx says that revolutions are the locomotive of world history. But perhaps it is quite otherwise. Perhaps revolutions are an attempt by the passengers on this train—namely, the human race—to pull the emergency brake."[10] More on this in a moment.

Spinozist is how Edwards describes his second category of Marx-inspired historical methodologies. Citing Daniel W. Smith's introduction to Vittorio Morfino's *Plural Temporalities*, Edwards presents this approach as one that replaces the seriality of cause and effect with a weave or web of nodes and nexuses.[11] Importantly, rather than exhibiting a dominant causative agency at work, this multitemporality has "no single driving contradiction, but durations, rhythms, and dissonances."[12] Here Morfino's description intriguingly resonates with Harney and Moten's jazzlike aesthetic fugitivity in the undercommons, where "art is practiced on and over the edge of politics, beneath its ground, in animative and improvisatory decomposition of its inert body."[13]

That said, aside from Baruch Spinoza, Morfino's primary influence has been Louis Althusser's structuralist Marxism, particularly his concept of overdetermination, in which all temporal elements play a role in deciding historical outcomes (as opposed to the economy being the final decisive factor). Still, with Althusser, major events, such as revolutions, are the result of material contradictions, even if these are multiple and overlapping as opposed to singular, as in a clash over the forces of economic production, for example. For Althusser the means of production remain crucial for historical change when it makes an abrupt appearance, whereas for Morfino the emphasis is on durational cycles, slowdowns and accelerations leading to the possibility of accidental encounters, which in turn implies that outcomes, including revolutions, are potentially random events. This also suggests, as though in a speculative time travel mode, that where historical events reoccur, things likely will conclude differently. In Spinozist Marxism we eliminate the inevitability of rigid historical stages, but another door opens to uncertain aleatory possibilities like those found in a dice-tossed musical piece by avant-garde composer John Cage, or the 2014 film *Edge of Tomorrow* in which characters become caught in looping alternative timelines.[14]

The influential postcolonial theorist Dipesh Chakrabarty is third on Edwards's list. Like Morfino, Chakrabarty embraces polytemporality, but for Edwards he retains a degree of primary causality—not from capitalism's developing mode of production per se, but from the entire zeitgeist of capitalist modernization. Key for Chakrabarty are those moments when this progress-oriented impulse collides with precapitalist societies: early mechanical industrialization in Europe, but also the many instances of imperialist modernization imposed upon the Global South in subsequent decades. These encounters generate both violence and resistance. In his major work, *Provincializing Europe* from 2000, Chakrabarty introduced this binary conflictual model of time as History #1, involving capital's influences, and History #2, involving all that remains outside the determinants of History #1.[15] And while there are still clearly specific forces driving how events unfold, in this schema they are far from predetermined since every clash between History #1 and #2 can have different and often unexpected outcomes, if always within limits. It is interesting here to pause and compare Chakrabarty's model with that of David Scott insofar as History #1 is shaped by materialist constraints, even if these are pre- or noncapitalist economic pressures stemming from forced slave labor that is tragically absent any specific destination or destiny, including, as Scott tells us above all, a romanticized and inevitable future emancipation. In any case, these horrific circumstances remain cruelly inscribed within current realities of politics, culture, and the economic forces of modern capitalist production. Put differently, as with Scott, Chakrabarty's History #1 is unshakably haunted and blocked by History #2, regardless of how much it attempts to surmount and move beyond it. In sum, the repetitive undying specter of a morally injurious past (Scott), or conversely, the political agency of a pre- or even nonmodern peasantry (Chakrabarty), serves to obstruct the present's passage into "the future."

The last of Edwards's theoretical foursome is Leon Trotsky's concept of uneven and combined development (UCD), which Edwards favorably describes as allowing "for great nuance."[16] Specifically, Trotsky's historical model provides for unexpected leaps of historical transformation, such as a late-developing state skipping right past capitalism by deploying current technologies and forces of production to bring about radical political socialization, while the model still retains an overall causality from capitalist forces of production operating at a broader, global level of influence. We could apply this formula to the inaugural ambitions of independent socialist governments in Algeria, Cuba, Egypt, Ghana, Indonesia, North Vietnam, and the Democratic Republic of Congo, among other postcolonial nations, particularly during the 1950s and early 1960s, including sovereignty for Trinidad and Tobago, as C. L. R. James allegorically celebrated in *The Black Jacobins* (see chapter 10). Here Edwards draws on his central theoretical interlocutor, the previously cited contemporary Marxist historian Banaji, who states that the key general distinction to grasp is "between relations of production and forms of exploitation," which may or may not overlap at any given moment.[17] What Banaji calls for instead is the study of how capitalism *articulates* different modes of production, as opposed to some inevitable ticking of history's fixed clockwork. With regard to art and culture, this nonlinear approach to causality "offers a way," Edwards explains, "of understanding how the centripetal forces of plural temporality are threaded together in particular conjunctures."[18] All the same, while citing Michael Hardt and Antonio Negri, Edwards cautions that this is not a "smooth space" but a "hierarchically ordered structure of power."[19] And at the end of the day, the developing forces of economic production do still remain dominant, if not always linear over time, even if this is expressed as junctures and jagged collisions rather than efficient and flowing evolutionary historical changes.

PREVENTED FUTURES

While all four methods outlined by Edwards complicate the sequential determinism of a linear stagist approach to historical change, some do so more than others, but sometimes at the expense of one of historical materialism's core political strengths: its conception of historical development as driven by transformations in the forces of production, forces that dialectically shape both material conditions and consciousness over time, bending history toward greater democracy, inclusion, and liberty. Of the historical concepts considered here, Benjamin's and Trotsky's theories remain closest to preserving this dynamic. Benjamin, however, shifts emphasis away from developmental seriality and onto that revelatory moment when the past is finally redeemed, either through a kind of secular-Messianic intervention or that hard, revolutionary tug on the emergency brake. Trotsky's UCD model, by contrast, retains a clear historical causality, though development proceeds neither smoothly nor strictly chronologically, remaining open to unexpected progressive surges as well as retreats. Applying UCD to the art historical record, Edwards explains how it accounts for anomalous modernisms: the Egyptian surrealists in 1930s Cairo, or earlier still, the Bengal Renaissance intellectuals of late nineteenth-century Calcutta who championed women's rights while challenging India's caste system. And perhaps this UCD approach also illuminates the retro-vanguardism of MAGA itself?

What unites these varied theoretical interventions—from Benjamin's messianic ruptures to Trotsky's uneven leaps—is their insistence that historical time need not unfold as a predetermined sequence of stages marching toward inevitable outcomes. Yet each still presumes some directionality, however discontinuous: Benjamin's redemptive moment that finally comes to pass, Morfino's aleatory encounters generating new possibilities, Chakrabarty's ongoing collisions producing resistant agency, and Trotsky's combined development enabling progressive surges. While each of these frameworks complicates linear stagism, none fully accounts for the condition I am describing: not interrupted progress, not layered temporalities, but the wholesale evacuation of futurity itself. Capitalism's totalizing process of abstraction has eliminated the very ground upon which emancipatory futures might be imagined, leaving only an eviscerated, spectral present haunted by phantoms of pasts that never were and futures that cannot be. The Unpresent represents not merely the disruption of linear progress but the wholesale evacuation of futurity itself as a credible category, even as it promises such advancement.

This is why both MAGA's retro-avant-garde and progressive nostalgia respond to the same underlying crisis: the untimeliness of the Unpresent is not a problem to be solved through better temporal models, but a condition to be reckoned with. The phantom archive emerges here, not as a repository of usable pasts but as a practice of conspicuous repair that marks the impossibility of seamless restoration while refusing to abandon the work of historical memory entirely. Where these Marxist temporalities offer tools for understanding how time might be complicated, the Unpresent requires us to think from within a moment when time itself appears to have run aground. Does this not necessitate another act of repair by seeking to repurpose what made Marx's investigation of class history so compelling in the first place, specifically his attention to what capitalism forecloses and renders impossible? These are what Bloch called prevented futures: possibilities that were blocked, not by historical inevitability but by capital's violent abstractions.

Edwards only mentions Marxist theoretician Ernst Bloch in passing, but Bloch's concept of *Ungleichzeitigkeit* (nonsimultaneity) offers still another analytical lens for interpreting the rise of the new nationalist right as a contemporary phenomenon today. In her book *Usable Pasts: Social Practice and State Formation in American Art*, art historian Larne Abse Gogarty explains that Bloch's idea of nonsimultaneous time under capitalism offers two opposite outcomes.[20] One sets the pace for history's apparent forward momentum such as technological change, while the other stimulates interest in past social formations that capital has already marginalized or even dissolved. Even though the latter is anachronistic and therefore seemingly a drag on ideologies of progress, this regressive fantasy serves capitalism, Bloch tells us, his primary example being twentieth-century European fascism. As with Adorno and Horkheimer's argument discussed earlier, this backward-looking mindset ultimately blocks genuine emancipatory transformation, including the outright dissolution of capitalism. But Bloch also proposes, so Gogarty lucidly explains, a nonsimultaneous but also revolutionary impulse regarding "prevented futures," not yet realized or fully envisioned, but also not yet weaponized as the "nostalgic longing for the past."[21]

ANOMALOUS TIME AND RETRO-AVANT-GARDISM

On balance, Edwards and his selective circle of Marx-inspired theorists, along with Gogarty and her use of Bloch, present a strong case within historical materialism for challenging long-held notions of deterministic causality. And yet some of these alternatives soften or fully undermine a central pillar of standard Marxian interpretations of history as a narrative about labor's social progress toward emancipation, peppered, of course, with temporary moments of regression in need of unblocking and surmounting. In this sense, these theorists might be said to be more aligned with an aesthetics of time than with standard notions of chronological or empirically determined history. Still, what can their theories tell us about the problem of a time severely out of joint, as in the Unpresent?

This assessment bears directly on an age in which temporality itself, not just modernism or progressive advancement, appears to have ceased as both idea and social fact. One of many things Edwards's useful outline offers is the capacity to expand the modernist cultural canvas to include reactionary avant-garde movements such as Italian futurism or British vorticism. And this insight might help us understand the peculiarly contemporary way MAGA similarly longs for "a past that never existed in conditions of crisis."[22] This is why, as Edwards maintains, we must study significant thinkers of conservative reaction, even more perhaps than those in the liberal center, because "the absolute modernity

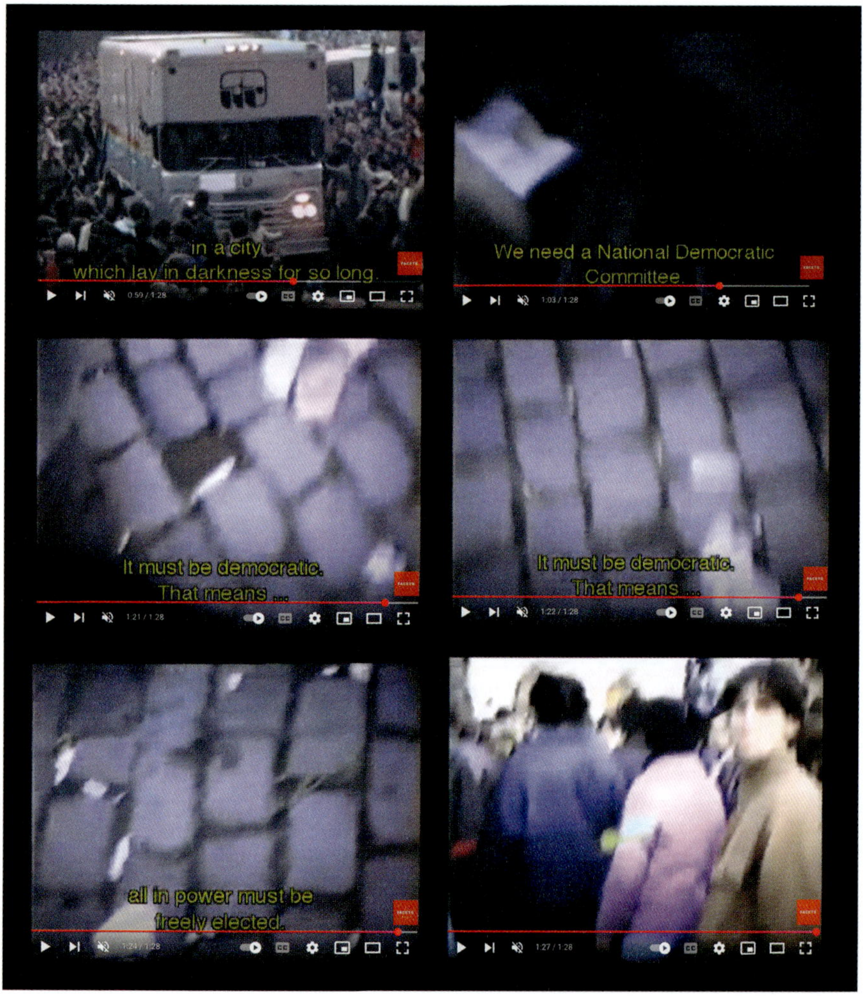
in a city
which lay in darkness for so long.
0:59 / 1:28
We need a National Democratic
Committee.
1:03 / 1:28
It must be democratic.
That means ...
1:21 / 1:28
It must be democratic.
That means ...
1:22 / 1:28
all in power must be
freely elected.
1:27 / 1:28

of conservative demagogues is a lesson we need to learn."[23] Let me note here too that the pro-MAGA American tech entrepreneur Marc Andreessen praises pro-fascist Filippo Marinetti's "Manifesto of Italian Futurism," leading scholars such as Becca Lewis to describe the dawning of what they label contemporary technofascism.[24] It is through these insights about archaic reactionary politics at work within the most allegedly contemporary of social phenomenon, and vice versa, that Marx's comment about time's carcass becomes most effective, even as it begs a new question: what would be required to repurpose the idea of history as a movement toward democratic, emancipatory justice in the radical Unpresent? In *Usable Pasts*, Gogarty suggested one possibility. Drawing on Bloch's concept of nonsimultaneity, she argued that the cooperative practices of contemporary socially engaged artists—Suzanne Lacy, Rick Lowe, Martha Rosler, Tania Bruguera, and the Austrian group WochenKlausur—echo historical models such as those of America's 1930s New Deal federal arts programs,

FIGURE 32

Stills from *Videograms of a Revolution* by Harun Farocki and Andrei Ujică (Berlin Harun Farocki Filmproduktion, 1992, 106 min.). Compiled from over 125 hours of amateur and television footage, the film documents the December 1989 overthrow of Romanian dictator Nicolae Ceaușescu. These frames capture demonstrators broadcasting live from the occupied state television station declaring the need for democracy in real time as revolution unfolded. The first still shows an ambulance advancing through protesters "in a city which lay in darkness for so long." What the footage could not capture was the ambiguous aftermath: the foreclosure of socialist futures, decades of neoliberal transformation, and ongoing struggles over what democracy might mean, all struggles that persist today. (Image courtesy of Farocki's estate / Green Naftali Gallery.)

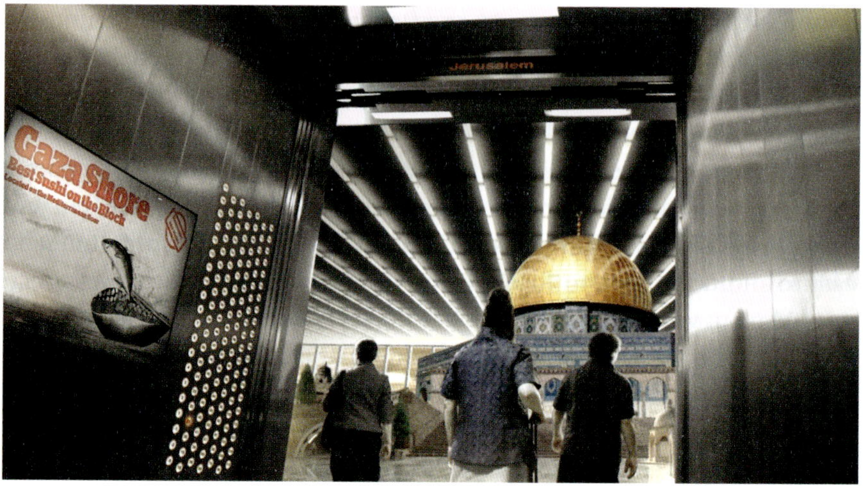

FIGURE 33

Larissa Sansour, *Nation Estate*, 2012, digital photograph. In this satirical vision, Palestine exists as a futuristic high-rise where each floor houses a different city. Here visitors arrive at the "Jerusalem" floor to find the Dome of the Rock relocated indoors under fluorescent lighting—sacred geography transformed into architectural exhibit. Through science fiction aesthetics glossy with high-tech promise yet shadowed by loss, Sansour imagines a future of vertical containment where national symbols become museumified artifacts. Yet resistance persists within this dystopia: the olive tree rooted in Palestinian soil, the artist's pregnant body—signs of *sumud* (steadfastness) that refuse complete foreclosure. It is heritage both curated and lived, a future simultaneously impossible and enduring. Image courtesy of the artist.

and inequity. Here I am drawing on Benjamin and Bloch, while seeking to press beyond Scott's diagnosis of our temporal predicament toward a more explicitly reparative practice. Still, I do not mean to suggest by this question that something metaphysical or theologically transcendent is in play, any more than I am proposing we become blindly euphoric. This is not about Hegel's spirit of time any more than that of Francis—Mr. *End of History*—Fukuyama's "last man."[27] Rather, history, if it is an ordinary linguistic signifier, must also be something else culturally speaking.

Call it a trope or a metaphor or a gift that is carried along, one passed from generation to generation and from struggle to struggle, often in the most run-of-the-mill way: history has been understood as a primary stand-in for the concept of justice, and needs to be considered so again. This is important, regardless of whether we sophisticated and skeptical academics object to grand narratives and universal conceptions of history, or choose to grumble along with Althusser that "the knowledge of history is no more historical than the knowledge of sugar is sweet."[28] Indeed, we might even go so far as to say that any liberatory, let alone Marxian, interpretation of history lacking a redemption narrative is not only bitter, it is surely also tragic. To cite Benjamin, "As flowers turn toward the sun, by dint of a secret heliotropism the past strives toward that sun which is rising in the sky of history. A historical materialist must be aware of this most inconspicuous of all transformations."[29] Or, in an inversion of this metaphor, Alex Callinicos cites Edward Thompson in proposing that "historical materialism, like the angel of history, faces backward, seeking to reconstruct and keep alive the 'tradition of the oppressed.'"[30] The surplus possibilities of the phantom archive emerge as a method for keeping alive history's emancipatory claim not through seamless restoration or mechanical determinism, but through marking what was or is obstructed while refusing abandonment of what persists.

STANDING UP BY ANY MEANS NECESSARY

"Time has been uncoupled," cultural theorist Marcus Verhagen warns us, "from the experiences that fill it, becoming an abstract and universal medium, like money."[31] What is to be done in response? Or more

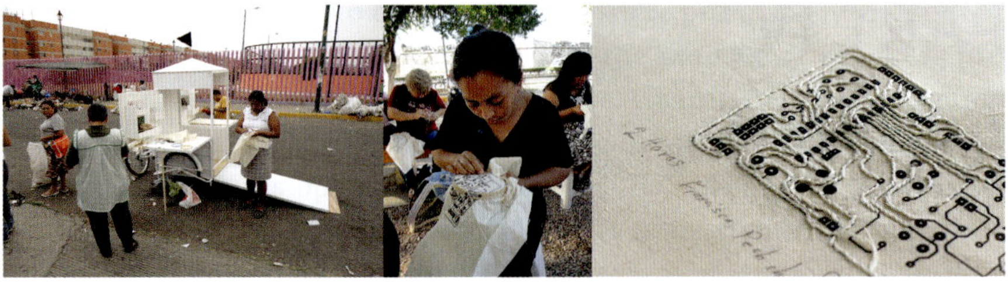

FIGURE 34

Amor Muñoz, *Maquila Región 4* or *MR4*, 2010/2013. Muñoz reimagines factory labor as aesthetic practice, employing local artisans to embroider functional electronic circuits on textiles, paying American minimum wage ($8 per hour vs. Mexico's $1.20) while connecting traditional craftsmanship with technology in economically marginalized communities in Mexico. By fusing textiles and electronics, the two central products of *maquiladora* factory exploitation, *MR4* restores a sense of dignity to what is primarily women's labor while making visible the human hands behind each circuit board. One cannot help but recall William Morris, who insisted that "all labour, even the commonest, must be made attractive" ("Useful Work versus Useless Toil," *The Collected Works of William Morris*, 23:98–120). Image courtesy of the artist.

12

CONSPICUOUS REPAIRS

Theorist Andreas Huyssen maintains that "rather than safeguarding some stable past, memory became a site of political battles, conflictual memories replacing what used to be vaguely called collective memory."[1] Art might be one if not the premier example of such memory politics. Drilling down into the spectral excess of the phantom archive reveals myriad core samples layered in dark genealogical veins. This cultural stratum haunts orthodox histories of modern and contemporary art, but also the broader sphere of culture within, marginal to, and willfully against capitalism. And yet what haunts the haunted, so to speak, is the distant nearness of the murmuring multitude's social collectivity. Efforts at apprehending this concrete, yet abstract, but also ubiquitous medium of social being has been central to artistic practice, especially in the modern era, and even more so since the introduction of lens-based mechanical image-making in the early nineteenth century. Born a few years after photography as a fixed medium was invented, poet and art critic Charles Baudelaire described the calotype or "sun picture" as potentially ruinous for art because of its "natural confederacy" with "the crowd," which he alternately eulogized and despised.[2]

For most others, what photography seemed to promise, followed by its cinematic, videographic, and digital progeny, was the accurate capture of the social being by and for itself. Each technological iteration, however, inevitably came up short, prodding artists to invent methods of

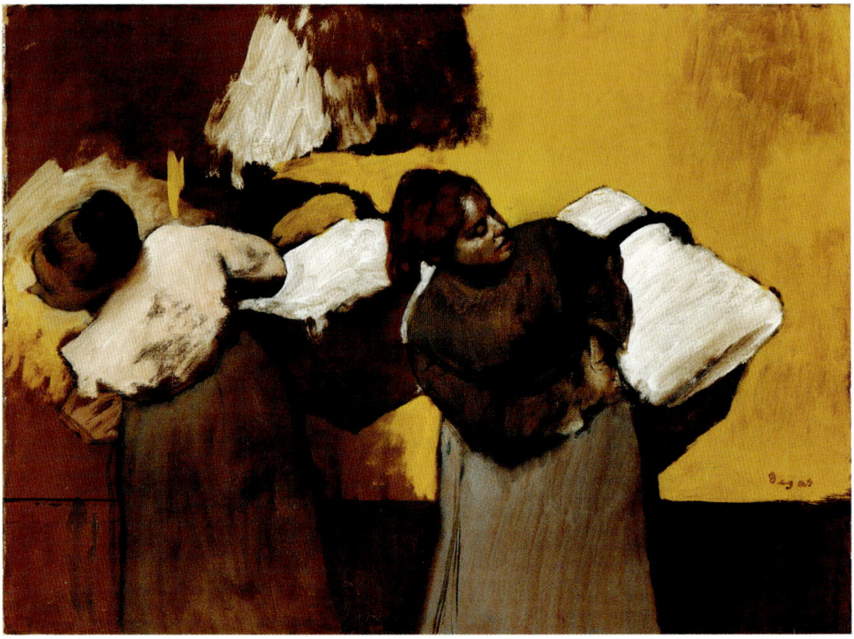

supplementation with words, special effects, and supplementary imagery in order to bring social collectivity into focus. Undoubtedly AI imaging will prove no different, despite its seemingly miraculous ability to fabricate images from mere word prompts. Indeed, AI's limitation may be the most revealing yet: trained exclusively on what has already been archived,

FIGURE 35

Edgar Degas, *Two Laundresses*, 1876, oil on paper, 46 × 61 cm. Five years after the Paris Commune, in an era when photography was beginning to make visible the lives of the laboring poor, Degas pursues a parallel ambition in paint: to arrest, if only briefly, the anonymous collective agency of working women whose labor animated—and largely disappeared into—the social fabric of modern Paris. Used with permission from Christie's Images, London/Scala, Florence.

it can only recombine existing representations, making the phantom archive's absences absolute. The murmuring multitude that was never photographed cannot be conjured by prompts. More fundamentally, AI produces aggregations of individual figures but cannot grasp collectivity itself—that temporal, rhythmical, lived quality of social being that resists reduction to visual stereotype.

Notably, a similar pattern also arises when artists attempt to represent time's passage in the form of historical events, periods, or moments of prefiguration. What remains evasive is the intangibility of human labor as a type of agency with the potential of transforming temporal circumstances. One can represent work, even monumentalize it as twentieth-century socialist realism often did. Monumentality is employed as a means of marking historical shifts in culture, politics, and society. However, as such, these types of representations also freeze the time-altering (or time-stopping) movement unique to living labor. Perhaps this is one reason public monuments are often the first to be toppled when radical historical conditions burst upon the scene? Still, it is a characteristic flaw that scars artistic representations, whether these are lens-based, painterly, or sculptural, although somewhat less so for time-based and performative portrayals addressed in part IV.

THE SPECTRAL AGENCY OF SOCIETY

The fragmented agency of the phantom archive might be grasped as the rhythmical and repetitive patterns of dissonance and disruption. This shadowy ligature represents neither a mere background nor foreground, but instead is a constitutive sequence with its own function of day-to-day resistance. For decades, artists, and especially those working with photography and lens-based practices, have grappled with how to render collective social agency visible. Subjects like factory workers or revolutionary masses, whether coerced to work together or working together through volition, elude conventional representation even as they collectively labor in time and space. From life painting and monumental sculpture to literature and contemporary socially engaged art, collective social agency remains a problem-space/time, with the most compelling efforts at portrayal making no effort to conceal this fact.

Yet within the Unpresent, this representational challenge intensifies considerably. We are no longer peering through a glass darkly; we are inside the unlit glass itself. From here, one can only catch an approximate rhythm of resistance, an indefinite anticipation of futures yet to come or pasts that may or may not have ever been. Within the Unpresent, both past and future exist as unrealized possibilities waiting to be reanimated, and the collective social formations artists seek to visualize become more spectral, ever more elusive. And rather than only making this enigma work for them, they make it their subject matter. As Tom Finkelpearl and Pablo Helguera have argued, contemporary socially engaged art emerges from a genealogy of participatory practices rooted in 1960s social movements, from civil rights organizing and the Port Huron Statement's vision of participatory democracy to feminist consciousness-raising that made the personal political. This practice understands art-making not as individual expression but as collaborative knowledge construction that produces social relations rather than merely representing them.[3]

One of the more compelling exemplars of this practice is what I term conspicuous repair. This concept echoes within much of the artwork presented in this book. It is also indebted to Theo Reeves-Evison's sophisticated theorization in *The Ethics of Contemporary Art* (2020) and his analysis of Kader Attia's work, which argues that "repair cannot be considered a static 'fix' to a breakage or problem, but rather invokes the potential for modification, transformation, and creative addition."[4] Building on Reeves-Evison's processual understanding, my notion of conspicuous repair draws on two further reference points. The first is Bertolt Brecht's alienation effect in theater; as the experimental director Akira Takayama puts it, the aim of projects like *Lehrstücke*, or learning plays, was to "create a situation, a paradox or a contradiction where learning can occur."[5] The second is the Japanese concept of *kintsugi*, the joining of cracked pottery using gold filler. Together, these inform an emphasis on the political function of making historical injuries visible in activist art's engagement with suppressed pasts. Conspicuous repairs and other related forms of self-evident repurposing, reuse, and reanimation do not seek to restore things as they "really were" but deliberately expose the stitching, the gaps, the impossibility of seamless restoration. (Chto Delat explicitly references a similar Brechtian practice; see figure 7.) These practices transform the profuse surplus of the phantom archive into a form of politically charged aesthetic practice, and this will be the focus of this section of the book as we continue to explore time and social agency in the Unpresent.

PHOTOGRAPHY, LABOR, AND THE SOCIAL PARADOX

Any effort made to repurpose or repair the archive by creating a time problem in the present, or, as I have proposed, in the Unpresent, is immediately challenged by one problem above all others: how to represent the agency of the social itself, how such representation has been attempted and in what ways, especially when artists seek to visualize those sectors of society that were systematically unseen or drastically underrepresented in the past. This includes labor in all its forms, human and nonhuman alike, for certainly animals too have been conscripted into productive capacity as extracted labor but seldom portrayed as such (contrarily, artistic attempts at portraying animals appear in images by Haapoja [figure 10], Michelson [figure 20], Toufic [figure 26], and Ryan and Hand [figure 36]). Consider especially the way subjects laboring inside early industrial factories vanish from sight in photographs depicting machinery and architecture absent living workers—and this includes the draft horses and mules whose hauling made those factories run, doubly erased from a record that struggled to capture human labor let alone animal.

In part, this focus on objects was due to the limitations of the medium, which required ample lighting and exposure times that blurred or erased moving elements, including people. Access to these premises was also tightly controlled by factory owners, who wanted both to prevent documentation of their operations for commercial reasons, and to exclude possible union organizers or government safety regulators. Many mills simply banned photography outright. When documentation did take place, it was carefully staged to produce ideal working conditions.

These and other limitations applied all the more severely to photographic representation of slave labor on plantations and domestic labor by slaves or free women, as well as child labor in general along with the photographic depiction of the nonhuman organic world. Photographer Jacob Riis did create a few indelible images of children at work (and play) in the late nineteenth century, including a photograph of a twelve-year-old boy pulling threads in a garment sweatshop in 1889, but it was not until the early twentieth century that Lewis Hine systematically documented child labor thanks to support from a private organization (the National Child Labor Committee) dedicated to exposing and reforming such working conditions.[6] Photographs of plantation work carried out by slave laborers are rarer still. And images of slaves engaged in the labor of liberating themselves appear to be completely nonexistent, an absence that artist Dread Scott has sought to conspicuously remedy, as explored in the next chapter.

THE MURMUR OF THE PHANTOM ARCHIVE

Capturing social agency remains elusive under any conditions. And yet seeking to visualize, interpret, and mobilize, but also, in some instances, to overtly reject the spectral agency of the *madding crowd* has been and continues to be a primary preoccupation of artists into present times, as we see with the activist, participatory, social practice, dialogical, and relational art of today. Simply put, along with efforts to remain autonomous and circumvent enclosure by the capitalist marketplace (more often a metaphorically oriented aspiration, a successful act of resistance), successive generations of artists have been possessed by a desire to grasp, render, or embody the social, in and for itself. Yet the social remains elusive and abstract, a hauntology motivated by the limitations of representational forms, which tend to reduce the multitude to a glimpse, a token, a metonym, or an ossified core sample of social time itself. After all, if anything about the phantom archive can be generalized, it is the tempo-setting role of social labor itself, as a collectivized rhythm or pulse that extends, withdraws, reasserts itself, while always constantly probing with intensity or even at times an obstinate resistance.

At the same time, isn't it the abstract repetitive redundancy of this surplus collective agency under capitalism, as much as it is the pockets and folds that puncture abstraction—the undercommons and dark matter spaces and times of withdrawal and defiance—that generates a kind of awe or even terror of the social itself? And is it not in the arts,

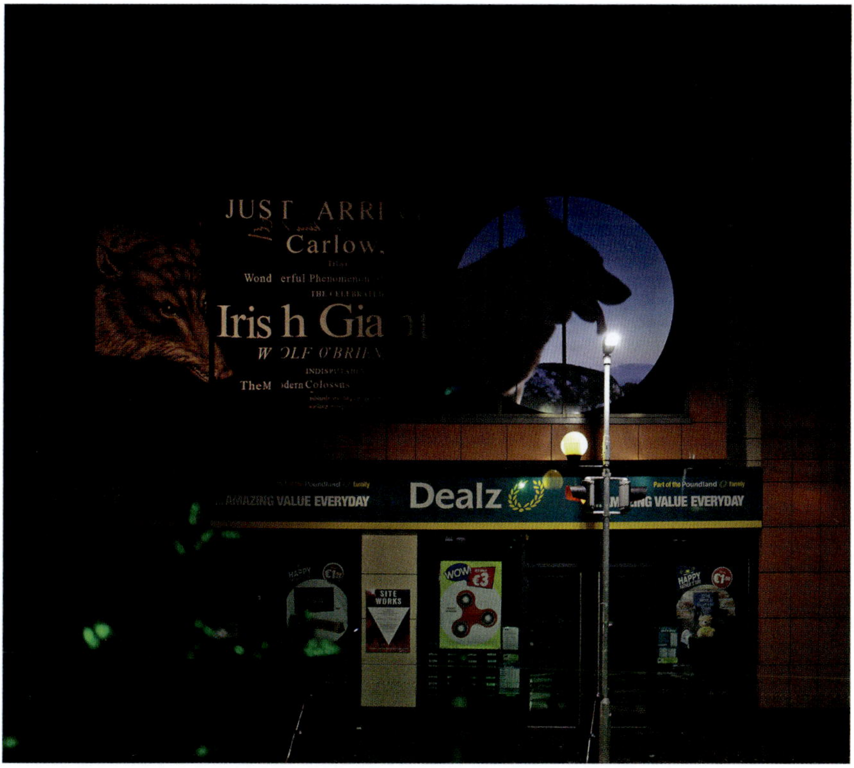

FIGURE 36

Orla Ryan and Brian Hand, *The Wolf O'Brien*, 2017. This installation in Carlow, Ireland, displayed outside a contemporary retail store, questions the mythology of the Irish wolfhound invented in the Victorian era and the fabricated connection between extinct wolves and the creation of an "authentic" Irish heritage. Here species themselves enter the phantom archive: wolves eliminated as capital cleared land, then mythologized through invented dog breeds that naturalize both colonial violence and nationalist authenticity as timeless Irish heritage (there is a similar romanticism at work in the "Neshaminy Indian" statue discussed in the introduction of this book). Image courtesy of the artists.

especially the visual arts, that, as Carol Duncan realized decades ago, redundant production is most evident and most essential?[7] This may be why attempts to represent collectivism through the arts typically take the form of metaphors, or metonyms, or barely glimpsed apparitions that can also appear as tormenting (think of the fascination today's popular culture has with swarms of purgatorial zombies). Given this challenge, just how have artists attempted to depict social collective labor in all of its specificity as well as abstractness? This has taken many forms, sometimes affirmative but at other times critical, or decidedly ambiguous. Still, the drive to capture social agency is unending among modern and contemporary artists. Consider the festive-turned-tragic photographs made of Parisian Communards celebrating their all too brief revolution atop improvised barricades, or surrealists aiming to capture on paper and canvas the workings of a presumed collective unconscious.

In the post-World War II era, *happenings* redeployed a ludic communal vehicle of erotic disengagement from disciplinary order, and Joseph Beuys co-organized the German Green Party while also working and shaping collectivity as "social sculpture." Years later, Rick Lowe regenerated affordable housing in an abandoned African American neighborhood in Houston using the rubric of social sculpture, while, years before Beuys's social sculpture, the Japanese group Hi Red Center had scrubbed Tokyo sidewalks while dressed as civic maintenance workers.[8] All three examples foreground the societal everyday, intimating that perhaps artistic efforts at visualizing social collectivity are really less about representation and mimesis than about utter redundancy as inevitable, invisible precepts of the abstraction and fungibility set forth by capital.

But artists pursued this ambition not only through photo-based or performative media. Think of the anonymous Parisian laundresses and washerwomen Edgar Degas portrayed in the middle of his career, including two laboring women depicted five years after the rise and fall of the Paris Commune (figure 35). The painter renders their dynamic movements hurriedly, almost in sketchbook fashion, emphasizing their powerful physical bodies with thick arms bending and stretching while pushing five- to nine-pound "sad irons" as they cross and cross again damp cotton sheets and muslin garments. Their labors literally stir the atmosphere surrounding them, animating a diffuse geometry of light and shadows, spaces and time, where women's unseen labor transpires. Degas's laundresses express both exhaustion and relief as they prepare to carry folded laundry straight off and out of the frame. Is this then a picture of work's thankful end? Almost certainly not. What we see is most likely a pause before work starts again, continuously, repetitively. But a pause in which the phantom archive's murmuring sociality breaks the surface, if only for an instant. For what else is at stake here other than attempting to apprehend that elusive, vital, and transformative capacity of everyday collective agency? It is, however, a goal that artists, with their repertoire of representational techniques and intellectual desires, share, albeit differently, with capital in its postindustrial form: the apprehension, disciplining, and monetization of life itself. When did this begin?

FROM INDUSTRIAL LABOR TO GLOBAL COMMODITY NETWORKS

A new type of social force, and a new representational necessity, emerged two centuries ago as the biopolitical forces of labor were marshaled into what would become the industrial working class via factory production. With the Fordist assembly line, labor becomes generalized, exchangeable, abstracted, and in a word, fungible. Time is transformed into a repetitive monotony of the same: the same action performed on the same commodity in the same, or ever-diminishing, amount of time. This was not, however, a universal condition as yet, and still is not today. As with Trotsky's uneven and combined development from the last chapter, and Chakrabarty's collision between History #1 and History #2, capital's expansion is uneven at best and patchy in its enlargement. For instance, Degas's female working bodies are engaged in preindustrial labor even as he embeds them within sketchy, abstract spaces as if prefiguring modes of mechanization that were not yet affecting such labor. Such mechanization would never entirely vanish, but would reappear in colonial spaces both within and outside of urban centers into the twenty-first century.

However, within the factory system, social time became its own kind of timeless abstraction and repetitive tedium of the same action. Today, this continuously unvarying labor is concentrated in Asia, Latin America, and Africa, where a largely female workforce turns out components for

13

DREAD SCOTT'S ARCHIVAL ACTIVISM

Between November 8 and 9, 2019, artist Dread Scott orchestrated an elaborate restaging of a (too-) little-known nineteenth-century slave uprising that took place in what is today Louisiana (see figure 37). Two hundred and eight years earlier, from January 8 to 10, 1811, just seven years after the conclusion of the Haitian uprising over 2,000 kilometers away, some 100 enslaved men and women walked off sugar plantations on the outskirts of New Orleans and began to march across the countryside. The runaways were soon joined by up to 500 others, including both men and women who armed themselves with hoes, shovels, and picks. As though anticipating Trotsky's future description of "the direct interference of the masses in historical events," this improvised "people's army" burned down several plantations before being attacked by a white militia two days into their campaign.[1] While a small portion of the rebels escaped capture, most were interrogated, tried, and then hung, shot, or in some instances, decapitated; their heads exhibited on pikes as a warning to other potential insurgent slaves. Only one of many traumas, but also only one of many insurrections that took place in the era of transatlantic slave trade and forced labor, the Louisiana Slave Revolt of 1811 reenters contemporary consciousness as an act of conspicuous archival repair by dozens of artisans, videographers, and performers organized by Dread Scott.

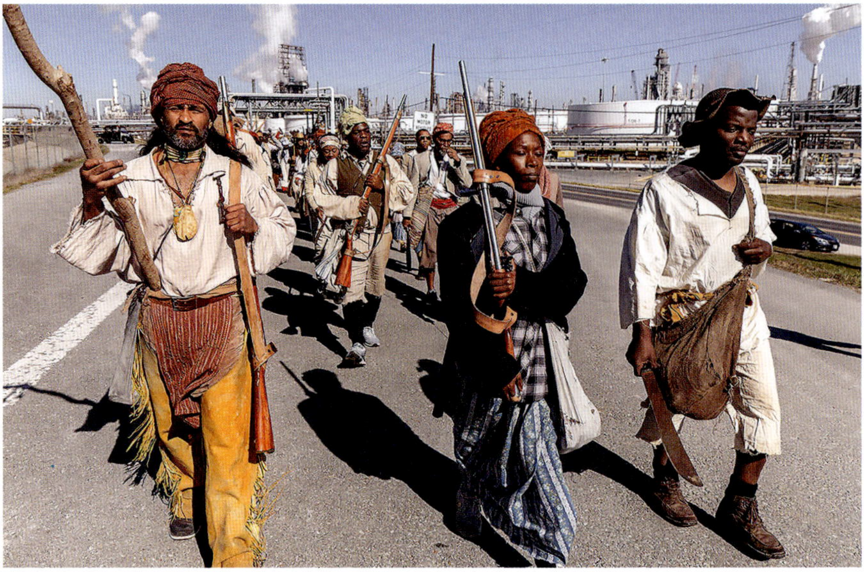

HEROIC TEMPOS, RADICAL MEASURES

Describing his own practice as "revolutionary art to propel history forward," Scott aimed in *Slave Rebellion Reenactment* to highlight "confluences between past and present" while generating "an ever-shifting dialogue that encourages viewers to rethink long-held assumptions."[2] Rather than recreating a march across a swampy rural Louisiana landscape, the artist acknowledged he would intentionally have the twenty-first-century performance pass by "heavy industry, gated communities, small businesses, low-income housing, big box-style stores, and other characteristics of everyday life."[3] Instead of attempting to create the

FIGURE 37

Dread Scott, *Slave Rebellion Reenactment*, with volunteer participants restaging the 1811 Louisiana slave uprising along its original route, New Orleans, 2019. Image courtesy of the artist.

illusion of time regained, Scott's reimagining explicitly sought to fold time back onto itself. The power of this archival haunting has even been testable. For a time after 2019, whenever one executed a Google image search using the phrase *slave uprising* or *slave insurgency*, among the first pictures to appear were those of Scott's 2019 *Slave Rebellion Reenactment* right alongside late eighteenth- and early nineteenth-century engravings and woodcuts from prephotographic newspapers (the images still appear in searches now, but less prominently). Think of this as hauntological activism in reverse, the future twisting about to trouble the past, or consider it the other way around, as an unconcealed act of restaging that troubles the present through its exposure of a fractured historical record, in what Tirza True Latimer describes as the mobilization of history's "gaps, absences, and apparitions."[4] Meanwhile, according to Scott, "a lot of my work looks at how the past sets the stage for the present, and how it exists in the present in new forms."[5]

Still, it took several years for the artist to marshal his reconstructed legion of volunteer Black troops for the reenactment, beginning with funds raised from a 2017 Kickstarter campaign launched in conjunction with the innovative New Orleans-based cultural organization Antenna. The men and women of Scott's infantry were costumed by Alison L. Parker, who founded ricRAK, a local not-for-profit offering community sewing classes that started by recycling and repurposing donated textiles typically disposed of after the conclusion of theatrical productions and Mardi Gras. Notably, Scott informs us that research for these garments was hampered not only by the absence of photographic documentation (the rebellion took place before photography was invented), but by the "racist assumptions and ideas" imbued in the representations of slave laborers that do exist in the woodcut illustrations used by newspapers in the early 1800s:

> This included things like big lips and pitch-black skin, but also happy dancing slaves and slaves being slovenly and not doing work. When we were looking to design costumes for Slave Rebellion Reenactment, we had to look at the painting, drawings, and prints from the French Atlantic world (Saint Domingue, Martinique, and Guadalupe) to get more "naturalistic" images of Africans and Afro-descendent people, including enslaved people.[6]

COLLABORATIVE PRODUCTION AND PEDAGOGY AS REVOLUTIONARY PRACTICE

Slave Rebellion Reenactment was produced by London-based artistic director Jennifer Crook and a team of location managers and assistants, and was ultimately captured on video by acclaimed Ghanaian-born British filmmaker John Akomfrah, a co-founder of the Black Audio Film Collective in the early 1980s. Scott's objective was to mirror the collective and clandestine preparations of the nineteenth-century uprising by initiating meetings of small volunteer groups with the goal that these would evolve into forms of self-organization in preparation for what he termed a "performative reenactment of history." Significantly, because these meetings and the conversations about the project were considered essential to the overall artwork, Scott's authorship is not absent but is certainly delimited to a degree by the collaborative structure of the work.

Along with its cooperative production and the way it salvages an underrepresented past, three other features of *Slave Rebellion Reenactment* especially draw my interest in relation to the concept of this book. First is the way the work's speculative imagination is performed via photography; second is Scott's focus on the agency of an anonymous multitude (as opposed to enshrining leading insurgent figures, in the way that François-Dominique Toussaint Louverture and Jacques Dessalines typically dominate reflections on the Haitian Revolution); and third is the work's prioritizing (in line with Lucy R. Lippard's definition of activist artists) of actively teaching.[7] Scott's considerable investment in pedagogy makes his reenactment project exemplary of Lippard's description as well as the archival repair methods being discussed here. This is thanks to his *Reenactment*'s important afterlife as distributed video documentation, but also happens more directly when the artist makes in-person visits to classrooms to engage with students. Consider also questions raised by a class at a historically Black college, which prompted the artist to reflect that

> the more that I talked with them, the more it became clear that they kinda felt . . . they would look at a situation was like, well, man, why are Black people . . . why are there 1.1 million Black people in prison? Why are we the ones that are poor? Why are the police shooting us down? Why are we the drug dealers? Why are our

families broken, as they like to say? And they really felt a sense of shame, actually, about being Black, but when they would learn about this slave revolt, suddenly they realized, that wait, our ancestors weren't slaves, they were people who were enslaved. And that there was this tremendous joy and uplifting sense that they had when they heard about people fighting back and resisting.[8]

THE TEXTURE OF EVERYDAY RESISTANCE

Scott's project builds up a sense of temporal resistance across time rather than in a particular time. The reenactment is made up not only of those spectacular moments of revolutionary uprising but, significantly, of the moments before, after, and in between. The hours spent working in the community, discussing the project with students and with future performers, the collaborations with garment and artifact makers: these are the typically shadowed temporal segments overlooked or only grasped by framing or interpreting them in direct relationship to the "real" event, the radical moment, the moment of rupture in which tables are turned and everything changes. Rather than mere background or foreground, they form a constitutive sequence with its own function in the everyday, akin to what Michel de Certeau theorized after May 1968 failed to produce sweeping social transformation.[9] It seems we are promised no significant sudden breaks from day-to-day unfreedom in the Unpresent, any more than from the bare nature of contemporary art and its institutions. For now, one can only glimpse this textural rhythm of resistance from a perspective of anticipation, making acts of repurposing, reusing, and repairing the phantom archive all the more indispensable.

REENACTMENT AS CONTEMPORARY ART

Reenactments have come to form an entire genre within contemporary art, Sven Lütticken tells us, dating this trend from 2000 with projects that include Jeremy Deller's *The Battle of Orgreave* produced by Howard Giles and filmed by Mike Figgis in 2001; as well as Rod Dickinson's *The Milgram*

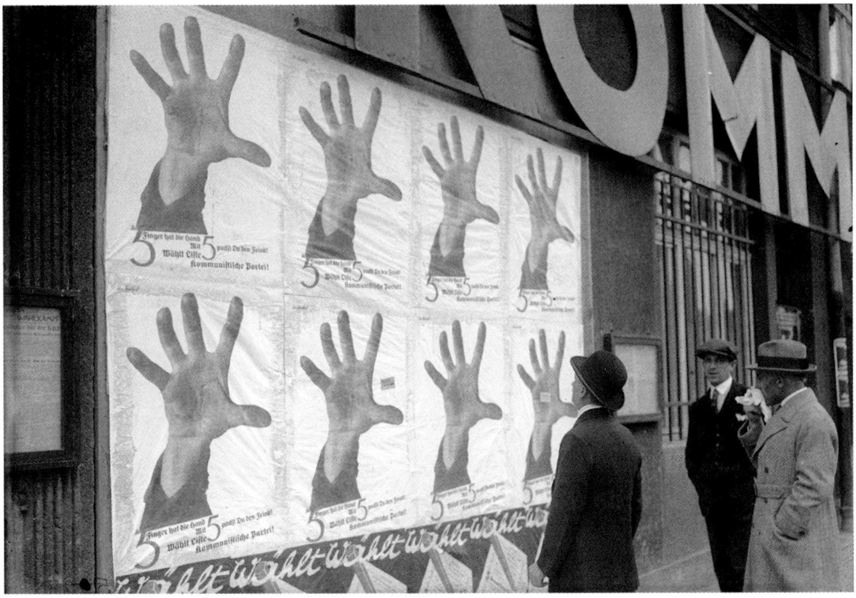

Reenactment (2002) and Omer Fast's *Godville* (2005).[10] Lütticken explains that this phenomenon approaches the concept of time in such a way that "history has increasingly been transformed into a deposit of potentially valuable materials to be mined by artists and other post-Fordist workers (i.e., creative and cognitive workers)."[11] Needless to say, this depository is quite similar to what I am referring to as the phantom archive of surplus ideas, tropes, images, and potentialities. Lütticken adds that this storeroom of possibilities is reanimated by "a productivist mobilization of the historical record."[12] Rephrasing this in terms of my argument, these processes of conspicuous reenactment, repurposing, and repair offer more than a theatrical period piece or spectacularization of the past;

FIGURE 38

John Heartfield, *The hand has 5 fingers! With these 5 grab the enemy!*, 1928, rotogravure montage posters, Berlin. Image used with permission from Bundesarchiv Federal Archives, Germany.

they provide a means for activist artists to reconstruct aspects of the archive that have been lost, exiled, or suppressed, what Bloch described as prevented futures. This includes picturing events that preceded photography's invention or which were never captured or only partially documented by the lens, such as workers' rebellions, anticolonial actions, the labor of women and children, and innumerable slave uprisings that took place throughout the seventeenth, eighteenth, and nineteenth centuries, including the Haitian Revolution.

Think of this fantastic juxtaposition in time and space as a twice-staged occurrence: the first time as an embodied event that still cleaves to the past and present, in which reenactment is corporally present; and the second time as a statement organized for the camera's eye. In this sense, Scott's project is a supplemental extension of lens-based technology both like and unlike that which Bertolt Brecht, Walter Benjamin, Gustav Klutsis, John Heartfield, and others theorized and practiced almost a century earlier. In this contemporary art practice, not space or images but time is what the artist juxtaposes, conjoins, and contrasts.

Reenactment and repurposing also have a peculiar effect on artistic egos and notions of the great work and singular authorship. Kate Valk, founding member of the Wooster Group, explains that reenactment dismisses ego-gratifying need, permitting performers to serve as vessels for the repetition of content, and therefore liberating them from the demands of individualistic artistic flourishes.[13] In fact, the closer one gets to the performative perfection of a scored reenactment, the more expansive this liberation becomes; think of this agency as that of a detached mimesis placed in the service of social transformation. Here, mimetic representation becomes an unlikely yet subtly powerful form of collective resistance, and reenactment an act of disruptive but self-evident repetition. What, then, of the desire to terminate repetition by restoring an ideal past, as I have proposed MAGA seeks to bring about?

THE POLITICS OF HISTORICAL REPETITION

If the MAGA focus on restoring a fantasy of America's ethnonationalist past is indeed our "new" retro-avant-garde, then it is precisely the

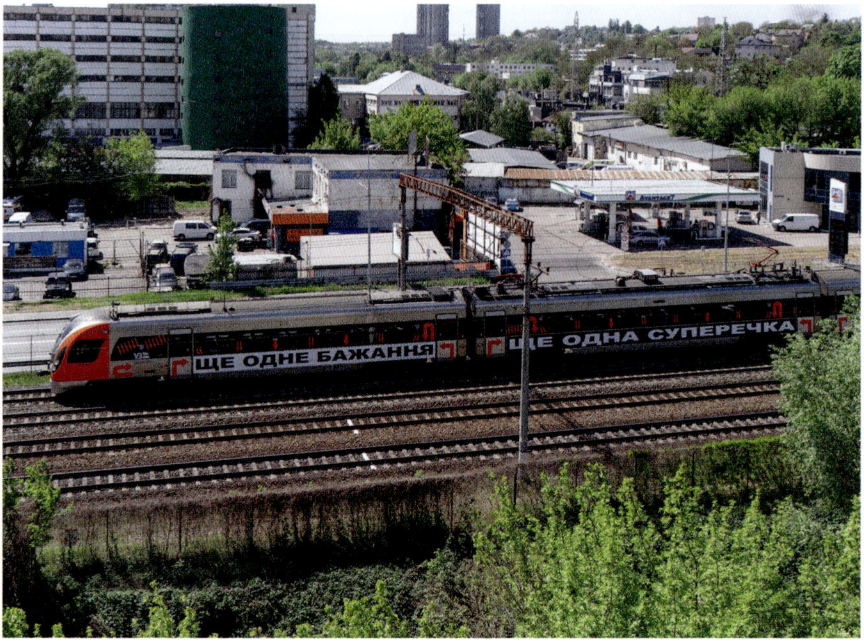

FIGURE 39

In Barbara Kruger's public installation *Untitled (Another Again)* (Commissioned by RIBBON International, 2025), a Ukrainian Railways Intercity train becomes a moving canvas for her distinctive bold typography in red, black, and white. The text, written in Ukrainian and visible in this aerial photograph, repeats the phrase "ЩЕ ОДНЕ БАЖАННЯ" [Another wish], among other poetic iterations of "another" paired with words like "day," "night," "fear," "hope," and "life." Traveling across war-affected Ukraine from May 1 to July 14, 2025, the artwork aimed to create a contemporary message of solidarity and resilience, while drawing inspiration from Ukraine's revolutionary-era "agit-trains" of the 1920s. Image courtesy of the artist.

opposite of Dread Scott's practice in *Slave Rebellion Reenactment*. For certainly the J6 insurrection was more than anything else an effort to actually experience something, to break with the uncanniness of the Unpresent, as attested to by such shouted comments as "I can't believe this is reality." Similarly, Rebecca Schneider, in her 2011 study *Performing Remains*, describes some reenactors of US Civil War or Revolutionary War battles undergoing "a physical collapse, or at least a profound confusion of time."[14] Schneider tells us the reenactors call the experience a "period rush" or a "wargasm," or they might say they are "seeing the elephant" or "touching time."[15] And yet, is this not a rendezvous with temporal repetition seemingly in the service of terminating repetition? The expression of a desire to step out of a collapsed experience of time under the unreal aesthetics of the Unpresent? Perhaps the truly disenchanting aspect of such a delusive quest is that, as the reenactors seek to escape such capitalist unrealism, the period rush merely reinstates it as a commodified, if selective, version of history as spectacle. Schneider reminds us that "many have noted how America has become a kind of theme park of itself—'The Past as a Theme Park' writes David Lowenthal in a simple, catchy phrase. And perhaps the present is a reality TV show taking place as the past."[16]

Schneider's observations became alarmingly accurate a decade after they were published. On one overcast afternoon in 2021, Washington, DC itself became a theme park. Nonetheless, from another perspective, we can also appreciate artist and theorist Hito Steyerl's musing, "I love history. But history doesn't love me back." She adds that certain invocations of the past are not "a noble endeavor, [but] something to be studied in the name of humankind so as to avoid being repeated."[17] Written during the year of Brexit and the first Trump presidency and focused on the beginning of the Russian war against Ukraine, Steyerl's summation of the way history is repurposed by militarized forces can apply to MAGA and Trump's invocation of America's manifest destiny as much as to Putin's yearning for a return to imperial Russia. "Frankly," she concludes, "this kind of history sucks."[18] Indeed, this version of history might be more accurately described as another example of time's carcass, whereby "history" is reduced to an unalloyed signifier of power, shorn of any latent reference to an all-embracing concept of emancipatory social, economic, and environmental justice.

14

TATLIN ET AL.: REVOLUTIONARY REPURPOSING

A "slap in the face of public taste" is how Vladimir Mayakovsky, Velimir Khlebnikov, and other early twentieth-century avant-garde provocateurs reassigned art's role in the year of the Russian Revolution, explicitly calling upon cultural producers to assist in the dismantling of bourgeois society. "The past is too tight," begins their manifesto; "the Academy and Pushkin are less intelligible than hieroglyphics. Throw Pushkin, Dostoevsky, Tolstoy, etc., etc., overboard from the Ship of Modernity."[1]

Putting cultural nostalgia to death is one way this slap is understood by contemporary philosopher and historian Boris Groys.[2] And rather than focus on the poetry and art of Mayakovsky, he cites Kazimir Malevich's 1915 painting *Black Square* as the epitome of this historical decontamination. Groys insists that what made the minimalist canvas so revolutionary was not its political or social intentions (after all, it had no recognizable content), but rather the painting's abandonment of all goals, revolutionary or otherwise. Since *Black Square* is anything but activist art, why is it even part of this study? For Groys, the radicalism of Malevich's work lies in its singular relationship to revolutionary time, a "non-teleological, potentially infinite process which the artist cannot and does not want to bring to an end."[3]

Put differently, this thread of avant-garde art linked with avant-garde politics is not situated in a moment, but across moments of time. To cite art historian Esther Leslie, the Russian constructivists, productivists,

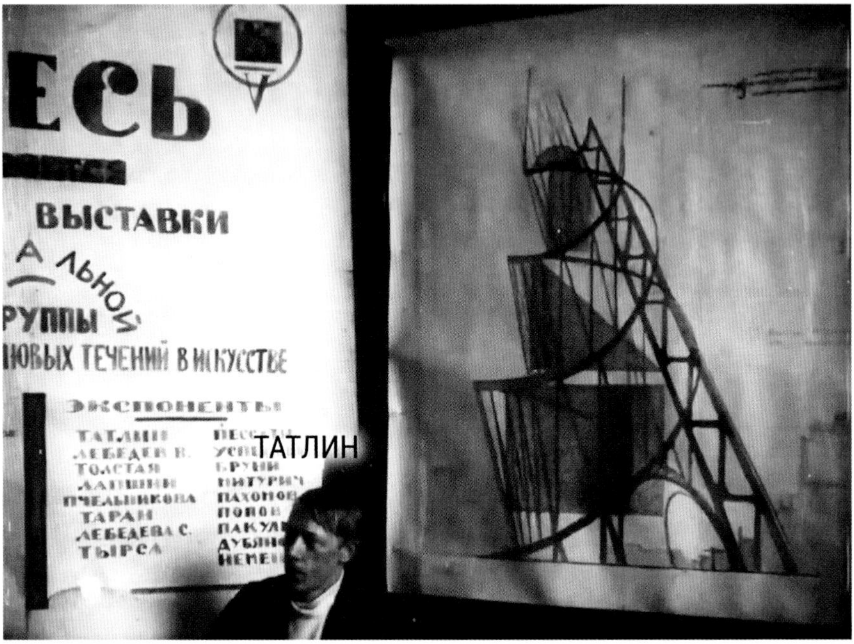

and futurists sought to represent the image of Lenin as "motile, mobile, in movement, unfixed," a figure who could only be represented through photomontage and seriality because any singular image would freeze what was fundamentally temporal.[4] "Lenin is in time, but has no time," she writes, capturing the avant-garde's attempt to represent revolutionary transformation as ongoing process rather than static monument, as fragmentation becomes both a necessity and a revolutionary method.[5]

FIGURE 41

Vladimir Tatlin, founder of Russian constructivism and author of *Monument to the Third International*, appearing in a newsreel from postrevolutionary Petrograd, Russia, 1923. Photo courtesy of Wikimedia Commons.

As Groys admits, the ferocity of dismantling history cannot be sustained. "What does it mean to continue the avant-garde?" he muses, then answers his own query by arguing that after the revolution, radical artistic form was transformed into a "pure decoration of power, or into a commodity."[6] In a still more audacious proposition, Groys argues that it was the unconditional aesthetic vision of Russia's artistic avant-garde that inadvertently laid the groundwork for the single-party communist state of Stalinism: "Under Stalin the dream of the avant-garde was in fact fulfilled and the life of society was organized in monolithic artistic forms, though of course not those that the avant-garde itself had favored."[7] In order to engineer a fresh aesthetic vocabulary for an entirely new Soviet society, the past had to be swept away. And yet, ironically, Groys maintains, this radical cultural restart was only truly fulfilled in the 1930s by socialist realism, a kitschy throwback, or so it seemed, to past academic styles. In truth, socialist realism was formulated for the masses, he argues, "by well-educated and experienced elites who had assimilated the experience of the avant-garde" by repeating its desire to "conquer and reorganize [society] in new forms."[8]

Whether or not we agree with the philosopher's severe interpretation of the Soviet avant-garde's devolution (and some scholars adamantly do not),[9] Groys's counterintuitive analysis opens a path to think about the relationship between vanguard experimentation, repurposing, and activist art. Building on the previous chapter's concepts of collectivism and repurposing via a phantom archive, this chapter begins with the travails of the postrevolutionary Soviet avant-garde, whose artists, as art historian Catherine Walworth perceptively observes, were paradoxically tasked (or tasked themselves) with creating "something novel, while in reality, they had to produce it out of nothing at all."[10] Overcoming this monumental reality gap, Walworth applies anthropologist Claude Lévi-Strauss's concept of bricolage, in which problems are solved by using whatever materials and processes are found at hand. Walworth proposes that while the USSR may have imagined itself to be engineering a new "radiant future," it was, in truth, repurposing the "bones of [Russia's] imperial past."[11]

While Marx provides insight into this phenomenon of repetition, as discussed in chapter 10, we can view the avant-garde's contradictions not as a revolutionary blind spot or an act of bad faith, but as a template for future socially engaged art insofar as it prefigures the necessary repurposing of a surplus-laden archive that is both material and conceptual. In other words, what might have been a necessary paradox in 1917 Russia has been productively hacked and reused since then; as we witnessed more recently with Dread Scott's *Slave Rebellion Reenactment*, for example, past events are repurposed as a critique of the present. Then again, doesn't capitalism often operate by way of repurposing? Yes, of course. However, unlike capitalism, which treats the past as time's carcass, as so much reified human labor waiting to be drained of value, but also unlike the MAGA movement's desire to restore wholesale an imagined past within the present, socially activist artists approach reuse and repair as a militant summoning of a spectral archive overflowing with hauntological potential. With this invocation, once-dead labor of all types rises again. And now, with the collapse of neoliberalism underway in the Unpresent, there is a new opportunity for investigating and reanimating this dead capital, which is, of course, simultaneously and importantly also dead labor. But such conspicuous resuscitation brings with it danger insofar as it establishes a new cultural scrimmage line where the forces of backlash and reaction will appear and must be confronted.

BRICOLAGE AND THE MATERIAL CONDITIONS OF REVOLUTION

Keeping pace with both Groys and Benjamin, British theorist John Roberts contends that radical art internalizes the retroactive and nonlinear latency of revolutionary time in order to unleash "the present from the necessities of chronological time."[12] Citing the contemporary Russian art collective Chto Delat, Roberts insists this same profane latency has allowed the avant-garde to survive into the present, despite capitalism's ultracommodified imposition of a stultifying, day-to-day sameness. This is where left-activist art enters. For, while the historical vanguard is typically defined as the cutting edge of historical development, activist artists self-consciously and without hesitation recapitulate and even cannibalize elements from the past that might be described as a site of both hope and repair, as well as repetition.

The metamorphic vortex of 1917 Russia gave way to nation-building, and the avant-garde was initially eager to be incorporated into this process. Even Malevich and his suprematist circle envisioned creating a collectivized "new architecture" using highly conceptual architectonic principles to propel abstract shapes "from the surface of canvas to space."[13] The challenge was how to repurpose a vanguard art experiment to establish socialism, presumably without merely decorating existing power, as Groys warns radical artists today. Nothing illustrates this adjustment from revolutionary art to that of a comradely state more dramatically than Vladimir Tatlin's startling Monument to the Third International: a proposed 400-meter tower to be built of steel struts that would harbor enormous geometric glass forms rotating at different speeds. Housed inside these suspended structures would be a broadcasting center and a massive headquarters for the Comintern made up of delegates from several dozen worldwide Communist parties. Tatlin described his approach as "uniting purely artistic forms with utilitarian intentions."[14] Other members of the Soviet cultural vanguard were even more expansive in their assessment. Mayakovsky insisted that Tatlin's tower was the "first monument without a beard."[15] Viktor Shklovsky described the structure as "made of steel, glass, and revolution."[16] The project continues to inspire artists, thinkers, and activists, with one recent book proposing that Tatlin's artistic practice "queers" the very idea of a masculine bourgeois subjectivity, thus generating a new Soviet social collectivity that is simultaneously universal and androgynous.[17] Still, by all accounts, as Christina Lodder has emphasized, Tatlin clearly demonstrated a "romanticization of technology" that led him to explore dynamic and spiraling abstract forms far beyond the material limitations of his day.[18]

POVERTY, IMPROVISATION, AND FOUND MATERIALS

Neither the constructivists nor their suprematist rivals would survive Stalin's imposition of socialist realism some ten years on, but in the immediate aftermath of the revolution both sides of this artistic divide were forced to contend with one imposing challenge above all others: the unprecedented communist society that seemed so visibly within reach

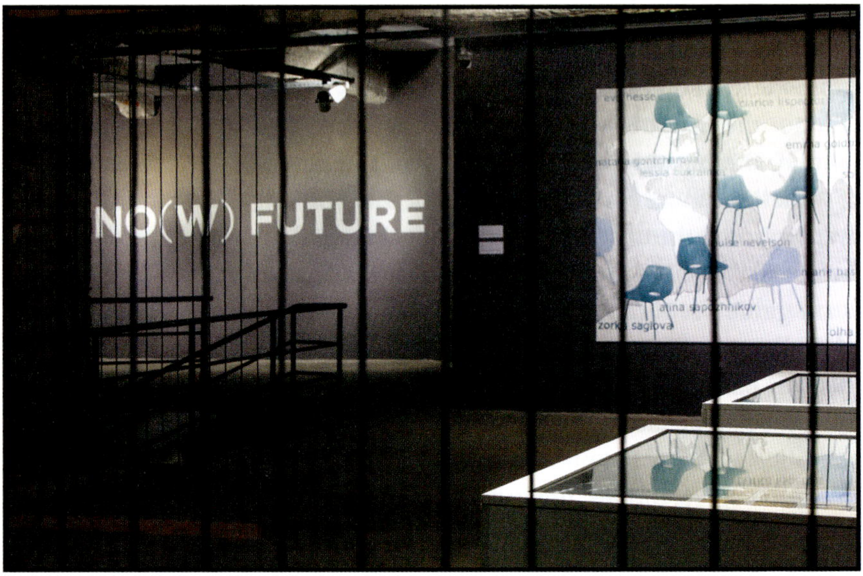

FIGURE 42

Yevgeniy Fiks's *In Edenia, a City of the Future* (2017) transforms a forgotten 1918 Yiddish utopian novella into a contemporary art exhibition, inviting international artists to create works as artifacts from an imaginary harmonious city. Set against Ukraine's political tensions between Soviet nostalgia and European aspirations, the project excavates suppressed multicultural histories while critically examining the seductive dangers of utopian thinking and contemporary art's own claims to social transformation. Image courtesy of the artist.

echoes of the 1871 Parisian uprising within it. Notably, Marx's own writings about the uprising in Paris were what later set the stage for situating the Commune not merely as a likeness or prefiguration of what was to come, but as both the practical and inexorable forerunner for twentieth-century proletarian revolt.[29] In his pamphlet *The State and Revolution*, Lenin draws heavily upon Marx's analysis of the Commune. As historian Jay Bergman observes, this introduces "a larger revolutionary teleology" which, as discussed in chapter 11, amounts to a stagist historical trajectory inevitably culminating in the founding of the USSR forty-six years later.[30] It is tempting to speculate what Lenin might have written had he considered the Haitian Revolution as another revolutionary precedent, a task that would be taken up differently by C. L. R. James two decades later, who saw in Toussaint's revolution a model for anticolonial liberation. Nonetheless, if the USSR was the summit of proletarian history up to that point, it was an evolutionary moment perforated with an indispensable DIY psyche in the form of *remont* (repair, renovation) culture.

Walter Benjamin himself characterized the 1920s Soviet Union as a "repair society," in which the owner-user of state-produced goods must "first work on them to make them fully functional, accommodating the object to their needs and themselves to the object's idiosyncrasies."[31] Labeling Moscow "the city of *remont*" (ремонт), Benjamin is said by Ekaterina Gerasimova and Sofia Chuikina to have adopted this difficult-to-translate Russian word, which also holds connotations of prolonging the life of objects, including "restoring to them their pragmatic or symbolic function."[32] Gerasimova and Chuikina also argue that this postrevolutionary *remont* reality did not limit itself solely to the repair of things or goods, but involved an entire range of informal practices such as "pulling strings, visiting flea markets, using homemade goods, pilfering products from factories, informally reallocating goods, etc."[33] Perhaps not coincidentally, there is also a similar word/concept for such DIY practices in Cuba that goes by the label *resolver*. With Cubans forced to improvise due to the US embargo, anyone who has visited the island can attest to the startling sight of American cars and the occasional Soviet Lada automobile still navigating Havana's streets with repurposed parts and engines all in perfectly good running order.

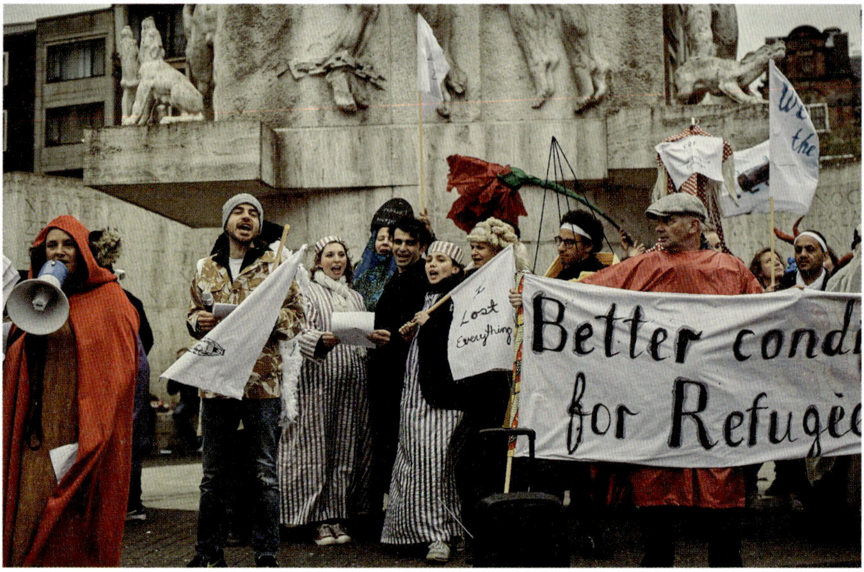

GUERNICA AND THE PHANTOM ARCHIVE OF PROTEST

The art of activism and its spectral archives overflow not just with reappropriated materials, but also with examples of high cultural imagery repurposed into contemporary forms of protest, including canonical paintings such as, above all others, Picasso's antifascist 1937 painting *Guernica*. What is being refunctioned is, of course, the iconic prestige of such pieces, even more than their appearance. A simple Google image

FIGURE 43

Portable art made by the artist Gluklya (Natalia Pershina-Yakimanskaya) from repurposed clothing and fabric and carried in a series of 2011–2012 demonstrations in St. Petersburg against the reelection of Vladimir Putin. Slogans include "Pension should be decent," "Bring Back Free Education!," and "We will all become like this drab piece of torn cloth soon!" Image courtesy of the artist.

search for "Guernica reused or reimagined" returns a multitude of recycled *Guernicas* from the predictable Lego, or dry pasta, or Post-It note interpretations, to full-scale murals decrying the plight of African immigrants crossing the Mediterranean Sea and Palestinian refugees denouncing Israeli walls surrounding camps near Bethlehem. Entire websites and class syllabi are devoted to such recreations. Relatedly, the physical site of Picasso's enormous painting has also been repurposed for activist ends. On January 8, 1970, members of the Art Workers' Coalition and Guerrilla Art Action Group unveiled an anti-Vietnam War poster in front of *Guernica* when it was still located in the Museum of Modern Art in New York. In this instance, the intervention was further amplified by leveraging the ideological power of the museum's global reputation.

But unquestionably the most startling twenty-first-century reactivation of Picasso's imagery took place on February 5, 2003, when the painting's charged antiwar imagery was made invisible on live television. During the lead-up to the US invasion of Iraq, a tapestry-style version of *Guernica*, which had hung inside the entrance to the United Nations' Security Council room since 1985, was covered over by a massive blue curtain. That day, US Secretary of State Colin Powell laid out the George W. Bush administration's case for the military takeover of Iraq, using what is now known to be forged evidence. The blue tarp ensured that televised broadcasts of the event avoided any symbolic contrast between Picasso's antifascist painting and Powell's militaristic performance. All the while, just outside, on the Plaza of the United Nations, groups of protesters held up copies of *Guernica* the painting in protest. In the months to come, variations of the work's imagery showed up as picket signs, puppets, and portable demonstration projects during the unprecedented antiwar rallies that soon rose up around the globe.

FROM IRELAND TO BELARUS: CONTEMPORARY REPURPOSING

The public activation of repurposed imagery also significantly contributed to the landmark 2018 repeal of Ireland's Eighth Amendment prohibiting abortion, which had forced women, even in the case of rape, to leave the country to end an unwanted pregnancy, or face up to a fourteen-year

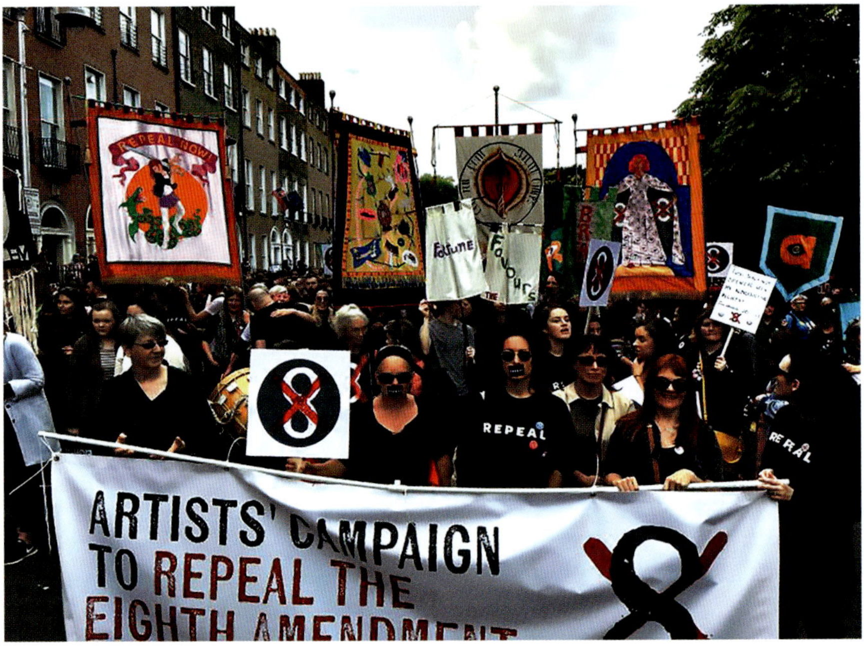

prison sentence. The Artists' Campaign to Repeal, begun in 2015, produced vividly colored, mobile protest banners styled after those created by left-wing trade unions dating back to the mid-1880s or earlier (see figure 44).[41] The banners also repurposed imagery by fifteenth- and sixteenth-century painters Piero della Francesca and Orazio Gentileschi. The activist art project by Alice Maher, Rachel Fallon, and Breda Mayock "opened up a space for discussion and reflection," writes cultural theorist Emma Mahoney, ultimately lending a "third dimension to the political discourse surrounding the abortion debate."[42]

FIGURE 44

Irish artists' campaign "Repeal the 8th" on September 30, 2017, with hand-painted fabric banners by Alice Maher, Rachel Fallon, and Breda Mayock. Image courtesy of the artists, photograph by Christian Kerskens.

And in 2020–2021, another poignant example of activist protest in the form of repurposed high art took place in the former Soviet republic of Belarus, a country where President Alexander Lukashenko—another election-rigging autocrat—has maintained dictatorial power for decades since first being elected in 1994. In the summer of 2020, opposition presidential candidate and banker Viktor Babariko was arrested in the lead-up to that year's elections. Babariko's art collection was also impounded by the state on allegations of tax evasion but was later returned to the gallery.[43] Whatever the reality of these charges may have been, most Belarusians and foreign observers consider his detention a political action. In a move that crosses from art to activism, protesters adopted images of paintings owned by Babariko for public demonstrations, including works by Ukrainian-born artist Chaim Soutine and Belarusian-born Marc Chagall. The works appear on T-shirts, picket sign placards, and social media, sometimes simply as reproductions and at other times as Photoshopped tableaus in which Chagall's wife Bella is abducted by a masked flying riot policeman over his snowy hometown of Vitebsk.

WHOSE MOTHERLAND IS CALLING?

Artist Anna Redko approached this targeted cultural reactivation differently, by repurposing a famous World War II Soviet antifascist poster by Irakliĭ M. Toidze, *The Motherland Is Calling You* (1941). Redko substitutes the figure of jailed Belarusian protest leader Maria Kolesnikova for that of the heroic maternal Russian woman who patriotically leads Red Army troops against Nazis in the original 1941 graphic (figure 45). For their safety, instigators of a four-story-high projection of Redko's image had to remain anonymous, yet their action transformed an entire apartment building in Minsk into a temporary public protest mural in 2020. Informally labeled a Flower Revolution, the all-too-brief moment of mass resistance in Belarus was primarily led by women. Belarus-born philosopher Olga Shparaga explains: "that women—or to be precise, a collective of women—have been at the head of the revolution also runs counter to the nationalist discourse, in which the role of women is to take care of the reproduction of the nation, by giving birth to and raising children."[44]

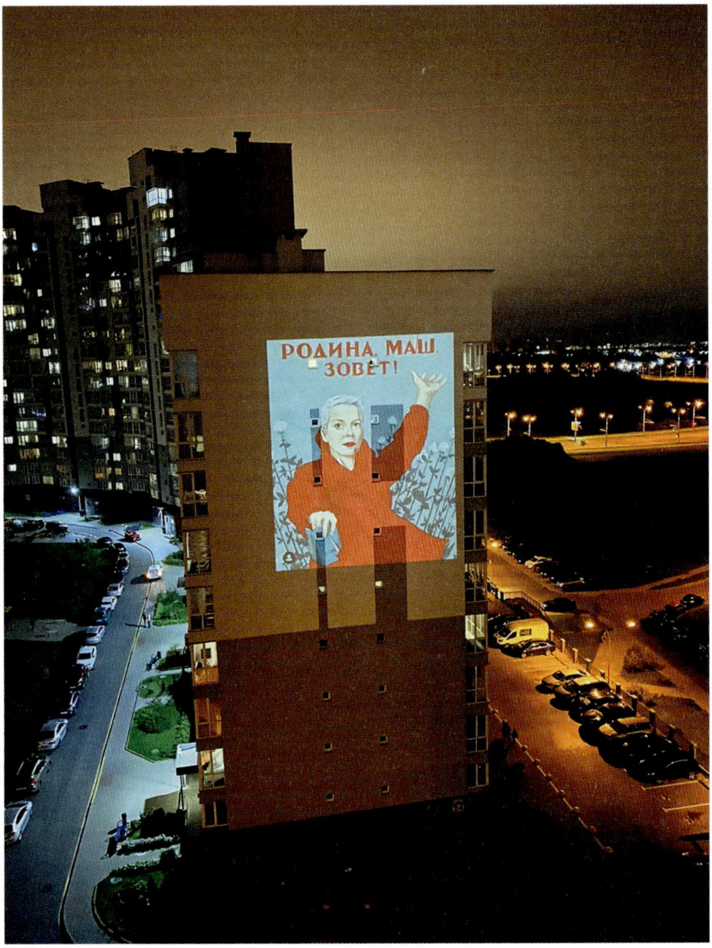

FIGURE 45

An illegal large-scale light projection appeared anonymously on an apartment building in Minsk, Belarus, in 2020. Featuring a poster created by artist Anna Redko, the image repurposes Irakliĭ Toidze's well-known 1941 antifascist poster *The Motherland Is Calling You*, except now substituting the currently jailed Belarusian dissident Maria Kolesnikova, who holds her own torn-up passport instead of the Soldier's Oath from the original World War II Soviet image. Photographer is anonymous.

Belarusian poet Dmitriy Strotsev described this feminist-political turn as generating ever new artistic and even carnivalesque Sunday protests in Minsk with banners, posters, costumes, traditional dance and music, and other acoustic elements. At times it was overwhelming, even as "the language of art . . . seems to be the driving force."[45] Following a days-long protest march, Belarusian-born artist Olia Sosnovskaya hurriedly chronicled her sensations of sudden ontological change brought about by the Flower Revolution. The future, she observes, appears to keep on coming but never arrives. Instead, it "stutters in constant anticipation of the post-, of the aftermath."[46] And yet the future, Sosnovskaya adds, "could only be canceled were we to have lived in linear time."[47] All of this energy, all this protest art, and all these reflections about temporal intervention were brought to a crushing termination in 2020, although sporadic protests continued across Belarus.[48]

CONSPICUOUS REUSE VERSUS SPECTACULAR NOSTALGIA

Conspicuous reuse returns frequently as a tactic of activist art, tapping into the phantom archive, often with a vengeance, to creatively hack cast-off materials and historic customs, as well as gender roles, revolutionary events, and ultimately the very experience of time itself. And while far more typical of the progressive left, it is also found, as discussed in chapter 8, within MAGA culture and the alt-right, who tend to employ reuse to lampoon what they term "elite liberal culture," such as a Keith Haring Pepe the Frog image, or recycled 1950s tradwife fashion. Consider also the "Deported Edition Labubu" AI image posted by the White House to X on September 9, 2025. But generally, MAGA's nationalist-right-oriented version of reuse lacks humor or conspicuousness or any noticeable reflexivity, such as when they display the Confederate flag or fly the US flag upside-down as a sign of distress (both in abundance on January 6), or when Proud Boys merch includes typographical designs using the date 1776 as though this was merely yesterday and nothing of any significance has occurred since then. And then there is the so-called Dark MAGA, in which Donald Trump is reimagined as an avenging Terminator or as a shadowy supernatural being with piercing blue Aryan laser-eyes. However, the problematic voids in time and space created by repressive government actions may not be simply cavities to be filled in with different content. Instead, no matter how socially progressive or regressive its subject matter might be, attempts to repair the temporal damage we are living through must retain the marking of that injury as scars of temporal discrepancy. This is one significant dissimilarity between a left-progressive utilization of the phantom archive and that of the right.

Now, our time traveling must be on the move once more, still further back this time, as we search for the most fugitive of all revelatory clues, that alleged wellspring where art met activism and activism met art. Not surprisingly, we have been there before.

15

KRISTEN ROSS: AFTERLIVES OF THE COMMUNE

The positioning of Gustave Courbet as the genius and ground-zero progenitor for both artistic innovation via the avant-garde and political engagement in the visual arts appears consistently throughout the growing art historical scholarship about protest aesthetics and activist art. Most notably, there are T. J. Clark's seminal companion volumes from 1973, *Image of the People: Gustave Courbet and the 1848 Revolution* and *The Absolute Bourgeois: Artists and Politics in France, 1848–1851*. In the latter, Clark declares that "if any artist came close to creating the conditions for revolutionary art, it was Courbet," while in the former he provocatively questions whether any truly revolutionary art has emerged in Courbet's wake.[1] More recently, Andre Mesquita, Charles Esche, and Will Bradley's comprehensive anthology *Art and Social Change: A Critical Reader* strategically opens with correspondence by Courbet during his Commune period, establishing him as a foundational figure in the lineage of socially engaged art.[2] This canonization is further reinforced in Gerald Raunig's challenging theoretical analysis *Art and Revolution: Transversal Activism in the Long Twentieth Century*, where he formulates "the Courbet model" through a philosophically Deleuzian framework.[3]

Courbet is not, however, a central figure in several other reflections on the Commune presented in this chapter and the next, including the book *Communal Luxury* by Kristin Ross and video documentations of staged performances by Zoe Beloff and Peter Watkins.[4] It is helpful here

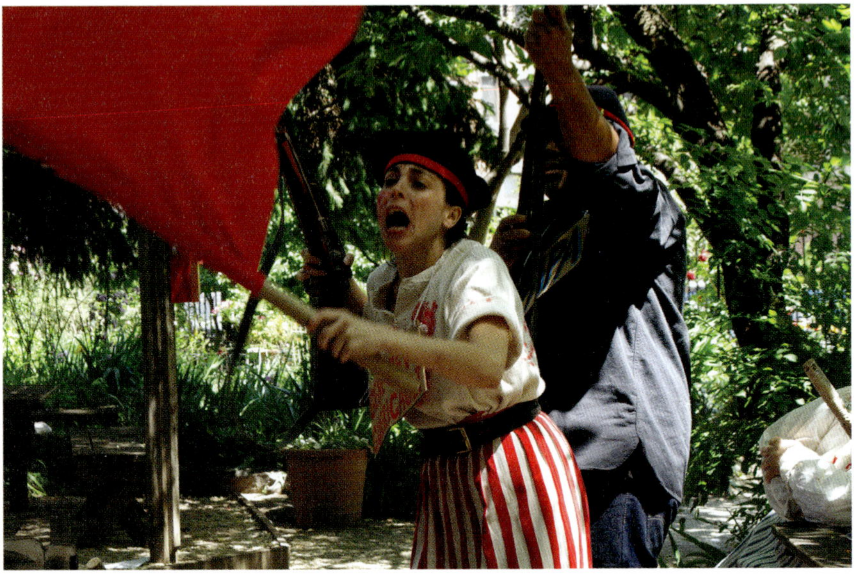

to think of Marxist theorist David Harvey's confrontation of collectivity itself when he stated that it took him many years "to understand why it was that the Parisian communards so readily put aside their pressing tasks of organizing for the defense of revolutionary Paris in 1871, in order to tear down the Vendôme column."[5] More will be said about this act of protest vandalism, but for now, consider how we might avoid elevating one individual artist into the role of ancestral patriarch for activist and protest art. Instead, we might seek to detect the recursive hauntings of an ensemble that incorporates singular persons, objects, images, and events, but also social being itself in all its profoundly everyday rhythms and

FIGURE 46

In the spring of 2012, artist and director Zoe Beloff restaged and produced a video piece of Bertolt Brecht's play *The Days of the Commune* at Zuccotti Park in New York City during Occupy Wall Street with some performers recruited from the Occupy participants. Image courtesy of the artist, photo by Julia Sherman.

tempos and evanescent collectivity. Think of this as the ontology of the phantom archive.

THE VENDÔME COLUMN: MONUMENT AND ANTI-MONUMENT

Let us return, one last time, to the revolutionary hopes of late nineteenth-century Paris and consider an audacious, if ultimately failed, attempt at puncturing the established space-time of a politically regressive regime: the Communards' toppling of the Vendôme Column that Harvey cites. It was (and still is) Napoleon I's protuberant monument to France's imperial conquests. The Communards' act might be summarized as a singular deed of protest, perhaps even a key forerunner of future protest aesthetics or perhaps a form of anti-aesthetics, but most importantly it was also a collective act of monumenticide whose significance continues to be debated, as we shall see. Indeed, the column's demolition continues to generate temporal echoes, some reflecting back to earlier events, others repeating forward, even in the untimely time of the Unpresent. I hardly need to add the rampant toppling of monuments, or acts of monumenticide, carried out in 2020 in parallel with Black Lives Matter following the murder of George Floyd (but also stemming from so many other similar murders and abuses of Black people globally). While this protest vandalism may not literally be intended as a reenactment, the sense of an onward-rolling shockwave of the Vendôme's obliteration cannot go unnoticed. Furthermore, the conscious and conspicuous encounter with such echoes is a central aspect of the artistic works running alongside this volume and forming a visual essay in their own right. One aim in this chapter, therefore, is to subsume, rather than displace, the singular figure of a begetting father of socially engaged art into the temporal pulse of these many rhythmic reverberations.

COURBET AND THE POLITICS OF MONUMENTICIDE

The 1871 Paris Commune has been described by cultural theorist Terry Eagleton as "a kind of Marxian sublime," while radical feminist theorist

most good bourgeois Parisians had, for some sixty years, passed by it and gradually unseen the memorial as they went about their daily routines, Courbet asserted that "the Vendôme Column is a monument devoid of all artistic value, tending to perpetuate by its expression the ideas of war and conquest of the past imperial dynasty," and thus "citizen Courbet expresses the wish . . . to disassemble this column."[14]

Less than a year after he submitted this letter to French authorities, the Executive Committee of the Paris Commune decreed that the column should be dismantled, an action Courbet was initially hesitant to perform, but in which the painter ultimately played his part. As fellow Communard Louis Barron commented, in its celebration of Napoleonic conquests the Vendôme Column was something "fragile, empty, miserable."[15] Once it was toppled on May 16, 1871, participants of the wrecking crew engaged in celebratory rituals, dancing around its debris and creating what might be termed a festival of liberation. However, the Paris Commune was itself attacked by French troops less than a week later. Courbet survived the state's murderous retribution but was arrested and charged with vandalizing French national property. When the artist fled to Switzerland, the restored government then seized his paintings, selling them off to pay for the reconstruction of the monument. In 1877, at the age of fifty-eight, Courbet died penniless. Ultimately, a copy of the original bronze statue of Napoleon that had previously topped the column was restored to its summit. This cycle of destruction and restoration is noteworthy considering events such as the J6 insurrection in 2021. For not only did the MAGA rioters seek to return a deposed Donald Trump to Washington, DC as their president, but in attempting to do so they also sought to erase a sense of ontic disorder, as if restaging the reactionary disciplining of time carried out by the post-Commune French authorities. And in fact they eventually succeeded in their first objective. Still, we might look at Trump's reelection as a second time that is less farce and more of a tragedy yet again.

GERALD RAUNIG'S CRITIQUE OF REVOLUTIONARY SPECTACLE

In Gerald Raunig's vigorous 2007 book *Art and Revolution*, the philosopher interprets the Communards' act of monumenticide as being just as

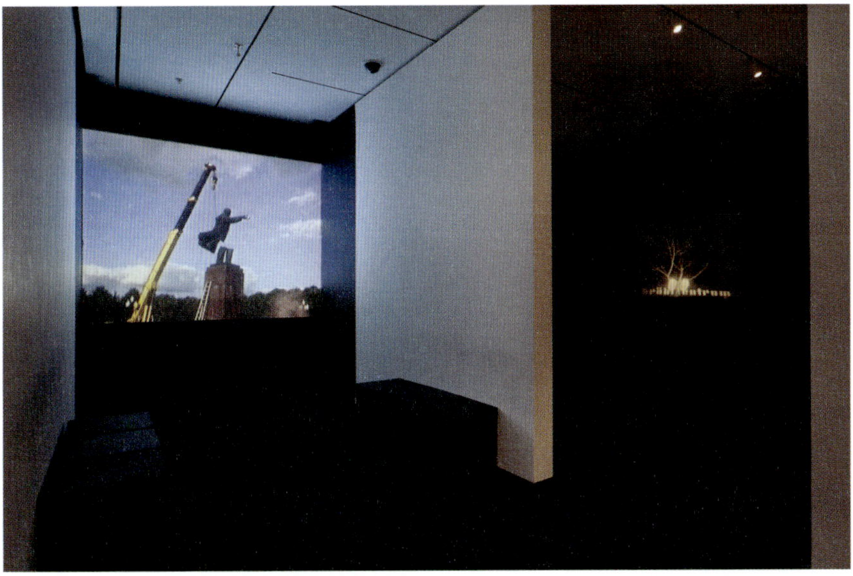

FIGURE 47

Deimantas Narkevičius's *Once in the XX Century* (2004), an eight-minute film originally shot on 16mm and converted to video, was featured in a 2012–2013 MoMA installation. Presented in a dark gallery, it seemingly portrays a grand statue of Vladimir Lenin being erected in Vilnius, celebrated by a cheering crowd. In reality, the film uses reverse footage of the Lenin monument's dismantling in the 1990s from the Lithuanian National TV archive. This clever editing merges two distinct historical moments, encouraging viewers to reflect on our complex relationship with history and how monuments symbolize shifting political ideologies. Image courtesy of the artist.

problematic as the bellicose iconography of the column itself. Raunig acknowledges, though, that the demolition of the column has subsequently been interpreted by many as a spontaneous, collective, and antihierarchical "attack on verticality," a view to which he demurs.[16] Countering that it was neither spontaneous nor a true assertion of political horizontality, he cites the concept of deterritorialized *transversality* as proposed by philosopher Félix Guattari. a concept proposing diagonal connections that cut across hierarchical structure (and later incorporated into his work with Gilles Deleuze).[17] "The construction and demolition of monuments are part of the same play," Raunig maintains, because "both operations organize the space around the monument, thus also serving to hierarchically organize the public."[18] Meticulously documenting how the demolition of the column had been discussed by the Communards in the months leading up to its demolition, he insists that the action falls into line with the type of grand spectacles he believes have marred other revolutionary movements since then. Furthermore, Courbet's indecisiveness is for Raunig a reflection of his artistic and anarchist outlook; the philosopher proposes that as an autonomous art producer, the painter must have had "great difficulty in finding a constructive position in the new setting of the Commune."[19] Indeed, Raunig advances the idea that this incommensurability between the demands of advanced art and that of organized radical politics is a dead end for art. The proof is found in the way Courbet transformed himself into a politician during the brief time of the Commune and only afterward became an artist once again. To put it another way, Raunig goes to lengths to present Courbet not as an artist-revolutionary, but as an artist and nonrevolutionary, turned non-artist revolutionary, and then back to artist as nonrevolutionary once more.

Here we might consider that like the Commune's destruction of the Vendôme Column itself, which the philosopher considers something of a political stunt performed for the masses by an emerging and centralized politburo, Courbet's anarchist-oriented sensibilities had to be set aside in order to meet the revolution's organizational demands. Such an analysis is unquestionably aimed at rejecting the vanguardism of Leninist party formations, in favor of the far more aesthetic vanguardism of antihierarchical desire in horizontal or rhizomatic networks proposed by Deleuze. For Raunig, the problem comes from the symbolic as well as perhaps structural similarities between the awe-inspiring demolition of the column as calculated public performance, on the one hand, and a complementary form of individual submission to collective discipline on the other. But what if we shifted our analysis from a primarily spatial form of intense action to that of a time-based cadence or tempo? This, I believe, is how Kristin Ross approaches the same event, describing the Commune's forms of political invention as available to contemporary rebels "not as lessons but as resources" useful for opening up a field of possible futures.[20] Suggestively, her concept cavorts imaginatively with an excessive and reworkable repository of social agency as rhythmic meter, especially when viewed in conjunction with David Scott's problem-space/time and Edwards's reinterpretations of historical materialism, or simply what I will describe as a phantom or surplus archive.

KRISTIN ROSS'S MULTITEMPORALITY AND COMMUNAL LUXURY

In most of her writings about 1871, Ross does not even mention Courbet. She does, however, convey that the Communards' destruction of the Napoleonic column, which Courbet participated in, was not merely an act of vandalism; it was a joyful rejection of "the dominant organization of social space and the supposed neutrality of monuments."[21] In this sense, the Vendôme monumenticide takes on its own aesthetic, but also an anti-aesthetic dimension as an act of public protest vandalism. Ross underscores this time and space inversion by describing the column's destruction as the creation of a "positive social void"[22]—a space of possibility rather than of mere negation, to which I will add that it was and remains also a time of possibility. Viewed differently, the column's removal was a reclamation of the public domain for the public, transforming a site dedicated to military conquest into one that might potentially foster collective social values. This includes the idea of communal wealth or communal luxury, as Ross interprets the Federation of Artists' declaration that "the committee will work towards our regeneration, the inauguration of communal wealth, the splendors of the future and the Universal Republic."[23]

Ross further interprets communal luxury as a radical alternative to private and exclusive notions of capitalist luxury that are reserved for the few. However, her interpretation of this term involves not merely the redistribution of existing wealth. Communal luxury requires reimagining wealth itself as something that could only be truly experienced collectively. The concept rejects, therefore, both bourgeois individualism and utilitarian socialism, proposing instead that true emancipation requires not just meeting basic needs but creating a world where beauty and pleasure and environmental justice are accessible to all through cooperative labor and shared resources. As the Communards called for, this includes the demolition of boundaries between manual and mental work, between the genders, and between artisans and artists. Indeed, prior to the Artists Federation statement, it was "simply illegal for a decorative artist or an artisan to sign their work," Ross tells us, adding that someone who produced metalwork, stained-glass windows, embroidery, or ceramics "could not aspire to either the status or the financial rewards that sculptors or painters possessed."[24]

WOMEN AND THE REVOLUTIONARY COMMONS

Significantly, the Paris Commune was notable for its unprecedented level of female participation in public life. Women played crucial roles in the revolution, forming organizations like the Union des Femmes pour la Défense de Paris et les Soins aux Blessés (Women's Union for the Defense of Paris and Aid to the Wounded), which was composed overwhelmingly of working-class women.[25] This organization, established on April 11, 1871, represented the most advanced revolutionary organization for women yet seen in France, combining working-class mobilization with feminist demands for equal work opportunities and wages.

Among many other women participants we find Elisabeth Dmitrieff, a twenty-year-old Russian aristocratic émigrée and friend of Marx who helped organize the Women's Union, as well as Louise Michel, a schoolteacher who fought in the ranks of the National Guard which defended the Commune "with remarkable composure" and later declared, "Barbarians that we are . . . I love cannon, the smell of powder, machine-gun bullets in the air!"[26] Nathalie Lemel, another female Communard, supervised the cooperative La Marmite that fed hundreds of starving people. Other significant women included André Leo, a journalist who formed a mutual benefit society called La Solidarité; Paule Minck, who established a girls' school in the chapel of St. Pierre de Montmartre; and Marguerite Tinayre, the first woman inspector of schools in French bureaucratic history, who also wrote novels under the male pseudonym Jules Paty. Like the members of the Guerrilla Girls collective over a century later, Tinayre and Louise Michel collaborated on a social realist novel about class misery, published under the joint pseudonym Jean Guêtré.[27]

The Communard women not only participated in traditional support roles but also took up arms and fought on the barricades. By May 1871, when the Versailles armies closed in on Paris, whole battalions of women fought together, for example as a company attached to the twelfth legion of the National Guard, led by Colonel Adelaïde Valentin and Captain Louise Neckbecker, a widowed lacemaker. As a contemporary journalist noted at the time, "I've seen three revolutions, and, for the first time, I've seen women getting resolutely involved, women and children. It seems that this revolution is precisely theirs and that by defending it, they are defending their own future."[28] Women also exercised an informal sovereignty through their participation in the thirty to fifty popular clubs that flourished during the Commune. By mid-May 1871, some clubs were reported to be overwhelmingly composed of women, such as the Club de la Délivrance in the Trinité church and the Club Lambert of Vaugirard. In these spaces, women voiced demands for the recognition of common-law marriages and the restoration of divorce and expressed their hatred for the Catholic Church and its sanctions. Michel presided over the Club de la Révolution in the church of St. Bernard de la Chapelle, where political discussions took place in a space previously controlled by religious authorities.

The Commune's defeat was followed by further brutal state repression. Approximately 17,000 people were massacred between May 22 and June 15, 1871, in what became known as Bloody Week (*la Semaine sanglante*). During the massacre and afterward, over a thousand women were arrested, with many sentenced to prison terms, exile, or deportation. Eight hundred women were initially imprisoned at the Gare de l'Ouest warehouses, while some, including Louise Michel and Nathalie Lemel, were sent to penal colonies in New Caledonia, along with other Communards including Louis Baron. Michel wrote her memoirs there. She also translated stories from the island's indigenous Kanak people into French, and later alleged that she encouraged the Kanak tribes, under their leader Ätaï, to revolt against their colonial oppressors, demonstrating how her revolutionary commitment transcended European contexts to embrace anticolonial struggles.[29] Still, few would have doubted this claim had they attended her trial in the winter of 1871 when Michel boldly declared: "I belong entirely to the social revolution and I declare that I will accept the responsibility of all my actions."[30] Demanding the death sentence for herself, Michel proclaimed, "If you aren't cowards, kill me."[31] Michel was granted amnesty in 1880 and died twenty-five years later, with thousands attending the funeral for "La Vierge Rouge" (The Red Virgin), which took the form of a procession marching through Paris on January 22, 1905.[32]

CONTESTED TIME: THEN AND NOW

The Commune represents a series of moments when collective action intentionally disrupted socially sanctioned divisions of class, labor, and gender, commencing a sense of time set against itself. If the felling of the Vendôme Column provides an emblematic figure for this revolutionary abundance of possibilities, then Michel embodied these ambitions by standing rather than groaning, to recall the words of Beckett quoted earlier. Following Ross, such events are never truly singular. The form is instead a cadence of reverberating spectral notes moving through the score of history. Rosa Luxemburg understood this temporal reverberation when she observed that "the grave of the Paris Commune ended the first phase of the European labor movement," not as tragic finale but as dialectical transformation.[33] The Commune's defeat became the ground for new forms of organizing, its phantom presence haunting subsequent movements.

Certainly, any effort at renarrating the spaces of the Commune as some form of self-affirmed budding state structure becomes a problem-space/time, to use David Scott's terminology. For, if we compare these

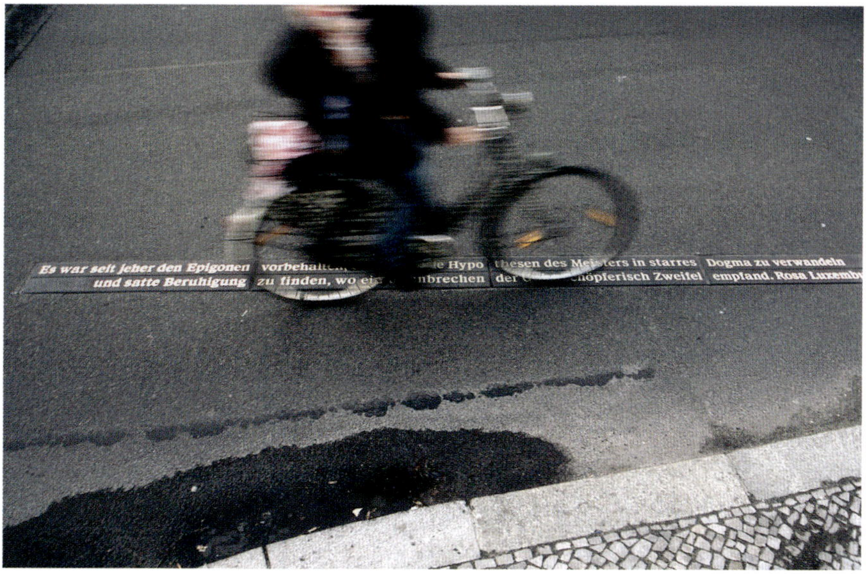

FIGURE 48

Hans Haacke's *Denkzeichen Rosa Luxemburg* (2006) integrates concrete strips with brass lettering displaying the revolutionary thinker's quotations dispersed across Berlin's Rosa-Luxemburg-Platz, in contrast to a traditional priapic monument. This subtle, easily overlooked approach reflects Luxemburg's complex legacy while refusing both nostalgic refuge in a ruinous past and contemporary spectacle. The memorial occupies a historically charged site that has witnessed significant political struggles, inviting pedestrians to encounter Luxemburg's words in fragments, building a multifaceted understanding of her political philosophy as they move through public space. Image courtesy of the artist; photograph by Hans Haacke.

archival echoes to those today calling for ethnonationalist supremacy, such as MAGA, the contrast is clearly striking. While the J6 insurgents demanded a simple reversal of time in order to restore a seemingly lost mastery or manifest destiny over the contingency of time itself, the Commune form, as Ross calls it—or communal time within the phantom archive, as I think of it—admits to no certainty other than a pulse or tempo busily dismantling divisions of class, gender, skills, and so forth. Revolutionary time's spectral and nearly incorporeal flow is epitomized by Communard Michel, who wrote in her memoirs: "Today, our destiny is the ghost ship that is advancing; it is the people, still convicts dragging their chains, who we deliver from the men who sacrificed us, and we will conquer our own freedoms. . . . Thought, rolling through life, transforms and grows, involving a thousand unknown forces. Yes, of course, the future man will have new meanings. We can feel them dawning in the being of our time."[34]

16

GHOST SHIPS

More than 150 years after its defeat, the Commune continues to inspire artists and activists, providing narrative shards like a ghostly currency for the imaginative and libidinal economy of the phantom archive of socially engaged art. Its archival wealth is tapped and retapped. It is, indeed, our historical communal luxury. The Russian avant-garde drew inspiration from the Commune's brief experiment in collective governance. Walter Benjamin saw in the Commune a revolutionary interruption of history's continuum. The Situationists in 1968 explicitly connected their movement to the Commune's legacy. More recently, the Occupy movement and various contemporary art collectives have invoked the Commune as a precedent for their own experiments in democratic practice. In 2012, artist Zoe Beloff tunneled backward from the present to restage Bertolt Brecht's 1949 play *The Days of the Commune* as part of the Occupy Wall Street encampment at Zuccotti Park (see figure 46). This multilayered temporal project involving a 2012 performance of a 1949 play about an 1871 event exemplifies the complex temporality of the phantom archive.

BELOFF: TIME'S STRATIFICATION AT OCCUPY WALL STREET

I spent some time at Occupy at Zuccotti Park and began to see it very much as a performance or a demonstration of how a radically democratic city should be,

laundresses, small shop owners, police officers, and a few specific men and women who represent a multitude of ordinary people radicalized by historical circumstances.[5]

Watkins's decentering tactic is as unorthodox for cinema as it is for art history, though it serves here by visualizing a nonlinear approach to representing the ghost ship of the past. And though his film never shows the tearing down of the Vendôme Column, we can cite Kristin Ross's important thesis that revolutionary moments like this one generate gaps and displacements in time and space.[6] Ultimately, neither Beloff nor Brecht nor Watkins represent the falling of the column in their work, preferring instead to focus on the day-to-day aspect of the revolution and its multitudes, which also counters the primacy of Courbet as heroic progenitor. Watkins's marathon duration refuses any degree of spectacular compression, insisting viewers experience something of the revolution's extended temporality, the meetings, debates, daily routines that constituted Communard life.

MAAMOUN: TIME TRAVEL AS REVOLUTIONARY PROPHECY

A third example of archival repurposing is not directly related to the Paris Commune but has similar formal features to the works by Beloff and Watkins. It also involves another insurrectionary iteration that might be thought of as echoing 1871, the Egyptian Revolution of 2011. In this case, however, the work focuses specifically on the challenge of time travel by reinterpreting the film *La Jetée* by Chris Marker (see chapter 11), in which a chrononaut from the future is sent on a mission into the past to alter events still to come. In Maha Maamoun's 2010 video entitled simply *2026*, a similar temporal displacement and temporal foreshadowing converge (see figure 50). For her remake of Marker's film, the artist recreated scenes from *La Jetée* with an Egyptian actor using dialogue taken from Mahmoud Osman's science fiction novel *Revolution 2053, the Beginning* (2007).[7] Both the book and Maamoun's movie remarkably predate the 2011 Egyptian Revolution that was centered in Tahrir Square and which ultimately ended the thirty-year reign of dictator Hosni Mubarak. And just as in Marker's work, the narrator's dialogue in Maamoun's remake rolls

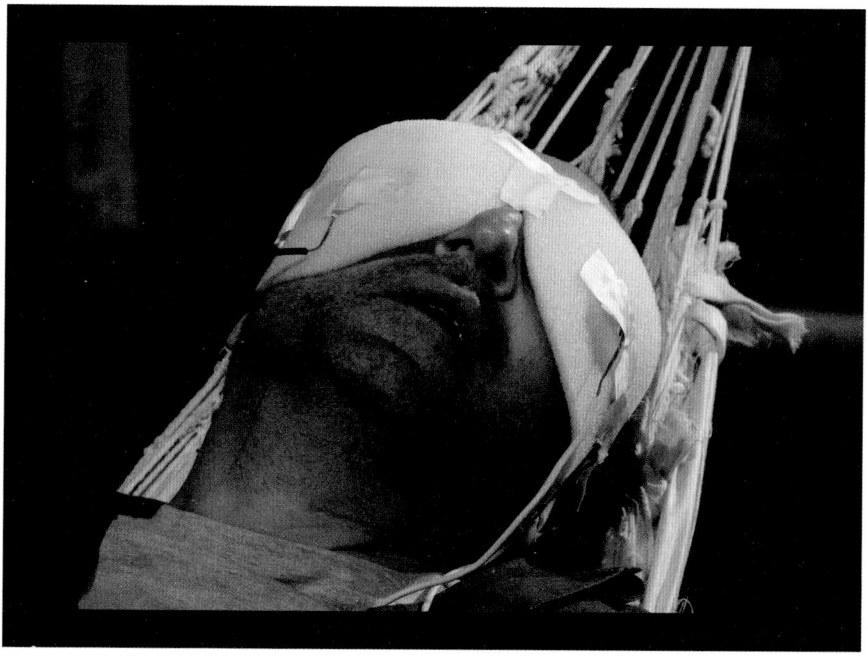

on as black-and-white still images scroll by. However, Maamoun selects just one key image from *La Jetée* to reenact, that of the time traveler lying in a hanging hammock with a large bandage over his eyes and two dangling wires running to whatever mysterious device is used to send him back in time.

As the narrative continues, we hear descriptions of a future Cairo in the year 2026 in which illuminated glass pyramids appear surrounded by fields of lush greenery. This utopian scenario soon becomes increasingly disturbing, and the narrator dry-mouthed and breathless. We discover that the paradise of the future is in fact a sham, and that the city is walled

FIGURE 50

Maha Maamoun, *2026*, 2010. Single-channel digital video, black-and-white, sound, 8 min., 21 sec. Art Jameel Fund, 2018.

in and surrounded by surveillance towers, with a crumbling city in the distance. An armored car with darkened windows approaches, followed by emaciated children wearing rags, who chase after the car as it kicks up dust. Suddenly, bags of food are catapulted toward them, and as the children scramble to get nourishment, fighting breaks out among them. The fabulous landscapes turn out to be mere projections. The time traveler's trauma is not to witness his own death, as in *La Jetée*, but the death of the future itself, or more accurately the future of a city, and not just any city but his own city. It becomes a space of bare life and near-death, gilded by illusions generated by the few against a backdrop of stark survival for the populace, in this case, that part of a populace representing its future, the children. Maamoun's project is uncanny for its time, and not simply because she foreshadowed the 2011 Revolution, which was already clearly in the air, but by glimpsing what was only a bit further ahead, when in 2013 a military coup d'état installed Abdel Fattah el-Sisi as a virtual Mubarak replacement, or restoration, and the Revolution collapsed into something horrific.

ANACHRONISM AS METHOD

Commenting on Marker's *La Jetée*, film theorist Nora M. Alter describes its plot as one in which the only hope for humanity in the future is via a "loophole through time."[8] I am reminded of Hito Steyerl's comment, quoted near the opening of this book, that history seems to have morphed into a loop. And perhaps the disquiet of the radical Unpresent is therefore also potentially liberatory, if for no other reason than that it forces into view the atemporality of our predicament as a time set against itself. In this case, the usefulness of the phantom archive becomes all the more important. As Kristin Ross observes regarding her hauntological concept of a usable archive, this transtemporal resource "could only be modeled on anachronisms land-locked in the present," as one way to "think oneself into the future."[9] To do so, however, requires thinking ourselves back into some version of historical time.

Similar sentiments have been expressed by Larne Abse Gogarty, Mark Fisher, and of course Walter Benjamin, all previously cited in these pages.

Without doubt, such attention to the outmoded, the anachronistic, the apparently obsolete also characterizes much contemporary activist art that reactivates forgotten or suppressed histories of resistance from different past moments currently coexisting in tension, or what Ernst Bloch described as "non-synchronous contradictions."[10] Put differently, these gaps and anachronisms, when appealed to as possibilities for reuse, repurposing, and conspicuous repair within the dominant temporality, or rather within the nontemporality of the Unpresent, as is the case now, become catalytic ordnance as time goes to war with itself.

17

CONCLUSIONS: TIME AGAINST ITSELF

THE TEMPORAL PARADOX

"Time," mused Jorge Luis Borges, is "such a respected subversive, so famous for its demolitions and ruins," yet it "also constructs."[1] As we reach the conclusion of this inquiry into the Unpresent and possibilities of resistance against it, reflecting once more on the strange temporality framing our moment seems only fitting. What began as an investigation of art's missing mass some twenty-five years ago has evolved into a broader analysis of how time itself has been warped, compressed, and ultimately made strange, but also militarized and battle-ready under postneoliberal ultranationalist capitalism. The archives of dark matter have split open, but not entirely in the way I anticipated, and yet not entirely irredeemably either. What has emerged is not only the creative surplus of marginalized cultural producers—artists' collectives, community practitioners, informal creatives, social movement dissidents, zinesters, knitivists, craftivists, and so forth—but also the darkest elements of that once obscure netherworld: reactionary fantasies, ultranationalist mythologies, and backward-facing visions that paradoxically present themselves as the impudent new vanguard of our time. Emancipatory, pro-democratic resistance also springs from this same illuminated region.

The MAGA movement, with its promise to "make America great again," exemplifies a key temporal contradiction of a retro-vanguard

organized labor banners and agit-prop of past centuries not as dead history to be either worshipped or forgotten, but as living provocations that interrupt our paralysis. It means refusing both the retro-vanguard's mythic restoration and neoliberalism's eternal present. It means keeping emancipatory embers alive without pretending we can simply reignite nineteenth-century flames in twenty-first-century conditions. The artists, collectives, and cultural workers explored in this book model this temporal solidarity through their conspicuous repairs, their reenactments that refuse exact replication, their repurposing that honors wounds rather than healing them seamlessly. They demonstrate that resistance in the Unpresent requires neither nostalgia nor utopian futurism, but rather a complex temporal choreography, reaching backward to reach forward, marking damage to imagine repair, inhabiting ruins to build something otherwise: a dark temporal solidarity for a dark time.

THE PHANTOM ARCHIVE AS PORTAL

Throughout the previous chapters, I have proposed the concept of a phantom archive as antithesis to the Unpresent condition. Drawing on many sources, including Walter Benjamin's *Jetztzeit* (messianic now time) as much as Tirza True Latimer's mobilized archival gaps, its excessive abundance and contingent hopes challenge notions of universal historical progress, but also engage with what Ernst Bloch called proto-revolutionary nonsimultaneity and what Kristin Ross describes as the Commune form—identifying and marking what remains blocked while refusing to abandon emancipatory embers never fully extinguished. Not merely a collection of ephemeral and often forgotten historical ideas and materials, our time traveling via the phantom archive develops a speculative methodology for engaging differently with time itself. By intentionally summoning specters from the past, it allows for alternatives to emerge, refusing both postmodern fragmentation and capitalist realism's foreclosure, while taking advantage of the uncanniness of the Unpresent's temporal disordering to reconsider history as a narrative reaching toward a future of inclusive justice. It is, if it is anything, as artist Michael Rakowitz asserts, that return of the past as ghostly surrogate—ancient forms remade in date syrup cans rather than stone—which interrupts the museological compulsion to put history in the past, seated safely on a plinth.[2] And all the while, these conspicuous procedures preserve the scars, intervals, and flaws of temporal dissonance rather than smoothing them into a fantasy like that of MAGA's retro-vanguard movement.

The practices examined in parts III and IV of this study—conspicuous repair, reenactment, repurposing—all share a commitment to keeping temporal wounds visible rather than sealed over. As I complete this book in the winter of 2026, the visual echoes of Covid-era landscapes dotted with empty monument pedestals remain vivid in my mind, as does, by contrast, the Bonapartist-like Capitol coup attempt of January 6, 2021, as well as the collectively liberatory ambitions of Parisians in 1871. The site of ruins around which these activist inclinations revolve must be considered: the shattered plinths of offensive racist monuments; the deaths, damaged interior, and obscene offal left behind by MAGA at the Capitol; the fallen Vendôme Column and fallen Communards of Paris, all forming a contrasting and obstinate apparition that punctuates history's rhythmic echoing. To cite Negt and Kluge once more, to be revolutionary is to become a "vessel for temporal states" in which a fragmented past is reassembled by "stitch[ing] it together at different times."[3] The ruin is also noticeably repaired, repurposed, or reused via scraps and splinters of the phantom archive, which is anything but a tidy repository of unproblematic solutions but instead a reservoir of questions, tactics, half-realized experiments, and partially blocked possibilities that remain available for different activation under different circumstances. As we confront the deepening crisis of the Unpresent—institutions hollowed from within, time at war with itself, reality fractured into competing unrealities—this archive offers not escape but engagement on different temporal terms.

Recall the aftermath of 2020's summer of monumenticides, which also included statue removal by states and municipalities. In both cases, the abhorred and defaced statuary left behind plinths and vacant perches, broken concrete, torn metal rebar, tagged and overwritten bronze and marble. Many of these leftovers reveal bare and rusted anchoring bolts jutting up and out of their graffiti-covered surfaces, supplemented with spray-painted tags such as "Black Lives Matter" and "George Floyd." These weird, uncanny, emotionally laden nothings drag our eyes and thoughts and sense of identity back to the holes torn into a phantasmagoric surplus archive of cultural time, a deep record overflowing with hopes and failures, possibilities and liberatory movements. It is here, right in these incisions and lacerations, that we glimpse remnants collectively transmuted into revenants, speculative possibilities ready to be repurposed into agents of social expectation and obstinate yet aesthetic resistance.

RESTORATION VERSUS REPURPOSING

At the very heart of our current crisis, therefore, exist two contrasting approaches to temporal mimicry, two types of time traveling, and two forms of coding error in the total aesthetic of neoliberalism that lingers in the Unpresent. It also gives birth to a dual form of repetition, one seeking return, the other accepting redundancy as excess and ellipsis. To simplify, we will describe them as restoration versus repurposing. Restoration seeks to *short the future* as if tomorrow was some type of tradable commodity, while emulating the past as it really was, but of course never *was*. Think of Donald Trump's alarmingly bizarre reference to the nineteenth-century racist notion of Manifest Destiny or his calls for returning to neoclassical architecture while sacking brutalism, much as the right-wing nationalist VMRO-DPMNE party in Skopje, North Macedonia, has done to that city's unique urban design aesthetic (see the left half of figure 52).

These are efforts to literally restore and impose an ethnonationalist and sanitized past on the past itself. By contrast, the kind of repurposing I'm describing allows the past to collaborate with us—or at times to antagonize us—in ways that remain spectral: not-present, unrestorable in their exactness, ultimately not fully representational. And yet this also generates another paradox. The brightening of cultural dark matter I celebrated decades ago has indeed proven double-edged, and in more ways than one. Not only has the illumination of a missing cultural mass emboldened some of its most antidemocratic and bigoted operatives, but what becomes visible also becomes available for extraction, manipulation, and control. In an age of near-total surveillance, visibility often means vulnerability. The Paris Commune itself offers a founding lesson in this predicament. As Allan Sekula astutely demonstrated in his 1986 breakthrough

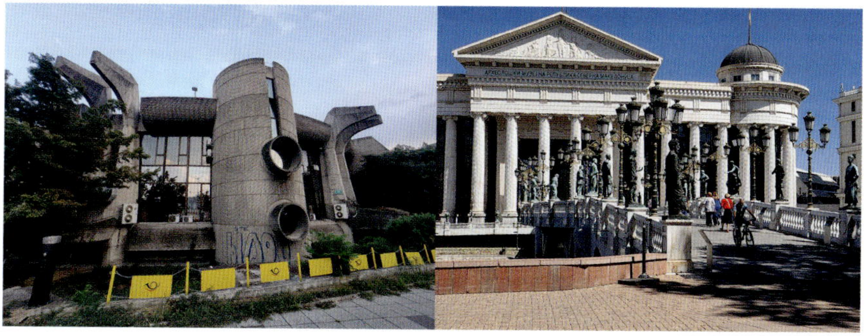

FIGURE 52

Skopje's split personality: on the left, Kenzō Tange's iconic brutalist Post Office building (1974) stands as a remnant of post-earthquake Yugoslav modernism; on the right, the Archaeological Museum exemplifies the government's "Skopje 2014" project, which spent over €560 million literally overwriting Tange's socialist-era structures with elaborate faux neoclassical facades reminiscent of Italian and German fascist monumental architecture of the 1930s, but also an act of historical rewriting that locals deride as "Disneyland" urbanism. Nonetheless, as Jon Blackwood and Jasmina Tumbas explain, "Yugoslavia's relics of antifascist and open-border socialism continue to haunt the present" (Blackwood and Tumbas, "Introduction: Yugoslav Hauntologies," 4). Photographs by Gregory Sholette, 2023.

essay on surveillance, "The Body and the Archive," the Communards who proudly posed for *cartes de visite* in 1871—early "selfies" taken atop their barricades and beside their captured cannon—unwittingly furnished the Versaillais police with the photographic evidence later used to identify, arrest, and execute them in the reprisals that followed.[4] The very movement whose afterlives have animated the preceding chapters was destroyed in part through the earliest systematic apparatus of photographic monitoring, in which the technologies of honorific portraiture and repressive identification proved to be one and the same.

VISIBILITY AND OPACITY

Consider Alex Karp, co-founder and CEO of the data analytics company Palantir, whose customers include government military and intelligence as well as private corporate entities. Karp, who studied with the esteemed Frankfurt School theorist Jürgen Habermas, deploys the language of artistic rebellion to justify bold technological innovation. "The challenge," he asserts, is to expect turmoil when one confronts old, out-of-date ideas, because "some of the most compelling and authentic nonconformists, the artists and iconoclasts, make for notoriously difficult colleagues."[5] His self-anointed heterodoxy has led him to develop a surveillance infrastructure tool called ELITE, or Enhanced Leads Identification & Targeting for Enforcement. The technology aims to provide ICE (US Immigration and Customs Enforcement) and other federal agencies with deportation "leads" drawn from Medicaid databases. As Karp's futurist forebear Marinetti asserted over a century ago, "there's nothing to match the splendor of the sun's red sword, slashing for the first time through our millennial gloom!"[6]

Palantir's reach now extends beyond its own proprietary systems. In 2024, the company partnered with the AI firm Anthropic to deploy its Claude language model within classified US defense and intelligence networks—the same model used by academics, writers, researchers, and by this author as an everyday tool for analysis and composition. As this book goes to press, Claude has reportedly been used in a US military operation in Venezuela in which dozens were killed, and the Pentagon

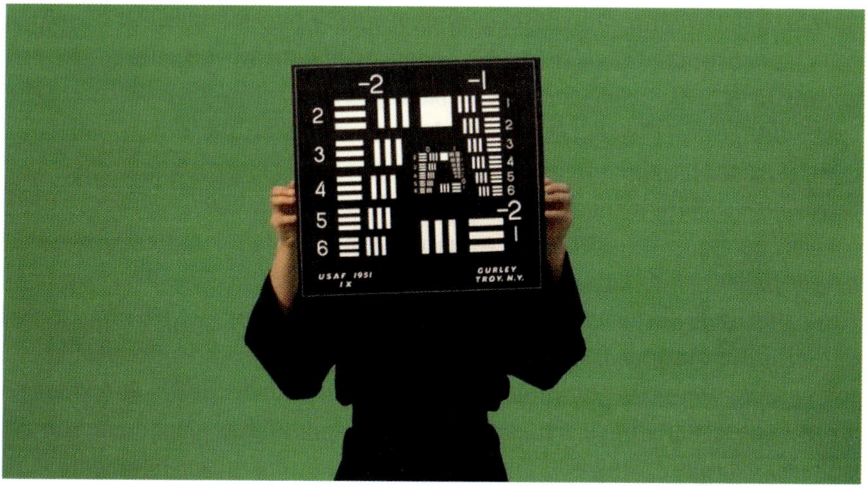

is actively reviewing its $200 million contract with Anthropic—not because the company abandoned its professed "hard limits" against autonomous weapons and mass surveillance, but because it has so far insisted on maintaining them.[7] Whether those limits represent durable ethical commitments or negotiating positions is a question being answered in real time, including by company researchers who have resigned in protest. Nevertheless one thing is clear: the infrastructure of the surveillance state now runs through the same AI platforms that intellectuals use to draft their critiques of it, thus closing down the escape routes in a way that

FIGURE 53

Hito Steyerl, *How Not to Be Seen: A Fucking Didactic Educational .MOV File*, 2013. Video still. A figure (the artist) is rendered unreadable to surveillance by holding a USAF optical resolution test chart—the very instrument designed to measure lens-based clarity—entirely blocking the face, thus paradoxically becoming hypervisible while remaining indecipherable. Image courtesy of the artist.

to earth in an act of glorious prosaicness. In its way, this refuses accelerationist time in favor of slow, iterative, perhaps even a rather routine aesthetic tempo. Such practices are not mere artifacts of resistance but temporal technologies in themselves. They operate by keeping alive what MAGA, the ethnonationalist right, and capitalist unrealism alike seek to foreclose: the possibility that time itself can be reorganized, that the future is not yet foreclosed, that certain pasts contain unrealized potentials still capable of disrupting our paralyzed present.

This returns us to our discussion of learning after neoliberalism. While universities face legislative purges, curricular censorship, and ideological litmus tests, some of the most unfettered critical pedagogy in America is unfolding in prison classrooms. This is not romanticization of captivity; the structural violence remains absolute. Rather, it points to how power's blind spots create provisional spaces of sanctuary. Carceral education, especially at the college level, exists below the sight line of MAGA specifically because the programs speak the language of recidivism reduction, not liberal arts and not critical consciousness. Theorists Gillian Harkins and Erica Meiners invoke Harney and Moten's undercommons to propose that "participation in education programs in prison holds the potential to redistribute economic, ethical, and aesthetic values associated with self- and community-determination," adding that "formal education is not the only pathway toward self-determination, and for many it is increasingly the vehicle least capable of supporting this goal."[10] What similar tactical opacity is possible with labor education programs, noncredit university classes, libraries, Community Land Trusts, and perhaps even art schools? The precedent is not only the Communards' repurposing of the National Guard but also Soviet-era samizdat—that clandestine circulation of typescript manuscripts which sustained an entire counterpublic sphere beneath the apparatus of state censorship, and whose hand-copied, carbon-smudged pages were themselves a form of conspicuous repair, preserving what power sought to erase.

Conspicuous repair is the *public-facing* practice, aimed at culture, memory, and solidarity. Tactical opacity or redarkening is the *organizational* practice, aimed at institutional survival under hostile power. They operate on different registers. The Communards built barricades visibly—but they also repurposed the National Guard under existing legal cover. Both at once. Organizing beyond the local under conditions of surveillance is hugely challenging, but this is where resistance scales up to its necessary magnitude. As Olúfẹ́mi Táíwò argues, purely oppositional politics—being "anticapitalist," "anticarceral," "antiracist"—however necessary, risks becoming a game of "Whac-A-Mole with injustice" unless coupled with constructive practices that build power through durable institutions and networks. The conspicuous repairs traced in this book represent one such constructive practice: not merely opposing the Unpresent but assembling, visibly and iteratively, temporal alternatives from the phantom archive's surplus.[11]

TIME WARS

The struggle ahead is no longer only about controlling space but recognizes that time itself has become contested terrain. Determining how time can be differently experienced, measured, valued, and regained has become a necessary struggle that the Unpresent has radically augmented. Although not the specific focus of this book, it is fair to say that the challenge reaches into deep planetary time, far beyond human society. Capital's war on time extends to geological scales, as extractive industries discount future catastrophe in favor of immediate profit, collapsing millions of years of accumulated carbon into a few centuries of combustion.

The archives of dark matter have split open. We stand amid their scattered contents, past and future interpenetrating our impossible present. The question is not whether we can return to some prior normalcy—we cannot—but whether we can forge temporal solidarities capable of surviving and resisting within the Unpresent while refusing its terms. The artwork and propositions in this book offer a set of ideas and models, some under way, others waiting to be realized, tested, shared. The work of conspicuous repair has already begun.

GLOSSARY OF TERMS

ARTIVISM: Art that prioritizes political outcomes over aesthetic concerns. The term emerged from a 1997 Chicano-Zapatista gathering and entered academic use by 2005, emphasizing equal importance of art and activism. Sometimes used interchangeably with "activist art," the preferred term used throughout most of this book.

BARE ART: Art stripped of claims to autonomy, with its economic and political contradictions exposed. Many in the art world choose to ignore this unvarnished reality.

BRICOLAGE: Problem-solving using whatever materials are at hand, as theorized by anthropologist Claude Lévi-Strauss.

CAPITALIST REALISM: Mark Fisher's concept describing post-Cold War conditions, where alternatives to capitalism seem unimaginable, making real change appear impossible.

CONSPICUOUS REPAIR: Act of repurposing that preserves traces of injury rather than erasing damage. The phantom archive supplies the materials; conspicuous repair is what you do with them.

TIME'S CARCASS: Marx's phrase for the reduction of human labor to abstract time under capitalism, where workers become mere vessels for labor time—"time is everything, man is nothing: he is at the most time's carcass" (*The Poverty of Philosophy*).

DARK MATTER: The invisible majority of cultural production which is left in the shadows of the mainstream art world but is nevertheless essential to its functioning.

HAUNTOLOGY: Jacques Derrida's concept (combining *haunting* and *ontology*) for unsettled obligations from the past or future that return as uncanny hauntings of the present.

MAGA AS DARK MATTER: Post-2024 Make America Great Again, and similar ethnonationalist movements, as retro-vanguardism—an avant-garde oriented toward imagined pasts rather than futures, mobilizing invisible resentments and nostalgic desires to escape the uncanny Unpresent through historical restoration.

MANIFEST DESTINY: Nineteenth-century American ideology justifying territorial expansion as divinely ordained.

MONUMENTICIDE: Symbolic acts of protest vandalism against material representations deemed politically offensive, such as the global toppling of racially offensive statues in 2020.

PHANTOM ARCHIVE: A surplus of alternative temporal possibilities existing as traces or remnants of suppressed histories overflowing with emancipatory interventions, experiments, repetitions, compromises, minor victories, and outright failures.

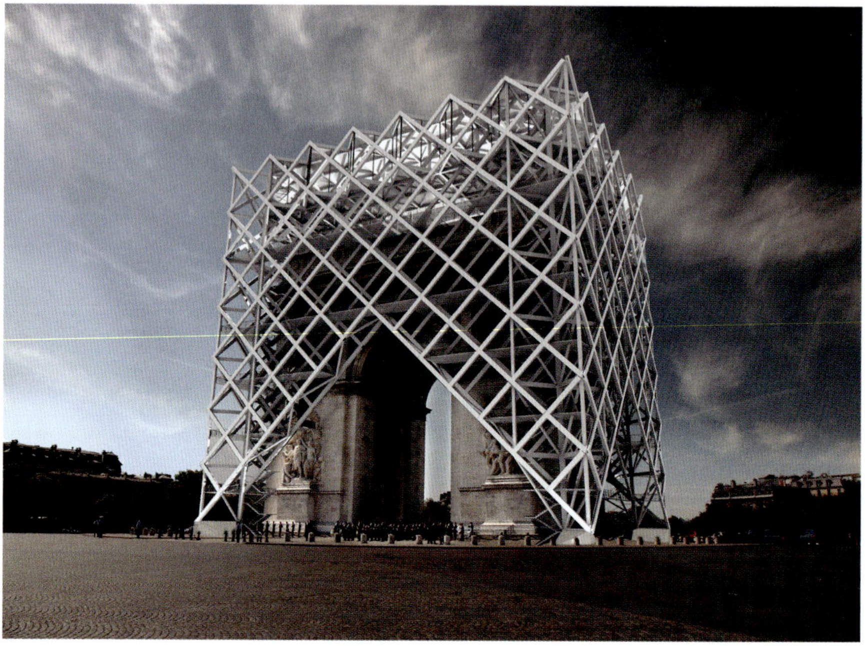

FIGURE 56

Krzysztof Wodiczko's provocative *Arc de Triomphe: World Institute for the Abolition of War* (2010) reenvisions Paris's iconic monument through a dramatic lattice-like scaffold structure. This conceptual intervention transforms one of history's most famous war memorials into its antithesis—a center for peace research and activism where historical time confronts its own contradictions, while challenging the monument's glorification of military conquest. First presented in *Harvard Design Magazine* and later exhibited at Galerie Gabrielle Maubrie in Paris, Wodiczko's proposal represents his career-long commitment to reclaiming public monuments as spaces for critical discourse on war trauma and displacement. Image courtesy of the artist.

PROBLEM-SPACE AND PROBLEM-TIME: David Scott's concept describing "an ensemble of questions and answers around which a horizon of identifiable stakes (conceptual as well as ideological-political stakes) hangs," including most importantly the future as inclusively emancipatory as well as economically and environmentally just.

REENACTMENT: Artistic practice restaging historical events to create temporal disruptions and activate suppressed possibilities. Unlike conventional historical reenactments, artistic versions deliberately introduce anachronisms and critical perspectives to challenge dominant narratives.

RESSENTIMENT: Friedrich Nietzsche's concept describing suppressed envy and hatred turning into a morality that devalues what one cannot obtain. It illuminates the psychological underpinnings of reactionary movements that seek to restore imagined pasts rather than create new futures.

RETRO-AVANT-GARDE: See MAGA.

SOCIAL PRACTICE: Art emphasizing collaborative, community-engaged processes over objects. Distinguished from artivism by institutional location and focus on dialogue as aesthetic material rather than direct political outcomes.

SOCIETY OF THE SPECTACLE: Guy Debord's concept of modern capitalist life organized through images rather than direct experience, "a social relationship between people mediated by images"—transforming participants into passive consumers.

STAGISM: The theory that history proceeds through materially determined historical stages by way of class struggle, from bourgeois-democratic, to socialist, and finally to communist.

TOTAL CAPITALIST SPECTACLE: The avant-garde's revolutionary aesthetic ambitions realized as consumerist spectacle rather than emancipatory social transformation, thus becoming a driver of neoliberal capitalism's comprehensive colonization of life itself.

UNCANNY VALLEY: The unsettling emotional response to objects (robots, CGI figures, simulations) that appear almost but not quite human, where increasing realism produces revulsion rather than affinity (Masahiro Mori, 1970).

UNDERCOMMONS: Stefano Harney and Fred Moten's concept of fugitive spaces of refuge within dominant educational institutions where marginalized groups create alternative forms of sociality.

***DAS UNHEIMLICHE*:** Sigmund Freud's concept of the uncanny—something familiar yet strange that produces discomfort.

THE UNPRESENT: Temporal condition where everything appears simultaneously the same yet completely transformed, without positive images of past or future. Unlike Orwell's dystopia of active historical erasure, the Unpresent involves spectral persistence, recursive hauntings and archival afterlives in a dislocated now time where past and present interpenetrate, resisting linear control.

INDEBTEDNESS

I am beholden to many people, including my remarkable life partner, wife, and intellectual companion, Olga Kopenkina, for helping me see this project to completion. My book editor, Victoria Hindley, along with Matthew Abbate and Paula Woolley, were indispensable for their insights and encouragement. I also thank my friend of many decades, David M. Stern, whose close critical reading of the early text helped remedy many jargon-laden passages—whatever remains is entirely on me. I greatly appreciate additional editorial assistance from Maliyah Mohamad, Jillian Steinhauer, Laura B. Thompson, and Jennie Yousef. The project could not have been completed without my unfailing friend and colleague Chloë Bass, who stepped up to manage our Mellon Foundation-funded social justice art para-institutional education project SPCUNY (Social Practice City University of New York) as I stepped back to focus on research and writing. The entire SPCUNY team also played a supporting role, including Nicolas Dumit Estevez Raful Espejo, Amir Farjoun, Tom Finkelpearl, Catherine LaSota, Ting Y. Lin, Jacquelyn Shannon, and Cory Tamler. Appreciation is also extended to my comrades at *Labor Art Review*, Keith Christensen, Barrie Cline, Noah Fischer, Robby Herbst, and to Dr. Grant Kester's *Field—A Journal of Socially-Engaged Art Criticism* and the many authors of the journal's Global Reports series, as well as friend, artist, and gallerist Leah Oats, a long-time supporter of my peculiar career as both a maker and a writer. I acknowledge also John Phillips and Georgia Perkins, whose forthcoming "Dark Matter" wing of the online Museum of Unrest intriguingly intersects with many of the concerns in this book. Furthermore, I sincerely thank Dr. Steven Nelson, former Dean of the Center for the Advanced Study of Visual Art, for providing me with a richly resourced research retreat in Washington, DC, in 2022 (within sight of the formerly besieged Capitol). Appreciation also goes to Tom (W. J. T.) Mitchell for calling attention to the history of the university as a long-conflicted institutional space in his 2026 lecture "The Academy in a State of Siege."

14. Mikhail Bakhtin, *Rabelais and His World*, trans. Hélène Iswolsky (Bloomington: Indiana University Press, 1984).

CHAPTER 1

1. Gregory Sholette, *Dark Matter: Art and Politics in the Age of Enterprise Culture* (London: Pluto Press, 2010), 188.
2. For example, Krylon produces industrial spray paint as well as products aimed at professional fine artists, as well as hobbyists, while Liquitex, a subsidiary of the Colart Group, produces both high-end and student-grade acrylic paints.
3. Carol Duncan, "Who Rules the Art World?," in *The Aesthetics of Power: Essays in Critical Art History* (New York: Cambridge University Press, 1983), 165–188.
4. Mario Tronti, "Factory and Society," in *Workers and Capital*, trans. David Broder (London: Verso, 2019), 12–35; Silvia Federici, *Caliban and the Witch: Women, the Body, and Primitive Accumulation* (Brooklyn, NY: Autonomedia, 2004).
5. Silvia Federici, *Wages against Housework* (Bristol: Falling Wall Press, 1975).
6. Angela Dimitrakaki, *Feminism. Art. Capitalism* (London: Pluto Press, 2025), ii.
7. Meanwhile, in an oppositional mode, the same multitude forms a new, anticapitalist agency in Michael Hardt and Antonio Negri's *Empire* (Cambridge, MA: Harvard University Press, 2001).
8. Dave Beech, *Art and Value: Art's Economic Exceptionalism in Classical, Neoclassical, and Marxist Economics* (Leiden: Brill, 2015).
9. John Roberts, *Revolutionary Time and the Avant-Garde* (London: Verso, 2015).
10. Yochai Benkler, *The Wealth of Networks: How Social Production Transforms Markets and Freedom* (New Haven, CT: Yale University Press, 2006), 130. For other similar early social media theorists, including Fukuyama and Lessig, see the bibliography.
11. Sholette, *Dark Matter*, 44.
12. Cornel West, *The Cornel West Reader* (New York: Basic Civitas Books, 1999), 275.
13. Friedrich Nietzsche, *On the Genealogy of Morality* (1887), trans. Carol Diethe (Cambridge: Cambridge University Press, 2006), Essay I.

CHAPTER 2

1. Kim Charnley, *Sociopolitical Aesthetics: Art, Crisis, and Neoliberalism* (London: Bloomsbury Academic, 2021), 144–145.
2. Wendy Brown, *In the Ruins of Neoliberalism: The Rise of Antidemocratic Politics in the West* (New York: Columbia University Press, 2019). See also Michael Premo's 2024 documentary *Homegrown*, which offers a rare vérité intimacy tracking three Proud Boys members from the 2020 Trump campaign through the January

6 Capitol attack. Michael Premo, dir., *Homegrown*, produced by Michael Premo and Rachel Falcone (2024; premiered Venice International Film Festival, Critics' Week).

3. Kriszti Fehérváry, "Christian Nationalism Goes Organic: Populist Politics and the Aesthetics of the Built Environment in Hungary," *Journal of the Association for Political and Legal Anthropology*, August 30, 2020, https://polarjournal.org/2022/08/30/christian-nationalism-goes-organic-populist-politics-and-the-aesthetics-of-the-built-environment-in-hungary/.
4. See Antonio Gramsci, *Prison Notebooks*, vol. 1–3, ed. and trans. Joseph A. Buttigieg and Antonio Callari (New York: Columbia University Press, 2011); see also Paul B. Jaskot, *The Architecture of Oppression: The SS, Forced Labor, and the Nazi Monumental Building Economy* (London: Routledge, 2002).
5. Marco Baravalle, "Laboratory Italy: The Meloni Government and Postfascist Intellectuals," *Field—A Journal of Socially-Engaged Art Criticism* 29 (Winter 2025), https://field-journal.com/issue-29-winter-2025/8591/.
6. Luc Boltanski and Ève Chiapello, *The New Spirit of Capitalism* (London: Verso, 2005). See also Thomas Frank, *The Conquest of Cool: Business Culture, Counterculture, and the Rise of Hip Consumerism* (Chicago: University of Chicago Press, 1997); Angela McRobbie, *Be Creative: Making a Living in the New Culture Industries* (Cambridge: Polity Press, 2016); Paolo Virno, *A Grammar of the Multitude: For an Analysis of Contemporary Forms of Life* (Los Angeles: Semiotext(e), 2004); and Maurizio Lazzarato, "Immaterial Labor," in *Radical Thought in Italy: A Potential Politics*, ed. Paolo Virno and Michael Hardt (Minneapolis: University of Minnesota Press, 1996), 133–147.
7. Quoted in Andrew Marantz, "The Tucker Carlson Road Show," *New Yorker*, September 11, 2024, 22–28.
8. On these specific growing nationalist temporalities as well as others, see the following global reports in *Field: A Journal of Socially Engaged Art Criticism* (field-journal.com): Kata Benedek and Ágnes Básthy, "Kulturkampf or Kulturchaos? New (Dis)orders in Contemporary Hungarian Cultural Politics," nos. 12–13; "A Discussion with the Residents of Rosa House of Culture (St. Petersburg)," nos. 12–13; Sandip K. Luis, "The Great Indian Hyperfascism: Art of Subjection and Survival among One-Fifth of the World's Population," no. 31 (Fall 2025); and Karen van den Berg, "Imagination Boosters against Hyperpolitics: Socially and Politically Engaged Art in Germany in 2025," no. 32 (Winter 2026).
9. Franco Berardi, *After the Future*, ed. Gary Genosko and Nicholas Thoburn (Oakland: AK Press, 2011), 12.
10. Catrina Doxee, "Examining Extremism: The Militia Movement," *Examining Extremism* (blog), Center for Strategic International Studies, August 12, 2021, https://www.csis.org/blogs/examining-extremism/examining-extremism-militia-movement.
11. Adar Primor, "The Veil? It Protects Us from Ugly Women," *Guardian*, November 26, 2017.

12. Vladan Jeremić and Rena Raedle, "Tools for Dismantling the Oligarchy—Student Protests in Serbia and Their Creativity," *Field—A Journal of Socially-Engaged Art Criticism* 30 (Spring 2025), https://field-journal.com/issue-30-spring-2025/tools-for-dismantling-the-oligarchy-student-protests-in-serbia-and-their-creativity/; Kuba Szreder, "The Authoritarian Turn: On the Crisis of the Polish Institutions of Contemporary Art," International Committee for Museums, March 6, 2023, https://cimam.org/news-archive/the-authoritarian-turn-on-the-crisis-of-the-polish-institutions-of-contemporary-art/ and "Between the Shitstorms," *Field—A Journal of Socially-Engaged Art Criticism* 32 (Winter 2026); Jonathan Blackwood and Bojan Ivanov, "Field Report—North Macedonia," *Field—A Journal of Socially-Engaged Art Criticism* 30 (Spring 2025), https://field-journal.com/issue-30-spring-2025/field-report-north-macedonia/.

13. Grant Kester, editorial in *Field—A Journal of Socially-Engaged Art Criticism* 30 (Spring 2025), https://field-journal.com/issue-30-spring-2025/test/

14. Mark Fisher, *The Weird and the Eerie* (London: Watkins Media, 2017), 9, emphasis in original.

15. Video documentation from January 6, 2021, is available from multiple sources: Lena V. Groeger, Jeff Kao, Al Shaw, Moiz Syed, and Maya Eliahou, "What Parler Saw during the Attack on the Capitol," ProPublica, January 17, 2021, https://projects.propublica.org/parler-capitol-videos/; Internet Archive, "Trump DC Insurrection and Coup Attempt—Jan 06 2021," https://archive.org/details/TrumpDCInsurrectionJan062021; and NPR, "The Jan. 6 Archive," https://apps.npr.org/jan-6-archive/.

16. John Sullivan, "The Insurrection of The United States Capitol," filmed January 6, 2021, 2:00 PM, Internet Archive, archived January 7, 2021, https://archive.org/details/nYiFQbNc65jwFYCWY. Sullivan's prosecution is discussed in Robert Mackey, "I Can't Believe This Is Reality!," *Columbia Journalism Review*, January 6, 2025, https://www.cjr.org/analysis/cant-believe-reality-mackey-capitol-january-6-insurrection-ashli-babbitt-tayler-hansen-john-sullivan.php.

17. ProPublica Archive, 3:12 PM EST.

18. See Christian Donlan and Keith Stuart, "Unreal Estate: The 12 Greatest Homes in Video Game History," *Guardian*, June 17, 2025.

19. Alexis de Tocqueville, quoted in Reinhart Koselleck, *Futures Past: On the Semantics of Historical Time*, trans. Keith Tribe (New York: Columbia University Press, 2004), 281n31.

20. Mark Fisher, "The Metaphysics of Crackle: Afrofuturism and Hauntology," *Dancecult: Journal of Electronic Dance Music Culture* 5, no. 2 (2013): 53.

21. Max Haiven, *The Player and the Played: From Gamed Capitalism to 21st-Century Fascism* (Cambridge, MA: MIT Press, 2026), 3, 8.

22. Kristóf Nagy, "Remaking Civil Society under Authoritarian Capitalism: The Case of the Orbán Regime's Hungarian Academy of Arts," *Intersections. East European Journal of Society and Politics* 9, no. 4 (2024): 80–100, https://doi.org/10.17356/ieejsp.v9i4.1127.

23. Oskar Negt and Alexander Kluge, *Public Sphere and Experience: Analysis of the Bourgeois and Proletarian Public Sphere*, trans. Peter Labanyi et al. (1993; London: Verso, 2016), 33.
24. Tom Dreisbach, "Donald Trump Calls Jan. 6 a 'Day of Love.' Here Are the Facts," NPR, October 29, 2024, https://www.npr.org/2024/10/29/nx-s1-5159868/2024-election-trump-harris-capitol-riot.
25. United States, White House, "National Security Strategy of the United States of America," December 4, 2025, https://www.whitehouse.gov/wp-content/uploads/2025/12/2025-National-Security-Strategy.pdf.
26. Hito Steyerl, "A Tank on a Pedestal: Museums in an Age of Planetary Civil War," *e-flux* 70 (February 2016), https://www.e-flux.com/journal/70/60543/a-tank-on-a-pedestal-museums-in-an-age-of-planetary-civil-war.

CHAPTER 3

1. Philip K. Dick, *Time Out of Joint* (New York: J. B. Lippincott, 1959), 32.
2. Dick, *Time Out of Joint*, 32.
3. Dick, *Time Out of Joint*, 32.
4. Dick, *Time Out of Joint*, 32.
5. Kevin Roose, "How the Biden Administration Can Help Solve Our Reality Crisis," *New York Times*, February 2, 2021.
6. Roose, "How the Biden Administration."
7. Roose, "How the Biden Administration."
8. Jason Farago, "Why Culture Has Come to a Standstill," *New York Times*, October 10, 2023.
9. Farago, "Why Culture Has Come to a Standstill."
10. Farago, "Why Culture Has Come to a Standstill."
11. Farago, "Why Culture Has Come to a Standstill."
12. Mark Fisher, *Ghosts of My Life: Writings on Depression, Hauntology and Lost Futures* (Winchester, UK: Zero Books, 2014), introduction.
13. Jeff Maskovsky and Sophie Bjork-James, introduction to *Beyond Populism: Angry Politics and the Twilight of Neoliberalism*, ed. Jeff Maskovsky and Sophie Bjork-James (Morgantown: West Virginia University Press, 2020), 4.
14. Roose, "How the Biden Administration."
15. Douglas Rushkoff, *Present Shock: When Everything Happens Now* (New York: Current, 2013), 2–3.
16. Rushkoff, *Present Shock*, 2–3.
17. Rushkoff, *Present Shock*, 49–50.
18. David Graeber, *The Utopia of Rules* (Brooklyn, NY: Melville House, 2015).

19. Anton Jäger, "Hyperpolitics in America," *New Left Review* 149 (September–October 2024), https://doi.org/10.64590/f5k; Jean Baudrillard, *Simulacra and Simulation*, trans. Sheila Faria Glaser (Ann Arbor: University of Michigan Press, 1994).
20. Mark Fisher, *Capitalist Realism: Is There No Alternative?* (Winchester, UK: Zero Books, 2009), 2. Fisher attributes the observation that "it is easier to imagine an end to the world than an end to capitalism" to both Fredric Jameson and Slavoj Žižek.

CHAPTER 4

1. Gregory Sholette, *The Art of Activism and the Activism of Art* (London: Lund Humphries, 2022), 123.
2. Peter Weibel, ed., *Global Activism: Art and Conflict in the 21st Century* (Cambridge: MIT Press, 2015), cover text.
3. Marc James Léger, "Revenge of the Surplus," review of *Dark Matter: Art and Politics in the Age of Enterprise Culture* by Gregory Sholette, *Monthly Review* 63, no. 8 (January 2012), https://monthlyreview.org/2012/01/01/revenge-of-the-surplus/.
4. Aidan McGarry et al., eds., introduction to *The Aesthetics of Global Protest: Visual Culture and Communication* (Amsterdam: Amsterdam University Press, 2019), 18.
5. Judith Butler, quoted in McGarry et al., introduction to *The Aesthetics of Global Protest*, 20.
6. Weibel, *Global Activism*, 24.
7. Boris Groys, "On Art Activism," *e-flux* 56 (2014), https://www.e-flux.com/journal/56/60343/on-art-activism.
8. Carol Duncan, *Civilizing Rituals: Inside Public Art Museums* (Abingdon, UK: Routledge, 2005), 8.
9. Groys, "On Art Activism."
10. Groys, "On Art Activism."
11. Lipovetsky, quoted in Oana Şerban, "The Critical Theory of Artistic Capitalism," *Hermenia* 18 (2017): 23.
12. Manfredo Tafuri, *Architecture and Utopia: Design and Capitalist Development* (Cambridge, MA: MIT Press, 1979).
13. Carin Kuoni, comp., *Energy Plan for the Western Man: Joseph Beuys in America* (New York: Four Walls Eight Windows, 1990), 19–25.
14. Regarding Apple's early advertising campaign, see Wikipedia, "Think Different," last modified August 18, 2025, https://en.wikipedia.org/wiki/Think_different.
15. David Cottington, *The Avant Garde: A Very Short Introduction* (Oxford: Oxford University Press, 2013); Marc James Léger, *The Neoliberal Undead: Essays on Contemporary Art and Politics* (Winchester, UK: Zero Books, 2013); John Roberts, "Revolutionary Pathos, Negation, and the Suspensive Avant-Garde," *New Literary History* 41, no. 4 (2010): 717–730.

16. Grant Kester, *Beyond the Sovereign Self: Aesthetic Autonomy from the Avant-garde to Socially Engaged Art* (Durham, NC: Duke University Press, 2023), 34–35.
17. Martha Rosler, "The Artistic Mode of Revolution: From Gentrification to Occupation," in Rosler, *Joy Forever: The Political Economy of Social Creativity* (London: MayFly Books, 2014), 194.
18. See Yoram Hazony's philosophical defense of nationalism for MAGA and other aligned ethnonationalist movements. Yoram Hazony, *The Virtue of Nationalism* (New York: Basic Books, 2018).

CHAPTER 5

1. Hal Foster, ed., *The Anti-Aesthetic: Essays on Postmodern Culture* (Port Townsend, WA: Bay Press, 1983). Jameson's essay "Postmodernism and Consumer Society" appears on pages 111–125.
2. Slavoj Žižek, *Living in the End Times* (London: Verso, 2011).
3. Claire Bishop, *Disordered Attention: Contemporary Art and Attention in the Twenty-First Century* (London: Verso, 2024), 36.
4. Bishop, *Disordered Attention*, 6.
5. Bishop, *Disordered Attention*, 6.
6. Bishop, *Disordered Attention*, 183.
7. Bishop, *Disordered Attention*, 183.
8. Bishop, *Disordered Attention*, 154.
9. Giorgio Agamben, *Homo Sacer: Sovereign Power and Bare Life*, trans. Daniel Heller-Roazen (Stanford, CA: Stanford University Press, 1998).
10. Ben Davis, *Art in the After-culture: Capitalist Crisis and Cultural Strategy* (Chicago: Haymarket Books, 2022), ix.
11. Boris Groys, "On Art Activism," *e-flux* 56 (2014), https://www.e-flux.com/journal/56/60343/on-art-activism; Gregory Sholette, *Delirium and Resistance: Activist Art and the Crisis of Capitalism*, ed. Kim Charnley (London: Pluto Press, 2017), postscript.
12. Jacques Rancière, *The Politics of Aesthetics: The Distribution of the Sensible*, trans. Gabriel Rockhill (London: Continuum, 2004), 43.
13. Jessica Zychowicz, "The Global Controversy over Pussy Riot: An Anti-Putin Women's Protest Group in Moscow," *InterDisciplinary Journal of Humanities and Arts* 2, no. 1 (Fall 2012), http://hdl.handle.net/2027/spo.11645653.0002.104.
14. Jeanne Vaccaro, "Art Collective Chto Delat's Members Fled Their Native Russia—But Kept Making Subversive Work," *Cultured*, May 10, 2023, https://www.culturedmag.com/article/2023/05/10/art-collective-chto-delat-russia/. The Canary Archive is further detailed at https://chtodelat.org/category/b8-newspapers/canary-archives-2022/.

15. Mimicry here denotes mimesis in the classical sense—art's representational approximation of reality. Wright's 1:1 marks mimesis's terminal point where the gap between art and the world closes entirely as representation dissolves but, paradoxically, so does capital's grip on art. Stephen Wright, *Toward a Lexicon of Usership* (Eindhoven: Van Abbemuseum, 2013).
16. Marina Vishmidt, *Speculation as a Mode of Production: Forms of Value Subjectivity in Art and Capital* (Leiden: Brill, 2018), 49.

CHAPTER 6

1. Carlos Garrido Castellano, "Living, Writing, Imagining (at) the End of Creative Capitalism," *Afterimage* 52, no. 2 (2025): 16.
2. Sigmund Freud, "The Uncanny," in *The Standard Edition of the Complete Psychological Works of Sigmund Freud*, vol. 17 (1917–1919), trans. James Strachey (London: Hogarth Press, 1955), 217–256.
3. Freud, "The Uncanny," 231.
4. Freud, "The Uncanny," 231.
5. Freud, "The Uncanny," 231.
6. Freud, "The Uncanny," 237.
7. Theodor W. Adorno and Max Horkheimer, *Dialectic of Enlightenment: Philosophical Fragments* (1944; Stanford, CA: Stanford University Press, 2002).
8. Adorno and Horkheimer, *Dialectic of Enlightenment*, 163.
9. Adorno and Horkheimer, *Dialectic of Enlightenment*, 162.
10. Adorno and Horkheimer, *Dialectic of Enlightenment*, 162.
11. Adorno and Horkheimer, *Dialectic of Enlightenment*, 162.
12. Jean-Paul Sartre, *Critique of Dialectical Reason: Theory of Practical Ensembles*, vol. 7, trans. Alan Sheridan-Smith (London: Verso, 2004), 401.
13. Adorno and Horkheimer, *Dialectic of Enlightenment*, 9.
14. Joseph Goebbels, speech at the Nazi Party Congress, Nuremberg, September 1935, United States Holocaust Memorial Museum, Holocaust Encyclopedia, https://encyclopedia.ushmm.org/content/en/film/goebbels-claims-jews-will-destroy-culture; Adolf Hitler, *Mein Kampf*, trans. Ralph Manheim (Boston: Houghton Mifflin, 1943), 366.
15. Sigmund Freud, *Totem and Taboo: Resemblances between the Mental Lives of Savages and Neurotics*, trans. James Strachey (New York: W. W. Norton, 1950).
16. Cited in Alan Feuer, "In Trump's Second Term, Far-Right Agenda Enters the Mainstream," *New York Times*, August 23, 2025.
17. Rebecca Bryant, *The Past in Pieces: Belonging in the New Cyprus* (Philadelphia: University of Pennsylvania Press, 2010), 3, emphasis added.
18. Bryant, *The Past in Pieces*, 2.

19. Bryant, *The Past in Pieces*, 11.
20. Bryant, *The Past in Pieces*, 12.
21. Mark Fisher, *The Weird and the Eerie* (London: Watkins Media, 2017), 9.
22. Bryant, *The Past in Pieces*, 17.
23. Guy Debord, *The Society of the Spectacle*, trans. Fredy Perlman and Jon Supak (Detroit: Black & Red, 1970; rev. ed. 1977).
24. Susan Buck-Morss, *The Dialectics of Seeing: Walter Benjamin and the Arcades Project* (Cambridge, MA: MIT Press, 1989), 86.
25. Mark Fisher, *Capitalist Realism: Is There No Alternative?* (Winchester, UK: Zero Books, 2009), 2.
26. Tao Leigh Goffe, *Dark Laboratory: On Columbus, the Caribbean, and the Origins of the Climate Crisis* (Garden City, NY: Doubleday, 2025), 159.
27. Mike DeBonis and John Hudson, "Trump Eyes Redevelopment of Gaza as a Real-Estate Opportunity," *Washington Post*, February 7, 2025.
28. Hannah Arendt, *The Portable Hannah Arendt* (London: Penguin, 2003), 568.
29. The Revelation of St. John the Divine 6:14, in The Holy Bible: King James Version (Oxford: Oxford University Press, 1769).

CHAPTER 7

1. Stefano Harney and Fred Moten, *The Undercommons: Fugitive Planning and Black Study* (London: Minor Compositions, 2013), 32.
2. Quoted in Thomas B. Edsall, "JD Vance Wanted to 'Aggressively Attack' American Universities. His Wish Has Been Trump's Command," *New York Times*, June 3, 2025.
3. Irit Rogoff, "Turning," *e-flux* 0 (November 2008), https://www.e-flux.com/journal/00/68470/turning/; Kristina Lee Podesva, "A Pedagogical Turn: Brief Notes on Education as Art," *Fillip* 6 (Summer 2007), https://fillip.ca/content/a-pedagogical-turn; Claire Bishop, "Pedagogic Projects: 'How Do You Bring a Classroom to Life as If It Were a Work of Art?,'" in Bishop, *Artificial Hells: Participatory Art and the Politics of Spectatorship* (London: Verso, 2012), 241–274. See also "MockstItutIons," chapter 7 of Sholette, *Dark Matter: Art and Politics in the Age of Enterprise Culture* (London: Pluto Press, 2010), 152–185, and Susanne Clausen, "Curating the Art School—Propositions for Developing a Collaborative Art Space in the Intersection between Art School and Community," November 6, 2020, https://www.researchcatalogue.net/view/542734/626649.
4. Mark Fisher, *Capitalist Realism: Is There No Alternative?* (Winchester, UK: Zero Books, 2009), 26.
5. Katherine Bell, "The MFA Is the New MBA," *Harvard Business Review*, April 14, 2008; https://hbr.org/2008/04/the-mfa-is-the-new-mba.
6. Edsall, "JD Vance Wanted to 'Aggressively Attack' American Universities."

7. Nick Land, *The Dark Enlightenment* (Imperium Press, 2022).
8. "Trump Signs Executive Action to Dismantle the Education Department," March 20, 2025, NPR, https://www.npr.org/2025/03/19/nx-s1-5333861/trump-executive-action-education-department.
9. "Pentagon Says It's Cutting Ties with 'Woke' Harvard, Ending Military Training," NPR, February 7, 2026, https://www.npr.org/2026/02/07/g-s1-109213/pentagon-says-its-cutting-ties-with-woke-harvard-ending-military-training.
10. John Power, "US Education Department to Halve Staff as Trump Pushes for Elimination," *Aljazeera*, March 12, 2025, https://www.aljazeera.com/news/2025/3/12/trump-slashes-us-education-department-staff-in-step-toward-dismantlement.
11. Mihir Zaveri, "No Plato: Texas University Pulls Readings on Gender Ideology in Philosophy Class," *Houston Chronicle*, January 8, 2026; Amy Reid, "Plato Has Been Censored; What Next?," press release, PEN America, January 7, 2026, https://pen.org/press-release/plato-has-been-censored-what-next/.
12. Harney and Moten, *The Undercommons*, 29.
13. Harney and Moten, *The Undercommons*, 26.
14. Jacques Derrida, "That Dangerous Supplement . . . ," in *Of Grammatology*, trans. Gayatri Chakravorty Spivak, corrected ed. (Baltimore: Johns Hopkins University Press, 1997), 141–164.
15. Key texts in this genealogy include: Immanuel Kant, *The Conflict of the Faculties* (1798); Herbert Marcuse, *One-Dimensional Man* (1964); Louis Althusser, "Ideology and Ideological State Apparatuses" (1970); Paulo Freire, *Pedagogy of the Oppressed* (1970); Ivan Illich, *Deschooling Society* (1971); Pierre Bourdieu, *Homo Academicus* (1984); Jacques Derrida, "Mochlos; or, The Conflict of the Faculties" (1992); Gayatri Chakravorty Spivak, *Outside in the Teaching Machine* (1993); bell hooks, *Teaching to Transgress* (1994); Bill Readings, *The University in Ruins* (1996); and Fred Moten and Stefano Harney, "The University and the Undercommons: Seven Theses" (2004), followed by Harney and Moten's 2013 *The Undercommons*, which is primarily cited in this chapter.
16. Harney and Moten, *The Undercommons*, 30.
17. Andrew Marantz, "Is It Happening Here?," *New Yorker*, May 5, 2025, 26–28.
18. Harney and Moten, *The Undercommons*, 122.
19. Harney and Moten, *The Undercommons*, 122.
20. Harney and Moten, *The Undercommons*, 122.
21. Harney and Moten, *The Undercommons*, 123.
22. Defense Advanced Research Projects Agency (DARPA), "Budgets and Testimony," US Department of Defense, 2024, https://www.darpa.mil/about/budgets-testimony; National Center for Science and Engineering Statistics (NCSES), "Higher Education R&D Expenditures Increased 11.2%, Exceeded $108 Billion in FY 2023," National Science Foundation, November 25, 2024, https://ncses.nsf.gov/pubs/nsf25313.

23. Karl Marx, *Capital: A Critique of Political Economy*, vol. 1, trans. Samuel Moore and Edward Aveling (1987; Moscow: Progress Publishers), 433.

24. See, for example, Susanne Clausen, "Curating the Art School—Propositions for Developing a Collaborative Art Space in the Intersection between Art School and Community," November 6, 2020, https://www.researchcatalogue.net/view/542734/626649.

25. For a detailed analysis of this era in relationship to art and education, see sections one and two of Andrew Hemingway, *Artists on the Left: American Artists and the Communist Movement, 1926–1956* (New Haven, CT: Yale University Press, 2002), 7–188.

CHAPTER 8

1. Adams writes for *Burlington Magazine*, *Apollo*, and *The Art Newspaper*; his paintings and drawings are in the collection of the Victoria & Albert Museum in London and the National Museum of Wales, among other institutions. All but one citation by Alexander Adams in this chapter come from his book *Artivism: The Battle for Museums in the Era of Postmodernism* (Exeter: Imprint Academic, 2022), with his comments about true art appearing on page 102.

2. Adams, *Artivism*, 41, 85.

3. "Art," Goldsmiths, University of London, accessed January 13, 2026, https://www.gold.ac.uk/subjects/art.

4. Márton Békés, *Cultural Warfare: The Theory and Practice of Cultural Power*, trans. Ferenc Sullivan (Budapest: ElektroPress, 2022), unpaginated.

5. Békés, *Cultural Warfare*.

6. Békés, *Cultural Warfare*.

7. David Goodhart, *The Road to Somewhere: The Populist Revolt and the Future of Politics* (New York: Oxford University Press, 2017).

8. Adams, *Artivism*, 4.

9. Adams, *Artivism*, 4.

10. Cindi Katz, "Vagabond Capitalism and the Necessity of Social Reproduction," *Antipode* 33, no. 4 (2001): 709–728.

11. Cuban artist and activist Luis Manuel Otero Alcántara, a student at Bruguera's school and founder of the San Isidro Movement, was arrested during the July 2021 protests and sentenced to five years in prison. He is expected to be released in July 2026. Fellow Cuban artist Tania Bruguera sought to negotiate his and others' release in exchange for her departure from Cuba in October 2021. Ultimately 25 other prisoners were set free. See Valentina Di Liscia, "Tania Bruguera Agreed to Leave Cuba in Exchange for Release of 25 Prisoners," *Hyperallergic*, October 7, 2021, https://hyperallergic.com/682889/tania-bruguera-agreed-to-leave-cuba-in-exchange-for-release-of-25-prisoners/.

20. Tomoshoi Murayama et al., "Mavo Manifesto" (1923), in Danchev, *100 Artists' Manifestos*, 235.

21. ProPublica Archive.

22. Stephen Eric Bronner, *Modernism at the Barricades: Aesthetics, Politics, Utopia* (New York: Columbia University Press, 2012), 69.

23. Marinetti, "The Foundation and Manifesto of Futurism."

24. Marc Andreessen, "The Techno-Optimist Manifesto," Andreessen Horowitz (a16z), October 16, 2023, https://a16z.com/the-techno-optimist-manifesto/.

25. Salvador Dalí et al., "The Yellow Manifesto" (1928), in Danchev, *100 Artists' Manifestos*, 257.

26. ProPublica Archive.

27. Przemysław Strożek, "Futurist Responses to African American Culture," in *Afromodernisms: Paris, Harlem, and the Avant-Garde*, ed. Fionnghuala Sweeney and Kate Marsh (Edinburgh: Edinburgh University Press, 2013). Similar analysis is found in Petrine Archer-Straw, *Negrophilia: Avant-Garde Paris and Black Culture in the 1920s* (New York: Thames, 2000).

28. Umberto Boccioni, *Gli scritti editi e inediti*, ed. Zeno Birolli (Milan: Feltrinelli, 1971), 87.

29. Valentine de Saint-Point, "Manifesto of the Futurist Woman: An Answer to F. T. Marinetti," Milan: Governing Group of the Futurist Movement, March 25, 1912, Library of Congress, https://www.loc.gov/item/2021667104/.

30. F. T. Marinetti and Fillia (Luigi Colombo), "Manifesto of Futurist Cuisine" (1930), in Danchev, *100 Artists' Manifestos*, 278.

31. ProPublica Archive.

32. Strożek, "Futurist Responses to African American Culture," 58.

33. Lebbeus Woods, "Manifesto" (1993), in Danchev, *100 Artists' Manifestos*, 411.

34. ProPublica Archive.

35. Steven S. Lee, *The Ethnic Avant-Garde: Minority Cultures and World Revolution* (New York: Columbia University Press, 2015), 64.

36. Art et Liberté, "Long Live Degenerate Art," in *Art in Theory: The West in the World—An Anthology of Changing Ideas*, ed. Charles Harrison and Paul Wood (Hoboken: John Wiley & Sons, 2021), 647–648.

37. The Dogme 95 group, "Manifesto 95" (1995), in Danchev, *100 Artists' Manifestos*, 415.

38. ProPublica Archive.

39. Cited in Claudia Calirman, *Brazilian Art under Dictatorship: Antonio Manuel, Artur Barrio, and Cildo Meireles* (Durham, NC: Duke University Press, 2012), 100.

40. Aimé Césaire, "Négreries: Black Youth and Assimilation," *L'Étudiant Noir*, March 1935, cited in *Black, Brown, and Beige: Surrealist Writings from Africa and the Diaspora*, ed. Franklin Rosemont and Robin D. G. Kelley (Austin: University of Texas Press, 2009), 58.

41. Billy Childish and Charles Thompson, "The Stuckist Manifesto" (1999), in Danchev, *100 Artists' Manifestos*, 429.

42. ProPublica Archive.

43. Mike Sell, *Avant-Garde Performance and the Limits of Criticism* (Ann Arbor: University of Michigan Press, 2005), 68.

44. For a useful overview of this movement, see Reiland Rabaka, *The Negritude Movement: W. E. B. Du Bois, Leon Damas, Aime Cesaire, Leopold Senghor, Frantz Fanon, and the Evolution of an Insurgent Idea* (Lanham, MD: Lexington Books, 2015).

45. Tristan Tzara et al., "Dada Excites Everything" (1921), in Danchev, *100 Artists' Manifestos*, 199.

46. ProPublica Archive.

47. Rosemont and Kelley, *Black, Brown, and Beige*; see also *Refusal of the Shadow: Surrealism and the Caribbean*, ed. Michael Richardson and Krzysztof Fijałkowski (London: Verso, 1996).

48. Étienne Léro, cited in Rosemont and Kelley, *Black, Brown, and Beige*, 37.

49. Kazimir Malevich, "From Cubism and Futurism to Suprematism: The New Realism in Painting" (Moscow, 1916), Monoskop PDF, 118, https://monoskop.org/images/b/bc/Malevich_Kazimir_1915_1976_From_Cubism_and_Futurism_to_Suprematism.pdf.

50. ProPublica Archive.

51. Mary Ann Al-Khatib, "Surrealism's America" (PhD diss., Johns Hopkins University, 2013), 28.

52. Marinetti, "The Foundation and Manifesto of Futurism."

53. ProPublica Archive.

54. Rafael Montañez Ortiz, "Destructivism: A Manifesto" (1962), in Danchev, *100 Artists' Manifestos*, 361.

55. Sullivan, *Full Video: The Seige*, 0:32.

CHAPTER 9

1. Aidan McGarry et al., eds., introduction to *The Aesthetics of Global Protest: Visual Culture and Communication* (Amsterdam: Amsterdam University Press, 2019), 18.

2. Jacques Derrida, *Specters of Marx: The State of the Debt, the Work of Mourning and the New International*, trans. Peggy Kamuf (New York: Routledge, 1994); also see "Why Hauntology" in Mark Fisher, *Ghosts of My Life: Writings on Depression, Hauntology and Lost Futures* (Winchester, UK: Zero Books, 2014).

3. Charnley cited in Gregory Sholette, *Delirium and Resistance: Activist Art and the Crisis of Capitalism* (London: Pluto Press, 2017), 149.

4. Kuba Szreder, *The ABC of the Projectariat: Living and Working in a Precarious Art World* (Manchester: Manchester University Press, 2021), 224–225.

5. Giorgio Agamben, *Homo Sacer: Sovereign Power and Bare Life*, trans. Daniel Heller-Roazen (Stanford, CA: Stanford University Press, 1998).
6. Jalal Toufic, *The Withdrawal of Tradition Past a Surpassing Disaster* (Beirut: Forthcoming Books, 2009).
7. Walter Benjamin, "Theses on the Philosophy of History," in *Illuminations: Essays and Reflections*, ed. Hannah Arendt, trans. Harry Zohn (New York: Harcourt, Brace & World, 1968), 254.
8. Ray Bradbury, "A Sound of Thunder," in *The Golden Apples of the Sun* (Garden City, NY: Doubleday, 1953); *La Jetée*, directed by Chris Marker (Paris: Argos Films, 1962); Octavia E. Butler, *Kindred* (Garden City, NY: Doubleday, 1979); *Primer*, directed by Shane Carruth (Los Angeles: THS Productions, 2004).
9. Philip K. Dick, *Time Out of Joint* (New York: J. B. Lippincott, 1959).
10. David Scott, *Conscripts of Modernity: The Tragedy of Colonial Enlightenment* (Durham, NC: Duke University Press, 2004), 221.
11. Carlos Garrido Castellano, *Beyond Representation in Contemporary Caribbean Art: Space, Politics, and the Public Sphere* (New Brunswick, NJ: Rutgers University Press, 2019), 4.
12. Giorgio Agamben, *What Is an Apparatus? and Other Essays*, trans. David Kishik and Stefan Pedatella (Stanford, CA: Stanford University Press, 2009), 5.

CHAPTER 10

1. Stuart Hall, "David Scott," *Bomb*, no. 90 (Winter 2005), bombmagazine.org/articles/2005/01/01/david-scott/.
2. David Scott, *Conscripts of Modernity: The Tragedy of Colonial Enlightenment* (Durham, NC: Duke University Press, 2004), 41.
3. Srimoyee Mitra, *Stephanie Dinkins: On Love and Data* (Ann Arbor: University of Michigan Press, 2024), 6.
4. Scott, *Conscripts of Modernity*, 41.
5. David Scott, "Black Futurities Past and Present: Thinking Reparations Through," paper read at "Colonial Repercussions: Sara Ahmed and David Scott, Opening Plenary Session," Akademie der Künste, Berlin, posted by the Akademie der Künste, June 23, 2018, YouTube, https://www.youtube.com/watch?v=OlzDe2rgfzs (1:44–2:25).
6. Scott, "Black Futurities Past and Present."
7. Scott, "Black Futurities Past and Present."
8. Scott, "Black Futurities Past and Present."
9. Scott, "Black Futurities Past and Present."
10. Scott, "Black Futurities Past and Present."
11. Scott, "Black Futurities Past and Present."

12. Scott, *Conscripts of Modernity*, 7.
13. Scott, *Conscripts of Modernity*, 8.
14. Scott, *Conscripts of Modernity*, 8.
15. Scott, *Conscripts of Modernity*, 8.
16. C. L. R. James, *The Black Jacobins: Toussaint L'Ouverture and the San Domingo Revolution* (New York: Vintage Books, 1989).
17. Scott, *Conscripts of Modernity*, 10.
18. Karl Marx, *Marx: Later Political Writings*, trans. T. Carver (Cambridge: Cambridge University Press, 1996), 31, 34.
19. It was Friedrich Engels, not Karl Marx, who coined the phrase "historical materialism," after his collaborator's death.

CHAPTER 11

1. *La Jetée*, directed by Chris Marker (Paris: Argos Films, 1962), English subtitles.
2. Steve Edwards, "'Time's Carcass': Art History, Capitalism, and Temporality," in *The Routledge Companion to Marxisms in Art History*, ed. Tijen Tunalı and Brian Winkenweder (Abingdon, UK: Taylor & Francis, 2025), 146–161.
3. Edwards, "'Time's Carcass,'" 148.
4. Stuart Hall, "The Problem of Ideology: Marxism without Guarantees," in *Stuart Hall: Critical Dialogues in Cultural Studies*, edited by David Morley and Kuan-Hsing Chen (London: Routledge, 1996), 25–46.
5. Jairus Banaji, *Theory as History: Essays on Modes of Production and Exploitation* (Leiden: Brill, 2010), 48.
6. Theodor W. Adorno, *Aesthetic Theory*, trans. Robert Hullot-Kentor (London: Continuum, 1997), 21.
7. Beech and Vishmidt don't agree on much else, however. See Dave Beech, *Art and Value: Art's Economic Exceptionalism in Classical, Neoclassical, and Marxist Economics* (Leiden: Brill, 2015); Marina Vishmidt, *Speculation as a Mode of Production: Forms of Value Subjectivity in Art and Capital* (Leiden: Brill, 2018).
8. Edwards, "'Time's Carcass,'" 146.
9. Walter Benjamin, "Theses on the Philosophy of History," in *Illuminations: Essays and Reflections*, ed. Hannah Arendt, trans. Harry Zohn (New York: Harcourt, Brace & World, 1968), 255.
10. Walter Benjamin, "On the Concept of History" (fragment/paralipomenon), in *Selected Writings*, vol. 4: *1938–1940*, ed. Howard Eiland and Michael W. Jennings (Cambridge, MA: Harvard University Press, 1996), 402.
11. Edwards, "'Time's Carcass,'" 151, citing Daniel W. Smith in Vittorio Morfino, *Plural Temporalities* (Leiden: Brill, 2014), xii.
12. Edwards, "'Time's Carcass,'" 151.

13. Stefano Harney and Fred Moten, *The Undercommons: Fugitive Planning and Black Study* (London: Minor Compositions, 2013), 73.
14. Doug Liman, director, *Edge of Tomorrow* (Warner Bros. Pictures, 2014).
15. Dipesh Chakrabarty, *Provincializing Europe: Postcolonial Thought and Historical Difference*, 2nd ed. (2000; Princeton, NJ: Princeton University Press, 2007).
16. Edwards, "'Time's Carcass,'" 151.
17. Banaji, *Theory as History*, 4–5, 359.
18. Edwards, "'Time's Carcass,'" 155.
19. Edwards, "'Time's Carcass,'" 151.
20. Larne Abse Gogarty, *Usable Pasts: Social Practice and State Formation in American Art* (Leiden: Brill, 2022), 17.
21. Gogarty, *Usable Pasts*, 17–18.
22. Edwards, "'Time's Carcass,'" 155.
23. Edwards, "'Time's Carcass,'" 155.
24. Becca Lewis, "Headed for Technofascism: The Rightwing Roots of Silicon Valley," *Guardian*, January 29, 2025.
25. Sylvain Duranton, "AI: The Return of Marxist Class Struggle?," *Forbes*, June 28, 2023.
26. Jean-Paul Sartre, *Search for a Method*, trans. Hazel E. Barnes (New York: Alfred A. Knopf, 1963), 45–46.
27. Francis Fukuyama, *The End of History and the Last Man* (New York: Free Press, 1992).
28. Louis Althusser and Étienne Balibar, *Reading Capital*, trans. Ben Brewster (London: New Left Books, 2024), 106.
29. Benjamin, "Theses on the Philosophy of History," 255.
30. Alex Callinicos, *Making History: Agency, Structure, and Change in Social Theory* (Leiden: Brill, 2004), 259.
31. Marcus Verhagen, *Viewing Velocities: Art and the Practice of Speed* (London: Verso, 2021), 7.
32. Samuel Beckett, *Nohow On: Company, Ill Seen Ill Said, Worstward Ho* (New York: Limited Editions Club, 1989), 156, 157.

CHAPTER 12

1. Andreas Huyssen, *Memory Art in the Contemporary World: Confronting Violence in the Global South* (London: Lund Humphries, 2022), 11.
2. "If photography is allowed to complement art in some of its functions, the latter will soon be ousted and ruined by it, thanks to the natural confederacy which will have grown up between photography and the crowd." Charles Baudelaire

from "The Salon of 1859: The Modern Public and Photography," cited in Walter Benjamin, "A Short History of Photography," *Screen* 13, no. 1 (1972): 25.

3. Tom Finkelpearl, "Introduction: The Art of Social Cooperation—An American Framework," in *What We Made: Conversations on Art and Social Cooperation* (Durham, NC: Duke University Press, 2013), 1–49; Pablo Helguera, *Education for Socially Engaged Art: A Materials and Techniques Handbook* (New York: Jorge Pint Books, 2011).
4. Theo Reeves-Evison, *Ethics of Contemporary Art in the Shadow of Transgression* (New York: Bloomsbury Visual Arts, 2020), 148.
5. Akira Takayama, interview by Mikala Tai, *Ocula*, April 17, 2018.
6. Jacob Riis, *How the Other Half Lives: Studies among the Tenements of New York* (New York: Charles Scribner's Sons, 1890); Lewis W. Hine, child labor photographs, 1908–1918, commissioned by the National Child Labor Committee, Library of Congress Prints and Photographs Division.
7. Carol Duncan, "Who Rules the Art World?," in *The Aesthetics of Power: Essays in Critical Art History* (New York: Cambridge University Press, 1983), 169–188.
8. Recommended reading includes Reiko Tomii, *Radicalism in the Wilderness: International Contemporaneity and 1960s Art in Japan* (Cambridge, MA: MIT Press, 2016); Christa-Maria Lerm Hayes and Victoria Walters, eds., *Beuysian Legacies in Ireland and Beyond: Art, Culture, and Politics* (Manchester: Manchester University Press, 2011); Finkelpearl, *What We Made*; and Gregory Sholette, *The Art of Activism and the Activism of Art* (London: Lund Humphries, 2022).
9. Guy Debord, *The Society of the Spectacle* (1967; Detroit: Black & Red, 1983).
10. Oskar Negt and Alexander Kluge, *Public Sphere and Experience: Analysis of the Bourgeois and Proletarian Public Sphere*, trans. Peter Labanyi et al. (1993; London: Verso, 2016), 33.
11. Friedrich Engels, *The Condition of the Working Class in England* (Oxford: Oxford University Press, 2009), 37, 40.
12. Riis, *How the Other Half Lives*, 1.
13. Katherine McKittrick, *Demonic Grounds: Black Women and the Cartographies of Struggle* (Minneapolis: University of Minnesota Press, 2006), 124.
14. Nicholas Mirzoeff and Carl Pope, *The Appearance of Black Lives Matter* (Miami: [NAME] Publications, 2017), 41.

CHAPTER 13

1. Leon Trotsky, *History of the Russian Revolution* (Chicago: Haymarket Books, 2008), xv.
2. Dread Scott, "Slave Rebellion Reenactment," Kickstarter campaign, last updated September 17, 2021, https://www.kickstarter.com/projects/antennaworks/slave-rebellion-reenactment?ref=a10dif.

3. Scott, “Slave Rebellion Reenactment.”
4. Tirza True Latimer, “Improper Objects: Performing Queer/Feminist Art/History,” in *Otherwise: Imagining Queer Feminist Art Histories*, ed. Amelia Jones and Erin Silver (Manchester: Manchester University Press, 2016), 93.
5. Quoted in Michael Slate, “Hundreds Trace the Path of the 1811 Slave Rebellion in Louisiana,” *The Michael Slate Show*, KPFK, November 11, 2019, https://revcom.us/a/621/michael-slate-interviews-dread-scott-en.html.
6. Dread Scott, email to the author, March 31, 2025.
7. Lucy R. Lippard, “Give and Take: Ideology in the Art of Suzanne Lacy and Jerry Kearns,” in *Art and Ideology*, exh. cat. (New York: New Museum, 1984).
8. Slate, “Hundreds Trace the Path.”
9. Michel de Certeau, *The Practice of Everyday Life*, trans. Steven Rendall (Berkeley: University of California Press, 1984).
10. Sven Lütticken, “From Re- to Pre- and Back Again,” in *Over and Over and Over Again: Reenactment Strategies in Contemporary Arts and Theory*, ed. Cristina Baldacci et al. (Berlin: ICI Berlin Press, 2022), 1.
11. Lütticken, “From Re- to Pre- and Back Again,” 12.
12. Lütticken, “From Re- to Pre- and Back Again,” 12.
13. Cited in Andrew Quick, *The Wooster Group Work Book* (New York: Routledge, 2007).
14. Rebecca Schneider, *Performing Remains: Art and War in Times of Theatrical Reenactment* (Abingdon, UK: Routledge, 2011), 35.
15. Schneider, *Performing Remains*, 35.
16. Schneider, *Performing Remains*, 25, referencing David Lowenthal, “The Past as a Theme Park,” in *The Heritage Crusade and the Spoils of History* (Cambridge: Cambridge University Press, 1998), 90–104.
17. Hito Steyerl, “A Tank on a Pedestal: Museums in an Age of Planetary Civil War,” *e-flux* 70 (February 2016), https://www.e-flux.com/journal/70/60543/a-tank-on-a-pedestal-museums-in-an-age-of-planetary-civil-war.
18. Steyerl, “A Tank on a Pedestal.”
19. An excellent analysis of the Soviet-era reenactments is found in Claire Bishop, *Artificial Hells: Participatory Art and the Politics of Spectatorship* (London: Verso, 2012), 30–37.

CHAPTER 14

1. Quoted in Mary Ann Caws, ed., *Manifesto: A Century of Isms* (Lincoln: University of Nebraska Press, 2001), 230.
2. Boris Groys, “Becoming Revolutionary: On Kazimir Malevich,” *e-flux* 47 (2013), https://www.e-flux.com/journal/47/60047/becoming-revolutionary-on-kazimir-malevich.

3. Groys, "Becoming Revolutionary."
4. Esther Leslie, "Lenin and the Image in Time," *Crisis and Critique* 11, no. 2 (2025): 240.
5. Leslie, "Lenin and the Image in Time," 240.
6. Boris Groys, *In the Flow* (London: Verso, 2016), 77.
7. Groys, *In the Flow*, 9.
8. Groys, *In the Flow*, 9.
9. For one such notable opposing view about the Soviet avant-garde, see Christina Kiaer, *Imagine No Possessions: The Socialist Objects of Russian Constructivism* (Cambridge, MA: MIT Press, 2005).
10. Catherine Walworth, *Soviet Salvage: Imperial Debris, Revolutionary Reuse, and Russian Constructivism* (University Park: Penn State Press, 2017), 10.
11. Walworth, *Soviet Salvage*, 185.
12. John Roberts, *Revolutionary Time and the Avant-Garde* (London: Verso, 2015), 48.
13. Caws, *Manifesto: A Century of Isms*, 412.
14. Vladimir Tatlin et al., "The Work Ahead of Us," in *Russian Art of the Avant-Garde: Theory and Criticism, 1902–1934*, ed. and trans. John Bowlt (New York: Viking, 1976), 206.
15. Norbert Lynton, *Tatlin's Tower: Monument to Revolution* (New Haven, CT: Yale University Press, 2009), 61.
16. Viktor Shklovsky, *Khod Konia* [Knight's Move] (Berlin: Gelikon, 1923), 69.
17. Yevgeniy Fiks, Brian James Baer, and Katherine Carl, *Queer(ing) Russian Art: Realism, Revolution, Performance* (Newton, MA: Academic Studies Press, 2023).
18. Christina Lodder, *Russian Constructivism* (New Haven, CT: Yale University Press, 1983), 56.
19. Anthony Heywood, "Post-war Economies (Russian Empire)," *International Encyclopedia of the First World War* (2014), https://encyclopedia.1914-1918-online.net/article/post-war-economies-russian-empire/.
20. I thank Maria Kokkori for this insight in an email to me from January 12, 2021.
21. Christina Lodder, email to the author, January 11, 2021.
22. Lodder, email to the author, January 11, 2021.
23. Walworth, *Soviet Salvage*, 19.
24. Larissa Alekseevna Zhadova, *Tatlin* (New York: Rizzoli, 1988), 145.
25. *The Marx-Engels Reader*, ed. Robert C. Tucker, 2nd ed. (New York: W. W. Norton, 1978), 32.
26. *The Marx-Engels Reader*, 595.
27. *The Marx-Engels Reader*, 633.
28. *The Marx-Engels Reader*, 633.

29. This is, for example, exactly the opposite of those claiming, as Gustave Flaubert did in a letter to George Sand, that the Commune was the "last manifestation of the Middle Ages." Gustave Flaubert, letter to George Sand, letter no. 188, 1871, Online-Literature.com, https://www.online-literature.com/gustave-flaubert/sand-flaubert-letters/4/.

30. Jay Bergman, *The French Revolutionary Tradition in Russian and Soviet Politics, Political Thought, and Culture* (Oxford: Oxford University Press, 2019), 464.

31. Ekaterina Gerasimova and Sofia Chuikina, "The Repair Society," *Russian Studies in History* 48, no. 1 (2009): 58.

32. Gerasimova and Chuikina, "The Repair Society," 61.

33. Gerasimova and Chuikina, "The Repair Society," 59.

34. Gerasimova and Chuikina, "The Repair Society," 62.

35. Walworth, *Soviet Salvage*, 8.

36. Christina Kiaer, "The Russian Constructivist Flapper Dress," *Critical Inquiry* 28, no. 1 (2001): 190.

37. Olga B. Vainshtein, "Designing the Future: Constructivist Laboratory of Fashion," in *Fashion and Modernism*, ed. Louise Wallenberg and Andrea Kollnitz (London: Bloomsbury, 2019), 101–124.

38. Factory of Found Clothes (Gluklya and Tsaplya), interview by Marina Vischmidt, "Interview with Marina Vischmidt for the 'Untitled' Magazine / London /2009," 2009, *Gluklya*, https://gluklya.com/interview/interview-with-marina-vischmidt/.

39. Factory of Found Clothes, interview by Vischmidt.

40. Gluklya (Natalia Pershina-Yakimanskaya), "Manifesto of the Utopian Unemployment Union, 2017," *Gluklya*, https://gluklya.com/manifest/manifesto-utopian/.

41. John Gorman, *Banner Bright: An Illustrated History of Trade Union Banners* (Essex: Scorpion Publishers, 1986).

42. Emma Mahoney, "Report from Ireland: Repealing the Eighth Amendment," *Field—A Journal of Socially-Engaged Art Criticism* (December 13, 2019), http://field-journal.com/issue-12.

43. Sophia Kishkovsky, "Belarus Art Collector Viktor Babariko, Rival to President Alexander Lukashenko, Jailed before Election," *Art Newspaper*, August 24, 2020, https://www.theartnewspaper.com/2020/08/24/belarus-art-collector-viktor-babariko-rival-to-president-alexander-lukashenko-jailed-before-election.

44. Quoted in Simon Garnet, "For a Belarusian Res Publica!," *Eurozine*, August 24, 2020, https://www.eurozine.com/for-a-belarusian-res-publica/.

45. Dmitriy Strotsev, "The Art of Popular Disobedience," *COLTA*, December 10, 2020, https://www.colta.ru/articles/specials/26156-dmitriy-strotsev-fenomen-belorusskogo-protesta.

46. Olia Sosnovskaya, "Future Perfect Continuous," *Zeitgeister* (Goethe-Institut), November 12, 2020.

47. Sosnovskaya, "Future Perfect Continuous."

48. For an in-depth analysis of this situation, see Olga Kopenkina, "No Time for Art? Strategies of Negation in Belarusian Art during the 2020 Anti-Government Uprising," *Field—A Journal of Socially-Engaged Art Criticism* 20 (Winter 2022), https://field-journal.com/issue-20/no-time-for-art-strategies-of-negation-in-belarusian-art-during-the-2020-anti-government-uprising/.

CHAPTER 15

1. T. J. Clark, *The Absolute Bourgeois: Artists and Politics in France, 1848–1851* (Berkeley: University of California Press, 1973), 180; T. J. Clark, *Image of the People: Gustave Courbet and the 1848 Revolution* (Berkeley: University of California Press, 1973), 154.
2. André Mesquita, Charles Esche, and Will Bradley, eds., *Arte e ativismo antologia* (Lisbon: MASP, 2021), 43, 44.
3. Gerald Raunig, *Art and Revolution: Transversal Activism in the Long Twentieth Century* (Cambridge, MA: MIT Press, 2007).
4. Kristin Ross, *Communal Luxury: The Political Imaginary of the Paris Commune* (London: Verso, 2016); Zoe Beloff speaking about her performative video *Days of the Commune* (2012), in a paper entitled "The Art of Reenactment," presentation at UnionDocs Center for Documentary Art, Queens, NY, January 27, 2023; Peter Watkins, director, *La Commune (Paris, 1871)* (13 Production, 2000), 345 min.
5. David Harvey, "Between Space and Time: Reflections on the Geographical Imagination," *Annals of the Association of American Geographers* 80, no. 3 (September 1990): 422.
6. Terry Eagleton, *The Ideology of the Aesthetic* (Oxford: Blackwell, 1990), 214; Silvia Federici, *Caliban and the Witch: Women, the Body, and Primitive Accumulation* (Brooklyn, NY: Autonomedia, 2004), 206.
7. Julian Coman, "Vive la Commune? The Working-Class Insurrection That Shook the World," *Guardian*, March 7, 2021.
8. W. Gibson, *Paris during the Commune, 1871: Being Letters from Paris and Its Neighbourhood, Written Chiefly during the Time of the Second Siege* (London: Whittaker, 1872), 117–118.
9. "Manifesto of the Paris Commune's Federation of Artists," Marxists Internet Archive, https://www.marxists.org/history/france/paris-commune/documents/artists.htm..
10. Art Workers' Coalition, "13 Demands," 1969, reprinted in Lucy R. Lippard, *A Different War: Vietnam in Art* (Seattle: Real Comet Press, 1990), 52–53; W.A.G.E. (Working Artists and the Greater Economy), "W.A.G.E. Certification," accessed November 28, 2025, https://www.wageforwork.com/
11. Andrew Hemingway, "Cultural Democracy by Default: The Politics of the New Deal Arts Programmes," *Oxford Art Journal* 30, no. 2 (2007): 269, 286–287.

12. Kristin Ross, "The Meaning of the Paris Commune," *Jacobin Magazine*, May 4, 2015, https://jacobin.com/2015/05/kristin-ross-communal-luxury-paris-commune.

13. Kristin Ross, "The Commune Form: A Conversation with Andreas Petrossiants," *e-flux Journal* 151 (February 2025), https://www.e-flux.com/journal/151/651825/the-commune-form-a-conversation, 63.

14. Gustave Courbet, "Letter to the Government of National Defense, September 4, 1870," in *The Communards of Paris 1871*, ed. Stewart Edwards (Ithaca, NY: Cornell University Press, 1973), 30–31.

15. Louis Barron, *Sous le drapeau rouge* [Under the red flag] (Paris: A. Savine, 1889), 167.

16. Raunig, *Art and Revolution*, 107–108.

17. Gilles Deleuze and Félix Guattari, *Anti-Oedipus: Capitalism and Schizophrenia*, trans. Robert Hurley et al. (Minneapolis: University of Minneapolis Press, 2004).

18. Raunig, *Art and Revolution*, 108.

19. Raunig, *Art and Revolution*, 110.

20. Ross, "The Meaning of the Paris Commune."

21. Kristin Ross, *The Emergence of Social Space: Rimbaud and the Paris Commune* (Minneapolis: University of Minnesota Press, 1988), 46.

22. Ross, *The Emergence of Social Space*, 46.

23. "Manifesto of the Paris Commune's Federation of Artists."

24. Ross, "The Commune Form."

25. Cécile Rimboud, "Women Fighters of the 1871 Paris Commune," *Socialist World*, March 5, 2021, https://www.socialistworld.net/2021/03/05/women-fighters-of-the-1871-paris-commune/.

26. Jade Maître, "The Memoirs of Louise Michel (in English)," *Louise Michel*, March 2, 2023, https://louisemichel.com/the-memoirs-of-louise-michel-in-english-read-free.

27. Louise Michel and Marguerite Tinayre, *La misère: roman*, ed. Daniel Armogathe and Xavière Gauthier (Paris: Éditions du Félin, 1999).

28. Editor of the newspaper *Le Vengeur*, quoted in Rimboud, "Women Fighters of the 1871 Paris Commune."

29. Mike Davis, *Late Victorian Holocausts: El Niño Famines and the Making of the Third World* (London: Verso, 2001).

30. Carolyn J. Eichner, *The Paris Commune: A Brief History* (New Brunswick, NJ: Rutgers University Press, 2020), 98.

31. Eichner, *The Paris Commune*, 98.

32. Photographs of the procession can be seen at "Funerailles Louise Michel," Wikimedia Commons, accessed November 29, 2025, https://commons.wikimedia.org/wiki/File:Funerailles_Louise_Michel.jpg; with illustrations of the event at Bridgeman Images, accessed November 29, 2025, https://www.bridgemanimages

.com/en-US/anonymous/funeral-of-clemence-louise-michel-january-22-1905-engraving/engraving/asset/904745.

33. Rosa Luxemburg, "The Junius Pamphlet: The Crisis in German Social Democracy" (1915), chap. 1, Marxists Internet Archive, https://www.marxists.org/archive/luxemburg/1915/junius/ch01.htm.
34. Maître, "The Memoirs of Louise Michel."

CHAPTER 16

1. Zoe Beloff, "The Art of Reenactment," presentation at UnionDocs Center for Documentary Art, Queens, NY, January 27, 2023.
2. Beloff, "The Art of Reenactment."
3. Beloff, "The Art of Reenactment."
4. Peter Watkins, director, *La Commune (Paris, 1871)* (13 Production, 2000), 345 min.
5. Michel de Certeau, *The Practice of Everyday Life*, trans. Steven Rendall (Berkeley: University of California Press, 1984), v.
6. Kristin Ross, *Communal Luxury: The Political Imaginary of the Paris Commune* (London: Verso, 2016).
7. Mahmoud Osman, *Revolution 2053, the Beginning* (self-published, 2007).
8. Nora M. Alter, *Chris Marker* (Champaign: University of Illinois Press, 2006), 94.
9. Ross, *Communal Luxury*, 94.
10. Quoted in Larne Abse Gogarty, *Usable Pasts: Social Practice and State Formation in American Art* (Leiden: Brill, 2022), 90.

CHAPTER 17

1. Jorge Luis Borges, *Selected Non-Fictions*, ed. Eliot Weinberger, trans. Esther Allen, Suzanne Jill Levine, and Eliot Weinberger (New York: Viking, 1999), 30.
2. Michael Rakowitz, "In the Studio: Michael Rakowitz," interview by Ian Forster, *Art21* (2023), https://art21.org/read/in-the-studio-michael-rakowitz/.
3. Oskar Negt and Alexander Kluge, *History and Obstinacy*, ed. Devin Fore, trans. Richard Langston et al. (New York: Zone Books, 2014), 66.
4. Allan Sekula, "The Body and the Archive," *October* 39 (Winter 1986): 3–64.
5. Alex Karp, "The Disapproval of the Crowd," Founders Tribune, accessed February 7, 2026, https://www.founderstribune.org/p/the-disapproval-of-the-crowd-by-alex-karp.
6. Filippo Tommaso Marinetti, "The Foundation and Manifesto of Futurism," in *100 Artists' Manifestos: From the Futurists to the Stuckists*, ed. Alex Danchev (London: Penguin, 2011), 1–8.

7. On February 9, 2026, Mrinank Sharma resigned as head of Anthropic's Safeguards Research Team; see "Pentagon Reviewing Anthropic Partnership over Terms of Use Dispute," *The Hill*, February 17, 2026, https://thehill.com/policy/defense/5740369-pentagon-anthropic-relationship-review/.

8. Simone Browne, *Dark Matters: On the Surveillance of Blackness* (Durham, NC: Duke University Press, 2015). Browne is currently working on a second book, *Like the Mixture of Charcoal and Darkness*, which examines artistic interventions in surveillance, from policing and AI to encryption and electronic waste.

9. Brianna Lyman, "The Halftime Show Was Literally about Erasing 'America,'" *The Federalist*, February 9, 2026, https://thefederalist.com/2026/02/09/the-super-bowl-halftime-show-was-literally-about-erasing-america/; Jorge Bonilla, "Bad Bunny's Polarizing Super Bowl Halftime Show Felt like a Slap at America," *Fox News*, February 9, 2026, https://www.foxnews.com/opinion/bad-bunnys-polarizing-super-bowl-halftime-show-felt-like-slap-america; and in support of the performance see Carl Wilson, "Bad Bunny's Super Bowl Halftime Show Was Part of a Whole Wave of Protest Music," *Slate*, February 10, 2026, https://slate.com/culture/2026/02/bad-bunny-super-bowl-halftime-show-bruce-springsteen-protest-songs.html.

10. Gillian Harkins and Erica Meiners, "Beyond Crisis: College in Prison through the Abolition Undercommons," *Lateral* 3 (2014), https://doi.org/10.25158/L3.1.24.

11. Olúfẹ́mi O. Táíwò, *Elite Capture: How the Powerful Took Over Identity Politics (and Everything Else)* (Chicago: Haymarket Books, 2022), 108.

BIBLIOGRAPHY

Abi-Mershed, Osama. *Apostles of Modernity: Saint-Simonians and the Civilizing Mission in Algeria*. Stanford, CA: Stanford University Press, 2010.

Adams, Alexander. *Artivism: The Battle for Museums in the Era of Postmodernism*. Exeter, UK: Imprint Academic, 2022.

Adorno, Theodor W. *Aesthetic Theory*. Translated by Robert Hullot-Kentor. London: Continuum, 1997.

Adorno, Theodor W., and Max Horkheimer. *Dialectic of Enlightenment: Philosophical Fragments*. Stanford, CA: Stanford University Press, 2002. Originally published 1944.

Agamben, Giorgio. *Homo Sacer: Sovereign Power and Bare Life*. Translated by Daniel Heller-Roazen. Stanford, CA: Stanford University Press, 1998.

Agamben, Giorgio. *What Is an Apparatus? and Other Essays*. Stanford, CA: Stanford University Press, 2009.

Akiba, Michiko. Afterword to *The Art of Activism and the Activism of Art*, by Gregory Sholette. Translated into Japanese by Michiko Akiba, 218–229. Tokyo: Film Art Co., 2025.

Alberro, Alexander. *Interstices: Negotiations at Contemporary Art's Boundaries*. Chicago: University of Chicago Press, 2025.

Al-Khatib, Mary. "Surrealism's America." PhD diss., Johns Hopkins University, 2013.

Alter, Nora M. *Chris Marker*. Champaign: University of Illinois Press, 2006.

Althusser, Louis. "Ideology and Ideological State Apparatuses (Notes towards an Investigation)." In *Lenin and Philosophy and Other Essays*, trans. Ben Brewster, 127–186. New York: Monthly Review Press, 1971.

Althusser, Louis, and Étienne Balibar. *Reading Capital*. Translated by Ben Brewster. London: New Left Books, 2024.

Andreessen, Marc. "The Techno-Optimist Manifesto." Andreessen Horowitz (a16z), October 16, 2023. https://a16z.com/the-techno-optimist-manifesto/.

Archer-Straw, Petrine. *Negrophilia: Avant-Garde Paris and Black Culture in the 1920s*. New York: Thames & Hudson, 2000.

Arendt, Hannah. *The Origins of Totalitarianism*. New edition with added prefaces. New York: Harcourt Brace Jovanovich, 1973.

Arendt, Hannah. *The Portable Hannah Arendt*. London: Penguin, 2003.

Art et Liberté. "Long Live Degenerate Art." In *Art in Theory: The West in the World—An Anthology of Changing Ideas*, edited by Charles Harrison and Paul Wood, 647–648. Hoboken, NJ: John Wiley & Sons, 2021.

Art Workers' Coalition. "The Art Workers' Coalition Demands." In *Art in Theory 1900–2000: An Anthology of Changing Ideas*, edited by Charles Harrison and Paul Wood, 896–897. Oxford: Blackwell, 2003.

Attia, Kader, and Léa Gauthier, eds. *RepaiR*. Paris: Blackjack éditions, 2014.

Aversa, Andrea. 2019. *ARCHIUM N°02: Un été italien*. With contributions by Luca Acquarelli, Guido Panvini, and Valentina Angeleri. Milan: DATA-Sharing Archives.

Ayoung, Todd. "Todd Ayoung." Interview by Curlee Raven Holton. *Bomb*, no. 38 (Winter 1992): 38–41. https://bombmagazine.org/articles/todd-ayoung.

Bakhtin, Mikhail. *Rabelais and His World*. Translated by Hélène Iswolsky. Bloomington: Indiana University Press, 1984.

Banaji, Jairus. *Theory as History: Essays on Modes of Production and Exploitation*. Leiden: Brill, 2010.

Baravalle, Marco. "Alter-institutions and Art. Between Governance and Autonomy. Capture, Subjectivity, Decolonization, Governance, Acceleration, Queering, Prefigurative Economics." In Kuba Szreder, ed., "Special PataInstitutional Online Issue." Special issue, *Journal of Aesthetics and Protest*. Accessed December 1, 2025. https://joaap.org/patainstitutional/marco.htm.

Baravalle, Marco. *The Battleground of Art: Alter-institutions and Radical Curating in the Neoliberal Era*. London: Verso, 2026.

Baravalle, Marco. "Laboratory Italy: The Meloni Government and Postfascist Intellectuals." *Field—A Journal of Socially-Engaged Art Criticism* 29 (Winter 2025). https://field-journal.com/issue-29-winter-2025/8591/.

Barron, Louis. *Sous le drapeau rouge* [Under the red flag]. Paris: A. Savine, 1889.

Bass, Chloë. "Artist Statement." *Chloë Bass* (website). Accessed January 4, 2026. https://www.chloebass.com/welcome.

Bastani, Aaron. *Fully Automated Luxury Communism: A Manifesto*. London: Verso, 2019.

Baudelaire, Charles. "The Salon of 1859: The Modern Public and Photography." In *Classic Essays on Photography*, edited by Alan Trachtenberg, 83–90. New Haven, CT: Leete's Island Books, 1980.

Baudrillard, Jean. *Simulacra and Simulation*. Translated by Sheila Faria Glaser. Ann Arbor: University of Michigan Press, 1994.

Bauman, Zygmunt. *Liquid Modernity*. Cambridge, UK: Polity Press, 2000.

Beckett, Samuel. *Nohow On: Company, Ill Seen Ill Said, Worstward Ho*. New York: Limited Editions Club, 1989.

Beech, Dave. *Art and Value: Art's Economic Exceptionalism in Classical, Neoclassical, and Marxist Economics*. Leiden: Brill, 2015.

Békés, Márton. *Cultural Warfare: The Theory and Practice of Cultural Power*. Translated by Ferenc Sullivan. Budapest: ElektroPress, 2022.

Bell, Katherine. "The MFA Is the New MBA." *Harvard Business Review*, April 14, 2008.

Beloff, Zoe. "The Art of Reenactment." Presentation at UnionDocs Center for Documentary Art, Queens, NY, January 27, 2023.

Benjamin, Walter. "The Author as Producer." In *Understanding Brecht*, translated by Anna Bostock, 85–103. London: NLB, 1973.

Benjamin, Walter. *Illuminations: Essays and Reflections*. Edited by Hannah Arendt and translated by Harry Zohn. New York: Harcourt, Brace & World, 1968.

Benjamin, Walter. *Moscow Diary*. Edited by Gary Smith. Translated by Richard Sieburth. Cambridge, MA: Harvard University Press, 1986.

Benjamin, Walter. *Selected Writings*. Volume 4, *1938–1940*, edited by Howard Eiland and Michael W. Jennings. Cambridge, MA: Harvard University Press, 1996.

Benjamin, Walter. "A Short History of Photography." *Screen* 13, no. 1 (1972): 5–26.

Benkler, Yochai. *The Wealth of Networks: How Social Production Transforms Markets and Freedom*. New Haven, CT: Yale University Press, 2006.

Berardi, Franco. *After the Future*. Oakland, CA: AK Press, 2011.

Berg, Karen van den, and Ursula Pasero, eds. *Art Production beyond the Art Market?* Translated by Wolfgang Astelbauer. Berlin: Sternberg Press, 2013.

Bergman, Jay. *The French Revolutionary Tradition in Russian and Soviet Politics, Political Thought, and Culture*. Oxford, UK: Oxford University Press, 2019.

Berlant, Lauren. *Cruel Optimism*. Durham, NC: Duke University Press, 2011.

Birolli, Zeno, ed. *Gli scritti editi e inediti* [by Umberto Boccioni]. Milan: Feltrinelli, 1971.

Bishop, Claire. *Disordered Attention: Contemporary Art and Attention in the Twenty-First Century*. London: Verso, 2024.

Blackwood, Jonathan, and Bojan Ivanov. "Field Report—North Macedonia." *Field—A Journal of Socially-Engaged Art Criticism* 30 (Spring 2025). https://field-journal.com/issue-30-spring-2025/field-report-north-macedonia/.

Blackwood, Jonathan, and Jasmina Tumbas. "Introduction: Yugoslav Hauntologies." In *Contemporary Art in the Post-Yugoslav Space: Case Studies in Hauntology*, edited by Jonathan Blackwood and Jasmina Tumbas, 1–16. London: Routledge, 2025.

Bloch, Ernst. *Heritage of Our Times*. Translated by Neville Plaice and Stephen Plaice. Berkeley: University of California Press, 1991.

Boltanski, Luc, and Ève Chiapello. *The New Spirit of Capitalism*. London: Verso, 2005.

Borges, Jorge Luis. *Selected Non-Fictions*. Edited by Eliot Weinberger. Translated by Esther Allen, Suzanne Jill Levine, and Eliot Weinberger. New York: Viking, 1999.

Bourdieu, Pierre. *Homo Academicus*. Translated by Peter Collier. Stanford, CA: Stanford University Press, 1988. Originally published 1984.

Bourdieu, Pierre, and Hans Haacke. *Free Exchange*. Stanford, CA: Stanford University Press, 1995.

Bourriaud, Nicolas. *Inclusions: Aesthetics of the Capitalocene*. Translated by Jeanine Herman. Berlin: Sternberg Press, 2022.

Brannen, Samuel J., Christian S. Haig, and Katherine Schmidt. "The Age of Mass Protests: Understanding an Escalating Global Trend." Center for Strategic and International Studies, March 2020. https://www.csis.org/analysis/age-mass-protests-understanding-escalating-global-trend.

Braziel, Jana Evans. *Street Art and Activism in the Greater Caribbean*. Jackson: University Press of Mississippi, 2022.

Brecht, Bertolt. *The Days of the Commune*. Translated by Clive Barker and Arno Reinfrank. London: Methuen, 1978. Originally published 1949.

Brecht, Bertolt. "The Threepenny Process: A Sociological Experiment." In *Bertolt Brecht on Film and Radio*. Translated by Marc Silberman. London: Methuen, 2000.

Breitbart, Andrew. *Righteous Indignation: Excuse Me While I Save the World*. New York: Grand Central Publishing, 2011.

Bronner, Stephen Eric. *Modernism at the Barricades: Aesthetics, Politics, Utopia*. New York: Columbia University Press, 2012.

Brown, Wendy. *In the Ruins of Neoliberalism: The Rise of Antidemocratic Politics in the West*. New York: Columbia University Press, 2019.

Browne, Simone. *Dark Matters: On the Surveillance of Blackness*. Durham, NC: Duke University Press, 2015.

Bru, Sascha. *The European Avant-Gardes, 1905–1935: A Portable Guide*. Edinburgh: Edinburgh University Press, 2018.

Bryant, Rebecca. *The Past in Pieces: Belonging in the New Cyprus*. Philadelphia: University of Pennsylvania Press, 2010.

Buck-Morss, Susan. *The Dialectics of Seeing: Walter Benjamin and the Arcades Project*. Cambridge, MA: MIT Press, 1989.

Buck-Morss, Susan. *Hegel, Haiti, and Universal History*. Pittsburgh: University of Pittsburgh Press, 2009.

Bürger, Peter. *Theory of the Avant-Garde*. Translated by Michael Shaw. Minneapolis: University of Minnesota Press, 1984.

Burns, Liz, ed. *Art and Activism*. With contributions by Helen Carey, Anthony Haughey and others. Dublin: Fire Station Artist Studios, 2014. https://www.firestation.ie/assets/uploads/2022/04/Art-and-Activism.pdf.

Butler, Octavia E. *Kindred*. Garden City, NY: Doubleday, 1979.

Calirman, Claudia. *Brazilian Art under Dictatorship: Antonio Manuel, Artur Barrio, and Cildo Meireles*. Durham, NC: Duke University Press, 2012.

Callinicos, Alex. *Making History: Agency, Structure, and Change in Social Theory*. Leiden: Brill, 2004.

Canclini, Néstor García. *Hybrid Cultures: Strategies for Entering and Leaving Modernity*. Minneapolis: University of Minnesota Press, 2005.

Carey, Helen, Anthony Haughey, Alan Grossman, and Ailbhe Murphy, eds. *Socially Engaged Art Practice in Ireland: Contested Narratives, Places and Futures*. Cork: Cork University Press, forthcoming.

Carruth, Shane, director. *Primer*. Los Angeles: THS Productions, 2004.

Caws, Mary Ann, ed. *Manifesto: A Century of Isms*. Lincoln: University of Nebraska Press, 2001.

Certeau, Michel de. *The Practice of Everyday Life*. Translated by Steven Rendall. Berkeley: University of California Press, 1984.

Césaire, Aimé. "Négreries: Black Youth and Assimilation." *L'étudiant Noir*. March 1935.

Chakrabarty, Dipesh. *Provincializing Europe: Postcolonial Thought and Historical Difference*. 2nd ed. Princeton, NJ: Princeton University Press, 2007.

Charnley, Kim. *Sociopolitical Aesthetics: Art, Crisis, and Neoliberalism*. London: Bloomsbury Academic, 2021.

Child, Danielle. *Working Aesthetics: Labour, Art, and Capitalism*. London: Bloomsbury Academic, 2019.

Clark, Timothy J. *The Absolute Bourgeois: Artists and Politics in France, 1848–1851*. Berkeley: University of California Press, 1973.

Clark, Timothy J. *Heaven on Earth: Painting and the Life to Come*. London: Thames & Hudson, 2018.

Clark, Timothy J. *Image of the People: Gustave Courbet and the 1848 Revolution*. Berkeley: University of California Press, 1973.

Clausen, Susanne. "Curating the Art School—Propositions for Developing a Collaborative Art Space . . ." November 6, 2020. https://www.researchcatalogue.net/view/542734/626649.

Clayson, S. Hollis. *Paris in Despair: Art and Everyday Life under Siege, 1870–1871*. Chicago: University of Chicago Press, 2002.

Coman, Julian. "Vive la Commune? The Working-Class Insurrection That Shook the World." *Guardian*, March 7, 2021. https://www.theguardian.com/world/2021/mar/07/vive-la-commune-the-working-class-insurrection-that-shook-the-world.

Corbet, David. *Trauma, Art, and Memory in the Postcolony*. London: Palgrave Macmillan, 2023.

Costanzo, Jim. "The Aaron Burr Society." *Journal of Aesthetics and Protest*, no. 7 (2010). https://joaap.org/7/Aaronburr.html.

Cottington, David. *The Avant Garde: A Very Short Introduction*. Oxford: Oxford University Press, 2013.

Courbet, Gustave. "Letter to the Government of National Defense, September 4, 1870." In *The Communards of Paris 1871*, edited by Stewart Edwards, 30–31. Ithaca, NY: Cornell University Press, 1973.

Crary, Jonathan. *24/7: Late Capitalism and the Ends of Sleep*. London: Verso, 2013.

Critical Art Ensemble. "Radiation Burn: A Temporary Monument to Public Safety." 2010. Project description. http://critical-art.net/radiation-burn-2010/.

Critical Art Ensemble. *Unreality and Its Discontents: The Struggle against Christian Nationalism*. Brooklyn, NY: Autonomedia, 2025.

Crombie, Isobel. *Re-View: 170 Years of Photography*. Melbourne, Victoria, Australia: National Gallery of Victoria, 2010.

Danchev, Alex, ed. *100 Artists' Manifestos: From the Futurists to the Stuckists*. London: Penguin, 2011.

Darío, Rubén. *Autobiografía*. Medellín, Colombia: Ediciones UNALUA, 2016.

Davis, Ben. *Art in the After-culture: Capitalist Crisis and Cultural Strategy*. Chicago: Haymarket Books, 2022.

Davis, Mike. *Late Victorian Holocausts: El Niño Famines and the Making of the Third World*. London: Verso, 2001.

Dawson, Ashley. *Environmentalism from Below: How Global People's Movements Are Leading the Fight for Our Planet*. Chicago: Haymarket Books, 2024.

Day, Gail. "The Fear of Heteronomy." *Third Text* 23, no. 4 (2009): 393–406.

Defense Advanced Research Projects Agency (DARPA). "Budgets and Testimony." US Department of Defense, 2024. https://www.darpa.mil/about/budgets-testimony.

Deleuze, Gilles. *Difference and Repetition*. New York: Columbia University Press, 1994.

Deleuze, Gilles, and Félix Guattari. *Anti-Oedipus: Capitalism and Schizophrenia*. Translated by Robert Hurley et al. Minneapolis: University of Minnesota Press, 2004.

Demos, T. J. *Radical Futurisms: Ecologies of Collapse, Chronopolitics, and Justice-to-Come*. Berlin: Sternberg Press, 2023.

Denning, Michael. *The Cultural Front: The Laboring of American Culture in the Twentieth Century*. London: Verso, 1997.

Derrida, Jacques. "Mochlos; or, The Conflict of the Faculties." In *Eyes of the University: Right to Philosophy 2*, translated by Jan Plug, 83–112. Stanford, CA: Stanford University Press, 2004. Originally published 1992.

Derrida, Jacques. *Archive Fever: A Freudian Impression*. Translated by Eric Prenowitz. Chicago: University of Chicago Press, 1995.

Derrida, Jacques. *Of Grammatology*. Trans. Gayatri Chakravorty Spivak. Corrected ed. Baltimore: Johns Hopkins University Press, 1997.

Derrida, Jacques. *Specters of Marx: The State of the Debt, the Work of Mourning and the New International*. Translated by Peggy Kamuf. New York: Routledge, 1994.

De Wachter, Ellen Mara. "Spectral Iconic Appearances: An Interview with Tony Chakar on De-sanctified Icons, the Space of Catastrophe and the Aftermath of the Lebanese Civil Wars." *springerin*, no. 4 (2008). https://springerin.at/en/2008/4/geisterhafte-ikonische-erscheinungen//.

Dick, Philip K. *Time Out of Joint*. New York: J. B. Lippincott, 1959.

Di Liscia, Valentina. "Tania Bruguera Agreed to Leave Cuba in Exchange for Release of 25 Prisoners." *Hyperallergic*, October 7, 2021. https://hyperallergic.com/682889/tania-bruguera-agreed-to-leave-cuba-in-exchange-for-release-of-25-prisoners/.

Dimitrakaki, Angela. *Feminism. Art. Capitalism*. London: Pluto Press, 2025.

Dimitrakaki, Angela. *Gender, ArtWork, and the Global Imperative: A Materialist Feminist Critique*. Manchester: Manchester University Press, 2013.

Dinkins, Stephanie. "Afro-now-ism: The Unencumbered Black Mind Is a Wellspring of Possibility." *Noema*, June 16, 2020. https://www.noemamag.com/afro-now-ism/

Doxee, Catrina. "Examining Extremism: The Militia Movement." *Examining Extremism* (blog). Center for Strategic International Studies. August 12, 2021. https://www.csis.org/blogs/examining-extremism/examining-extremism-militia-movement.

D'Souza, Aruna. *Whitewalling: Art, Race & Protest in 3 Acts*. New York: Badlands Unlimited, 2018.

Duncan, Carol. *Civilizing Rituals: Inside Public Art Museums*. Abingdon, UK: Routledge, 2005.

Duncan, Carol. "Who Rules the Art World?" In *The Aesthetics of Power: Essays in Critical Art History*, 165–188. New York: Cambridge University Press, 1983.

Duranton, Sylvain. "AI: The Return of Marxist Class Struggle?" *Forbes*, June 28, 2023. https://www.forbes.com/sites/sylvainduranton/2023/06/28/ai-the-return-of-marxist-class-struggle/?sh=7c45f491139a.

Eagleton, Terry. *The Ideology of the Aesthetic*. Oxford: Blackwell, 1997.

Edsall, Thomas B. "JD Vance Wanted to 'Aggressively Attack' American Universities. His Wish Has Been Trump's Command." *New York Times*, June 3, 2025.

Edwards, Steve. "Commons and Crowds: Figuring Photography from Above and Below." *Third Text* 23, no. 4 (2009): 447–464.

Edwards, Steve. "Time's Carcass: Art History, Capitalism, and Temporality." In *The Routledge Companion to Marxisms in Art History*, edited by Tijen Tunalı and Brian Winkenweder, 146–161. Abingdon, UK: Taylor & Francis, 2025.

Egbert, Donald Drew. "The Idea of Avant-Garde in Art and Politics." *Leonardo* 3, no. 1 (1970): 75–86.

Egbert, Donald Drew. *Social Radicalism and the Arts*. New York: Knopf, 1970.

Eichner, Carolyn J. *The Paris Commune: A Brief History*. New Brunswick, NJ: Rutgers University Press, 2020.

Eichner, Carolyn J. *Surmounting the Barricades: Women in the Paris Commune*. Bloomington: Indiana University Press, 2004.

Eisenberg, Daniel, and Ellen Rothenberg, eds. *Re:Working Labor*. Chicago: School of the Art Institute of Chicago, 2023.

Engels, Friedrich. *The Condition of the Working Class in England*. Oxford: Oxford University Press, 2009.

Erlich, Gábor. "Update from Hungary, the Semi-core of the Illiberal International." *Field—A Journal of Socially-Engaged Art Criticism* 30 (Spring 2025). https://field-journal.com/issue-30-spring-2025/update-from-hungary/.

Ermida, Raquel. "The Rise of Porto Artist Collectives and the Birth of Democratic Collaboration over Fifteen Years of Daily Art Practice." *Journal of Visual Art Practice* 23, no. 3 (2024): 327–354.

Evans, Richard J. *The Third Reich in Power, 1933–1939*. New York: Penguin, 2005.

Farago, Jason. "Why Culture Has Come to a Standstill." *New York Times*, October 10, 2023.

Federici, Silvia. *Caliban and the Witch: Women, the Body, and Primitive Accumulation*. Brooklyn, NY: Autonomedia, 2004.

Federici, Silvia. *Wages against Housework*. Bristol: Falling Wall Press, 1975.

Fehérváry, Kriszti. "Christian Nationalism Goes Organic: Populist Politics and the Aesthetics of the Built Environment in Hungary." *Journal of the Association for Political and Legal Anthropology*, August 30, 2020. https://polarjournal.org/2022/08/30/christian-nationalism-goes-organic-populist-politics-and-the-aesthetics-of-the-built-environment-in-hungary/.

Felton-Dansky, Miriam. *Viral Performance: Contagious Theaters from Modernism to the Digital Age*. Evanston, IL: Northwestern University Press, 2018.

Feuer, Alan. "In Trump's Second Term, Far-Right Agenda Enters the Mainstream." *New York Times*, August 23, 2025.

Fiks, Yevgeniy, Brian James Baer, and Katherine Carl. *Queer(ing) Russian Art: Realism, Revolution, Performance*. Newton, MA: Academic Studies Press, 2023.

Finkelpearl, Tom. *What We Made: Conversations on Art and Social Cooperation*. Durham, NC: Duke University Press, 2013.

Fisher, Mark. *Capitalist Realism: Is There No Alternative?* Winchester, UK: Zero Books, 2009.

Fisher, Mark. *Ghosts of My Life: Writings on Depression, Hauntology and Lost Futures*. Winchester, UK: Zero Books, 2014.

Fisher, Mark. "The Metaphysics of Crackle: Afrofuturism and Hauntology." *Dancecult: Journal of Electronic Dance Music Culture* 5, no. 2 (2013): 42–55.

Fisher, Mark. *The Weird and the Eerie*. London: Watkins Media, 2017.

Flaubert, Gustave. Letter to George Sand, letter no. 188, 1871. Online-Literature.com. Accessed July 11, 2025. https://www.online-literature.com/gustave-flaubert/sand-flaubert-letters/4/.

Foster, Hal, ed. *The Anti-Aesthetic: Essays on Postmodern Culture*. Port Townsend, WA: Bay Press, 1983.

Fraenkel, Ernst. *The Dual State: A Contribution to the Theory of Dictatorship*. Translated by E. A. Shils, in collaboration with Edith Lowenstein and Klaus Knorr. New York: Oxford University Press, 1941.

Frank, Thomas. *The Conquest of Cool: Business Culture, Counterculture, and the Rise of Hip Consumerism*. Chicago: University of Chicago Press, 1997.

Freeman, Elizabeth. *Time Binds: Queer Temporalities, Queer Histories*. Durham, NC: Duke University Press, 2010.

Freire, Paulo. *Pedagogy of the Oppressed*. Translated by Myra Bergman Ramos. New York: Herder and Herder, 1970.

Freud, Sigmund. *Totem and Taboo: Resemblances between the Mental Lives of Savages and Neurotics*. Translated by James Strachey. New York: W. W. Norton, 1950.

Freud, Sigmund. "The Uncanny." In *The Standard Edition of the Complete Psychological Works of Sigmund Freud*, vol. 17 (1917–1919), translated by James Strachey, 217–256. London: Hogarth Press, 1955.

Fukuyama, Francis. *The End of History and the Last Man*. New York: Free Press, 1992.

Galimberti, Jacopo. *Individuals against Individualism: Art Collectives in Western Europe, 1956–1969*. Liverpool: Liverpool University Press, 2017.

Garnet, Simon. "For a Belarusian Res Publica!" *Eurozine*, August 24, 2020. https://www.eurozine.com/for-a-belarusian-res-publica/.

Garrett, Marc, and Yiannis Colakides, eds. *Frankenstein Reanimated: Creation and Technology in the 21st Century*. Liverpool: Torque Editions, 2022.

Garrido Castellano, Carlos. *Beyond Representation in Contemporary Caribbean Art: Space, Politics, and the Public Sphere*. New Brunswick, NJ: Rutgers University Press, 2019.

Garrido Castellano, Carlos. "Living, Writing, Imagining (at) the End of Creative Capitalism." *Afterimage* 52, no. 2 (2025): 16–23.

Gerasimova, Ekaterina, and Sofia Chuikina. "The Repair Society." *Russian Studies in History* 48, no. 1 (2009): 58–74.

Gibson, W. *Paris during the Commune, 1871: Being Letters from Paris and Its Neighbourhood, Written Chiefly during the Time of the Second Siege*. London: Whittaker, 1872.

Glahn, Philip, and Cary Levine. *The Future Is Present: Art, Technology, and the Work of Mobile Image*. Cambridge, MA: MIT Press, 2024.

Goebbels, Joseph. Speech at the Nazi Party Congress, Nuremberg, September 1935. Holocaust Encyclopedia, United States Holocaust Memorial Museum. https://encyclopedia.ushmm.org/content/en/film/goebbels-claims-jews-will-destroy-culture.

Goffe, Tao Leigh. *Dark Laboratory: On Columbus, the Caribbean, and the Origins of the Climate Crisis*. Garden City, NY: Doubleday, 2025.

Gogarty, Larne Abse. *Usable Pasts: Social Practice and State Formation in American Art*. Leiden: Brill, 2022.

Gogarty, Larne Abse. *What We Do Is Secret: Contemporary Art and the Antinomies of Conspiracy*. Berlin: Sternberg Press, 2023.

Goodhart, David. *The Road to Somewhere: The Populist Revolt and the Future of Politics*. New York: Oxford University Press, 2017.

Gordon, Avery. *Ghostly Matters: Haunting and the Sociological Imagination*. Minneapolis: University of Minnesota Press, 2008.

Gorin, Jean-Pierre. "Jean-Pierre Gorin on Marker's *La Jetée*." 2005. *The Criterion Channel*. Video. https://www.criterionchannel.com/la-jetee/videos/jean-pierre-gorin-on-la-jetee.

Gorman, John. *Banner Bright: An Illustrated History of Trade Union Banners*. Essex, UK: Scorpion Publishers, 1986.

Gough, Maria. "Back in the USSR: John Heartfield, Gustavs Klucis, and the Medium of Soviet Propaganda." *New German Critique*, no. 107 (2009): 133–183.

Graeber, David. *The Utopia of Rules: On Technology, Stupidity, and the Secret Joys of Bureaucracy*. Brooklyn, NY: Melville House, 2015.

Gramsci, Antonio. *Prison Notebooks*. Vols. 1–3. Edited and translated by Joseph A. Buttigieg and Antonio Callari. New York: Columbia University Press, 2011.

Greenwald, Dara, and Josh MacPhee, eds. *Signs of Change: Social Movement Cultures 1960s to Now*. Oakland: AK Press; New York: Exit Art, 2010.

Groeger, Lena V., Jeff Kao, Al Shaw, Moiz Syed, and Maya Eliahou. "What Parler Saw during the Attack on the Capitol." *ProPublica*, January 17, 2021. https://projects.propublica.org/parler-capitol-videos/.

Groys, Boris. "Becoming Revolutionary: On Kazimir Malevich." *e-flux* 47 (2013). https://www.e-flux.com/journal/47/60047/becoming-revolutionary-on-kazimir-malevich.

Groys, Boris. *In the Flow*. London: Verso, 2016.

Groys, Boris. "On Art Activism." *e-flux* 56 (2014). https://www.e-flux.com/journal/56/60343/on-art-activism.

Groys, Boris. *The Total Art of Stalinism: Avant-garde, Aesthetic Dictatorship, and Beyond*. London: Verso, 2014.

Haiven, Max. *Art after Money, Money after Art: Creative Strategies against Financialization*. London: Pluto Press, 2018.

Haiven, Max. *The Player and the Played: From Gamed Capitalism to 21st-Century Fascism*. Cambridge, MA: MIT Press, 2026.

Hall, Stuart. "David Scott." *Bomb*, no. 90 (Winter 2005). bombmagazine.org/articles/2005/01/01/david-scott/.

Hall, Stuart. "The Problem of Ideology: Marxism without Guarantees." In *Stuart Hall: Critical Dialogues in Cultural Studies*, edited by David Morley and Kuan-Hsing Chen, 25–46. London: Routledge, 1996.

Hardt, Michael, and Antonio Negri. *Empire*. Cambridge, MA: Harvard University Press, 2001.

Harkins, Gillian, and Erica Meiners. "Beyond Crisis: College in Prison through the Abolition Undercommons." *Lateral* 3 (2014). https://doi.org/10.25158/L3.1.24.

Harney, Stefano, and Fred Moten. *The Undercommons: Fugitive Planning and Black Study*. London: Minor Compositions, 2013.

Harney, Stefano, and Fred Moten. "The University and the Undercommons: Seven Theses." *Social Text* 22, no. 2 (2004): 101–115.

Hartog, François. *Regimes of Historicity: Presentism and Experiences of Time*. New York: Columbia University Press, 2015.

Harvey, David. "Between Space and Time: Reflections on the Geographical Imagination." *Annals of the Association of American Geographers* 80, no. 3 (1990): 418–434.

Harvey, David. *The Condition of Postmodernity: An Enquiry into the Origins of Cultural Change*. Oxford, UK: Basil Blackwell, 1989.

Harvey, David. *Marx, Capital, and the Madness of Economic Reason*. New York: Oxford University Press, 2018.

Hazony, Yoram. *The Virtue of Nationalism*. New York: Basic Books, 2018.

Helguera, Pablo. *Education for Socially Engaged Art: A Materials and Techniques Handbook*. New York: Jorge Pint Books, 2011.

Hemingway, Andrew. *Artists on the Left: American Artists and the Communist Movement, 1926–1956*. New Haven, CT: Yale University Press, 2002.

Hemingway, Andrew. "Cultural Democracy by Default: The Politics of the New Deal Arts Programmes." *Oxford Art Journal* 30, no. 2 (2007): 269–287.

Herbst, Robby. "What Was Liberalism: Affective Policy in the Art of Citizen Participation." *Landscapes, A Blade of Grass*, 2024. https://www.abladeofgrass.pub/contributions/what-was-liberalism-affective-policy-in-the-art-of-citizen-participation.

Heywood, Anthony. "Post-war Economies (Russian Empire)." *International Encyclopedia of the First World War* (2014). https://encyclopedia.1914-1918-online.net/article/post-war-economies-russian-empire/.

Hicks, John, and Robert Tucker, eds. *Revolution and Reaction: The Paris Commune 1871*. Amherst: University of Massachusetts Press, 1973.

Hitler, Adolf. *Mein Kampf*. Translated by Ralph Manheim. Boston: Houghton Mifflin, 1943.

Hlavajova, Maria, and Simon Sheikh, eds. *Former West: Art and the Contemporary after 1989*. Cambridge, MA: MIT Press, 2016.

Holmes, Brian. *Hieroglyphs of the Future: Art and Politics in a Networked Era*. Zagreb: Arkzin/What, How, and for Whom, 2003.

hooks, bell. *Teaching to Transgress: Education as the Practice of Freedom*. New York: Routledge, 1994.

Houellebecq, Michel. *The Map and the Territory*. New York: Vintage, 2012.

Huyssen, Andreas. *After the Great Divide: Modernism, Mass Culture, Postmodernism*. Bloomington: Indiana University Press, 1986.

Huyssen, Andreas. *Memory Art in the Contemporary World: Confronting Violence in the Global South*. London: Lund Humphries, 2022.

Ibrahim, Habiba, and Badia Ahad. "Introduction: Black Temporality in Times of Crisis." *South Atlantic Quarterly* 121, no. 1 (2022): 1–10.

Illich, Ivan. *Deschooling Society*. New York: Harper & Row, 1971.

Jäger, Anton. "Hyperpolitics in America." *New Left Review* 149 (September–October 2024). https://doi.org/10.64590/f5k.

James, C. L. R. *The Black Jacobins: Toussaint L'Ouverture and the San Domingo Revolution*. New York: Vintage Books, 1989.

Jameson, Fredric. "Postmodernism and Consumer Society." In *The Anti-Aesthetic: Essays on Postmodern Culture*, edited by Hal Foster, 111–125. Port Townsend, WA: Bay Press, 1983.

Jameson, Fredric. *Postmodernism, or, The Cultural Logic of Late Capitalism*. Durham, NC: Duke University Press, 1991.

Jameson, Fredric. *Representing Capital: A Reading of Volume One*. London: Verso, 2011.

Janes, Robert R., and Richard Sandell, eds. *Museum Activism*. London: Routledge, 2019.

Jaskot, Paul B. *The Architecture of Oppression: The SS, Forced Labor, and the Nazi Monumental Building Economy*. London: Routledge, 2002.

Jeremić, Vladan, and Rena Raedle. "Tools for Dismantling the Oligarchy—Student Protests in Serbia and Their Creativity." *Field—A Journal of Socially-Engaged Art Criticism* 30 (Spring 2025). https://field-journal.com/issue-30-spring-2025/tools-for-dismantling-the-oligarchy-student-protests-in-serbia-and-their-creativity/.

Joselit, David. *After Art*. Princeton, NJ: Princeton University Press, 2013.

Kant, Immanuel. *The Conflict of the Faculties*. Translated by Mary J. Gregor. Lincoln: University of Nebraska Press, 1992. Originally published 1798.

Karimi, Pamela. *Alternative Iran: Contemporary Art and Critical Spatial Practice*. Stanford, CA: Stanford University Press, 2022.

"Karl Beveridge Reflects." *Labor Art Review*, October 2, 2025. https://laborartreview.net/karl-beverege-reflects/.

Karp, Alex. "The Disapproval of the Crowd." Founders Tribune. Accessed February 7, 2026. https://www.founderstribune.org/p/the-disapproval-of-the-crowd-by-alex-karp.

Karp, Alexander C., and Nicholas W. Zamiska. *The Technological Republic: Hard Power, Soft Belief, and the Future of the West*. New York: Crown Currency, 2025.

Katz, Cindi. *Growing Up Global: Economic Restructuring and Children's Everyday Lives*. Minneapolis: University of Minnesota Press, 2004.

Katz, Cindi. "Vagabond Capitalism and the Necessity of Social Reproduction." *Antipode* 33, no. 4 (2001): 709–728.

Kester, Grant. *Beyond the Sovereign Self: Aesthetic Autonomy from the Avant-Garde to Socially Engaged Art*. Durham, NC: Duke University Press, 2023.

Kester, Grant. Editorial. *Field—A Journal of Socially-Engaged Art Criticism* 29 (Winter 2025). https://field-journal.com/issue-30-spring-2025/test/.

Kester, Grant. *The One and the Many: Contemporary Collaborative Art in a Global Context*. Durham, NC: Duke University Press, 2011.

Kiaer, Christina. *Imagine No Possessions: The Socialist Objects of Russian Constructivism*. Cambridge, MA: MIT Press, 2005.

Kiaer, Christina. "The Russian Constructivist Flapper Dress." *Critical Inquiry* 28, no. 1 (2001): 185–243.

Kishkovsky, Sophia. "Belarus Art Collector Viktor Babariko, Rival to President Alexander Lukashenko, Jailed before Election." *Art Newspaper*, August 24, 2020. https://www.theartnewspaper.com/2020/08/24/belarus-art-collector-viktor-babariko-rival-to-president-alexander-lukashenko-jailed-before-election.

Klein, Naomi. *Doppelganger: A Trip into the Mirror World*. New York: Farrar, Straus and Giroux, 2023.

Koselleck, Reinhart. *Futures Past: On the Semantics of Historical Time*. Translated by Keith Tribe. New York: Columbia University Press, 2004.

Kuoni, Carin, comp. *Energy Plan for the Western Man: Joseph Beuys in America*. New York: Four Walls Eight Windows, 1990.

Land, Nick. *The Dark Enlightenment*. 2013. Reprint, Imperium Press, 2022.

Lambert-Beatty, Carrie. "Make-Believe: Parafiction and Plausibility." *October* 129 (2009): 51–84.

Lang, Martin. *Militant Aesthetics: Art Activism in the 21st Century*. London: Bloomsbury Academic, 2024.

"Latest Trafalgar Square Fourth Plinth Artwork Unveiled." BBC News, March 28, 2018. https://www.bbc.com/news/uk-england-london-43565870.

Latimer, Tirza True. "Improper Objects: Performing Queer/Feminist Art/History." In *Otherwise: Imagining Queer Feminist Art Histories*, edited by Amelia Jones and Erin Silver, 93–109. Manchester: Manchester University Press, 2016.

Lavine, Steven D., and Ivan Karp, eds. *Exhibiting Cultures: The Poetics and Politics of Museum Display*. Washington, DC: Smithsonian Institution Press, 1991.

Lawton, Anna, and Herbert Eagle, trans. and eds. *Words in Revolution: Russian Futurist Manifestos, 1912–1928*. Washington, DC: New Academia Publishing, 2005.

Lazzarato, Maurizio. "Immaterial Labor." Translated by Paul Colilli and Ed Emory. In *Radical Thought in Italy: A Potential Politics*, edited by Paolo Virno and Michael Hardt, 133–147. Minneapolis: University of Minnesota Press, 1996.

Lee, Steven S. *The Ethnic Avant-Garde: Minority Cultures and World Revolution*. New York: Columbia University Press, 2015.

Lefebvre, Henri. *The Production of Space*. Translated by Donald Nicholson-Smith. Hoboken, NJ: Wiley-Blackwell, 1991.

Lefebvre, Henri. *Rhythmanalysis: Space, Time and Everyday Life*. Translated by Stuart Elden and Gerald Moore. London: Continuum, 2004.

Léger, Marc James, ed. *The Idea of the Avant Garde: And What It Means Today*. Vol. 2. Bristol, UK: Intellect Books, 2019.

Léger, Marc James. *The Neoliberal Undead: Essays on Contemporary Art and Politics*. Winchester, UK: Zero Books, 2013.

Léger, Marc James. "Revenge of the Surplus." Review of *Dark Matter: Art and Politics in the Age of Enterprise Culture* by Gregory Sholette. *Monthly Review* 63, no. 8 (January 2012). https://monthlyreview.org/2012/01/01/revenge-of-the-surplus/.

Legrás, Horacio. "Seeing Women Photographed in Revolutionary Mexico." *Discourse* 38, no. 1 (2016): 3–21.

Lenin, Vladimir Ilyich. *The State and Revolution: The Marxist Theory of the State and the Tasks of the Proletariat in the Revolution*. London: Verso, 2024.

Lerm-Hayes, Christa-Maria. *Post-War Germany and "Objective Chance": W. G. Sebald, Joseph Beuys, and Tacita Dean*. Göttingen: Steidl, 2011.

Leslie, Esther. "Lenin and the Image in Time." *Crisis and Critique* 11, no. 2 (2025): 239–253.

Lessig, Lawrence. *The Future of Ideas: The Fate of the Commons in a Connected World*. New York: Vintage, 2002.

Lewis, Becca. "Headed for Technofascism: The Rightwing Roots of Silicon Valley." *Guardian*, January 29, 2025.

Liman, Doug, director. *Edge of Tomorrow*. Warner Bros. Pictures, 2014. 113 min.

Lipovetsky, Gilles. "On Artistic Capitalism." *Crash* 65 (2018). https://www.crash.fr/on-artistic-capitalism-by-gilles-lipovetsky-crash-65/.

Lippard, Lucy R. *A Different War: Vietnam in Art*. Seattle: Real Comet Press, 1990.

Lippard, Lucy R. *Get the Message? A Decade of Art for Social Change*. New York: E. P. Dutton, 1984.

Lippard, Lucy R. *The Lure of the Local: Senses of Place in a Multicentered Society*. New York: New Press, 1997.

Lippard, Lucy R. *Overlay: Contemporary Art and the Art of Prehistory*. New York: Pantheon Books, 1983.

Little, Adrian. *Temporal Politics: Contested Pasts, Uncertain Futures*. Edinburgh: Edinburgh University Press, 2022.

Lodder, Christina. *Russian Constructivism*. New Haven, CT: Yale University Press, 1983.

Lovink, Geert. *Networks without a Cause: A Critique of Social Media*. Cambridge: Polity, 2012.

Lovink, Geert. *Social Media Abyss: Critical Internet Cultures and the Force of Negation*. Cambridge: Polity, 2016.

Lowenthal, David. "The Past as a Theme Park." In *The Heritage Crusade and the Spoils of History*, 90–104. Cambridge: Cambridge University Press, 1998.

Lütticken, Sven. "From Re- to Pre- and Back Again." In *Over and Over and Over Again: Reenactment Strategies in Contemporary Arts and Theory*, edited by Cristina Baldacci et al., 1–16. Berlin: ICI Berlin Press, 2022.

Luxemburg, Rosa. "The Junius Pamphlet: The Crisis in German Social Democracy." 1915. Marxists Internet Archive. https://www.marxists.org/archive/luxemburg/1915/junius/ch01.htm.

Lynn, Jennifer M. "Contesting Images: Representations of the Modern Woman in the German Illustrated Press, 1924–1933." PhD diss., University of North Carolina at Chapel Hill, 2008.

Lynton, Norbert. *Tatlin's Tower: Monument to Revolution*. New Haven, CT: Yale University Press, 2009.

Mahoney, Emma. "Report from Ireland: Repealing the Eighth Amendment." *Field—A Journal of Socially-Engaged Art Criticism* (December 13, 2019). http://field-journal.com/issue-12.

Maître, Jade. "The Memoirs of Louise Michel (in English)." Louise Michel, March 2, 2023. https://louisemichel.com/the-memoirs-of-louise-michel-in-english-read-free.

Malzacher, Florian. *The Art of Assembly: Political Theatre Today*. Berlin: Alexander Verlag; New York: Martin E. Segal Theatre Center, 2023.

"Manifesto of the Paris Commune's Federation of Artists." Marxists Internet Archive. Accessed February 15, 2026. https://www.marxists.org/history/france/paris-commune/documents/artists.htm.

Marantz, Andrew. "Is It Happening Here?" *New Yorker*, May 5, 2025, 28–26.

Marantz, Andrew. "The Tucker Carlson Road Show." *New Yorker*, September 11, 2024, 22–28.

Marche, Stephen. "'Profound and Abiding Rage': Canada's Answer to America's Abandonment." Guest essay, *New York Times*, August 19, 2025.

Marcuse, Herbert. *One-Dimensional Man: Studies in the Ideology of Advanced Industrial Society*. Boston: Beacon Press, 1964.

Marinetti, Filippo Tommaso. "The Manifesto of Futurism." *Le Figaro*, February 20, 1909.

Marker, Chris, director. *La jetée: Sans soleil*. With Jean-Pierre Gorin, commentator, and Anatole Dauman, producer. Special edition DVD. New York: Criterion Collection, 2007.

Marsh, Kate, and Fionnghuala Sweeney, eds. *Afromodernisms: Paris, Harlem, and the Avant-Garde*. Edinburgh: Edinburgh University Press, 2013.

Martínez, Francisco. *Remains of a Soviet Past in Estonia: An Anthropology of Forgetting, Repair, and Urban Traces*. London: UCL Press, 2018.

Marx, Karl. *Capital: A Critique of Political Economy*. Vol. 1. Translated by Samuel Moore and Edward Aveling. 1887; Moscow: Progress Publishers.

Marx, Karl. *Grundrisse: Foundations of the Critique of Political Economy*. Translated by Martin Nicolaus. London: Penguin, 1993.

Marx, Karl. *Later Political Writings*. Translated by T. Carver. Cambridge: Cambridge University Press, 1996.

Maskovsky, Jeff, and Sophie Bjork-James, eds. *Beyond Populism: Angry Politics and the Twilight of Neoliberalism*. Morgantown: West Virginia University Press, 2020.

Matei, Adrienne. "Systems Are Crumbling—But Daily Life Continues. The Dissonance Is Real." *Guardian*, May 22, 2025.

Mbembe, Achille. *Necropolitics*. Durham, NC: Duke University Press, 2019.

McGarry, Aidan, Itir Erhart, Hande Eslen-Ziya, Olu Jenzen, and Umut Korkut, eds. *The Aesthetics of Global Protest: Visual Culture and Communication*. Amsterdam: Amsterdam University Press, 2019.

McKee, Yates. *Strike Art: Contemporary Art and the Post-Occupy Condition*. London: Verso Books, 2016.

McKittrick, Katherine. *Demonic Grounds: Black Women and the Cartographies of Struggle*. Minneapolis: University of Minnesota Press, 2006.

McKittrick, Katherine, ed. *Sylvia Wynter: On Being Human as Praxis*. Durham, NC: Duke University Press, 2015.

McRobbie, Angela. *Be Creative: Making a Living in the New Culture Industries*. Cambridge: Polity Press, 2016.

Meitin, Alejandro. 2009. Interview by Marcela Fuentes. Hemispheric Institute Encuentro, Bogotá, Colombia, August 26, 2009. Hemispheric Institute Digital Video Library. http://hdl.handle.net/2333.1/c59zw5f5.

Melucci, Alberto. *Nomads of the Present: Social Movements and Individual Needs in Contemporary Society*. Philadelphia: Temple University Press, 1989.

Mesquita, André, Charles Esche, and Will Bradley, eds. *Arte e ativismo antologia*. Lisbon: MASP, 2021. Originally published as Will Bradley and Charles Esche, eds., *Art and Social Change: A Critical Reader* (London: Tate Publishing, 2007).

Michel, Louise, and Marguerite Tinayre. *La misère: roman*. Edited by Daniel Armogathe and Xavière Gauthier. Paris: Éditions du Félin, 1999.

Militz, Marlene. "Perspectives on Institutional Capture and the Artification of Climate Activism." *21: Inquiries into Art, History, and the Visual* 6, no. 1 (2025): 99–131.

Miller, Tyrus. "Retro-Avant-Garde: Aesthetic Revival and the Con/Figuration of Twentieth-Century Time." *Filozofski vestnik* 28, no. 2 (2007): 253–265.

Mirzoeff, Nicholas. *The Right to Look: A Counterhistory of Visuality*. Durham, NC: Duke University Press, 2011.

Mirzoeff, Nicholas, and Carl Pope. *The Appearance of Black Lives Matter*. Miami: [NAME] Publications, 2017.

Mitchell, W. J. T., Bernard E. Harcourt, and Michael Taussig. *Occupy: Three Inquiries in Disobedience*. Chicago: University of Chicago Press, 2013.

Mitra, Srimoyee. *Stephanie Dinkins: On Love and Data*. Ann Arbor: University of Michigan Press, 2024.

Moore, Alan W. *Occupation Culture: Art and Squatting in the City from Below*. London: Minor Compositions, 2015.

Morfino, Vittorio. *Plural Temporalities: Transindividuality and the Aleatory between Spinoza and Althusser*. Translated by Max Henninger. Leiden: Brill, 2014.

Morris, William. *The Collected Works of William Morris*, vol. 23. Edited by May Morris. London: Longmans Green, 1915.

Nagy, Kristóf. "Remaking Civil Society under Authoritarian Capitalism: The Case of the Orbán Regime's Hungarian Academy of Arts." *Intersections. East European Journal of Society and Politics* 9, no. 4 (2024): 80–100. https://doi.org/10.17356/ieejsp.v9i4.1127.

National Center for Science and Engineering Statistics (NCSES). "Higher Education R&D Expenditures Increased 11.2%, Exceeded $108 Billion in FY 2023." National Science Foundation, 2024. https://ncses.nsf.gov/pubs/nsf25313.

NCTV. "Memes as an Online Weapon: An Analysis into the Use of Memes by the Far Right." Ministry of Justice and Security, Netherlands, 2024. https://english.nctv.nl/documents/publications/2024/08/01/far-right-memes-undermining-and-far-from-recognizable.

Negt, Oskar, and Alexander Kluge. *History and Obstinacy*. Edited by Devin Fore. Translated by Richard Langston et al. New York: Zone Books, 2014.

Negt, Oskar, and Alexander Kluge. *Public Sphere and Experience: Analysis of the Bourgeois and Proletarian Public Sphere*. Translated by Peter Labanyi et al. 1993; London: Verso, 2016.

Neidich, Warren, and Arne De Boever, eds. *The Psychopathologies of Cognitive Capitalism*. Berlin: Archive Books, 2013.

Nicholls, Julia. *Revolutionary Thought after the Paris Commune, 1871–1885*. Cambridge: Cambridge University Press, 2019.

Nietzsche, Friedrich. *On the Genealogy of Morality*. 1887. Translated by Carol Diethe. Cambridge: Cambridge University Press, 2006.

Osborne, Peter. *Anywhere or Not at All: Philosophy of Contemporary Art*. London: Verso, 2013.

Osman, Mahmoud. *Revolution 2053, the Beginning*. Self-published, 2007.

PAD Issue 1. February 1981. https://www.darkmatterarchives.net/wp-content/uploads/2011/01/PADD.FirstIssue.1981.No_.1.pdf.

Paulson, Ronald. *Representations of Revolution, 1789–1820*. New Haven, CT: Yale University Press, 1983.

Perraudin, Frances. "Labour Leadership Race: Tories Back Jeremy Corbyn in Bid to Damage Party." *Guardian*, June 16, 2015.

Pershina-Yakimanskaya, Natalia. "Interview with Marina Vishmidt for the 'Untitled' Magazine / London /2009." *Gluklya*. http://gluklya.com/interview/interview-with-marina-vischmidt.

Pershina-Yakimanskaya, Natalia. "Manifesto of the Utopian Unemployment Union, 2017." *Gluklya*. https://gluklya.com/manifest/manifesto-utopian/.

Podesva, Kristina Lee. "A Pedagogical Turn: Brief Notes on Education as Art." *Fillip* 6 (Summer 2007). https://fillip.ca/content/a-pedagogical-turn.

Power, John. "US Education Department to Halve Staff as Trump Pushes for Elimination." *Aljazeera*, March 12, 2025. https://www.aljazeera.com/news/2025/3/12/trump-slashes-us-education-department-staff-in-step-toward-dismantlement.

Premo, Michael, dir. *Homegrown*. Produced by Michael Premo and Rachel Falcone. 2024.

Primor, Adar. "The Veil? It Protects Us from Ugly Women." *Guardian*, November 26, 2017.

Puchner, Martin. *Poetry of the Revolution: Marx, Manifestos, and the Avant-Gardes*. Princeton, NJ: Princeton University Press, 2005.

Purdie, Bernard Lee. "Bernard Purdie Explains Ghost Notes." Facebook, uploaded by Stephen Taylor. @StephenTaylorDrums, March 10, 2017. www.facebook.com/watch/?v=1451029534941071.

Quick, Andrew. *The Wooster Group Work Book*. New York: Routledge, 2007.

Rabaka, Reiland. *The Negritude Movement: W. E. B. Du Bois, Leon Damas, Aime Cesaire, Leopold Senghor, Frantz Fanon, and the Evolution of an Insurgent Idea*. Lanham, MD: Lexington Books, 2015.

Raicovich, Laura. *Culture Strike: Art and Museums in an Age of Protest*. London: Verso, 2021.

Raicovich, Laura, Carin Kuoni, and Kareem Estefan, eds. *Assuming Boycott: Resistance, Agency, and Cultural Production*. New York: OR Books, 2017.

Rancière, Jacques. *The Politics of Aesthetics: The Distribution of the Sensible*. Translated by Gabriel Rockhill. London: Continuum, 2004.

Raunig, Gerald. *Art and Revolution: Transversal Activism in the Long Twentieth Century*. Cambridge, MA: MIT Press, 2007.

Readings, Bill. *The University in Ruins*. Cambridge, MA: Harvard University Press, 1996.

Reeves-Evison, Theo. *Ethics of Contemporary Art in the Shadow of Transgression*. New York: Bloomsbury Visual Arts, 2020.

Reitan, Ruth. *Global Activism*. London: Routledge, 2007.

Remešová, Anna. "Mykola Ridnyi: Any War Is a War of Images." *Blok*, October 28, 2022. https://blokmagazine.com/mykola-ridnyi-any-war-is-a-war-of-images/.

Revelation of St. John the Divine. In *The Holy Bible: King James Version*. Oxford: Oxford University Press, 1769.

Richards, Jill. *The Fury Archives: Female Citizenship, Human Rights, and the International Avant-Gardes*. New York: Columbia University Press, 2020.

Richardson, Michael, and Krzysztof Fijałkowski, eds. *Refusal of the Shadow: Surrealism and the Caribbean*. London: Verso, 1996.

Ricoeur, Paul. *Memory, History, Forgetting*. Translated by Kathleen Blamey and David Pellauer. Chicago: University of Chicago Press, 2004.

Rifkin, Adrian. *Communards and Other Cultural Histories: Essays by Adrian Rifkin*. Edited by Steve Edwards. Chicago: Haymarket Books, 2018.

Riis, Jacob. *How the Other Half Lives: Studies among the Tenements of New York*. New York: Charles Scribner's Sons, 1890.

Rimboud, Cécile. "Women Fighters of the 1871 Paris Commune." *Socialist World*, March 5, 2021. https://www.socialistworld.net/2021/03/05/women-fighters-of-the-1871-paris-commune/.

Roberts, John. "Revolutionary Pathos, Negation, and the Suspensive Avant-Garde." *New Literary History* 41, no. 4 (2010): 717–730.

Roberts, John. *Revolutionary Time and the Avant-Garde*. London: Verso, 2015.

Robinson, Cedric J. *Black Marxism: The Making of the Black Radical Tradition*. Chapel Hill: University of North Carolina Press, 2000.

Rogoff, Irit. "Turning." *e-flux* 0 (November 2008). https://www.e-flux.com/journal/00/68470/turning/.

Romik, Natalia. 2024. *Hideouts: Architecture of Survival*. Edited by Mirjam Wenzel et al. Berlin: Hatje Cantz.

Roose, Kevin. "How the Biden Administration Can Help Solve Our Reality Crisis." *New York Times*, February 2, 2021.

Rosemont, Franklin, and Robin D. G. Kelley, eds. *Black, Brown, and Beige: Surrealist Writings from Africa and the Diaspora*. Austin: University of Texas Press, 2009.

Rosler, Martha. *Decoys and Disruptions: Selected Writings, 1975–2001*. Cambridge, MA: MIT Press, 2004.

Rosler, Martha. *Joy Forever: The Political Economy of Social Creativity*. London: MayFly Books, 2014.

Ross, Andrew. *The Weather Report: A Journey through Unsettled Climates*. Brooklyn: Common Notions, 2025.

Ross, Kristin. "Communal Luxury: Kristin Ross." *Verso Blog*, April 30, 2019. https://www.versobooks.com/blogs/news/3169-communal-luxury-kristin-ross.

Ross, Kristin. *Communal Luxury: The Political Imaginary of the Paris Commune*. London: Verso, 2016.

Ross, Kristin. "The Commune Form: A Conversation with Andreas Petrossiants." *e-flux Journal*, no. 151 (February 2025). https://www.e-flux.com/journal/151/651825/the-commune-form-a-conversation.

Ross, Kristin. *The Emergence of Social Space: Rimbaud and the Paris Commune*. Minneapolis: University of Minnesota Press, 1988.

Ross, Kristin. "The Meaning of the Paris Commune." *Jacobin Magazine*, May 4, 2015. https://jacobin.com/2015/05/kristin-ross-communal-luxury-paris-commune.

Ross, Kristin. "Rimbaud and Spatial History." *Assemblage*, no. 6 (1988): 49–61.

Rushkoff, Douglas. *Present Shock: When Everything Happens Now*. New York: Current, 2013.

Saito, Kohei. *Karl Marx's Ecosocialism: Capital, Nature, and the Unfinished Critique of Political Economy*. New York: Monthly Review Press, 2017.

Saito, Kohei. *Slow Down: The Degrowth Manifesto*. Translated by Brian Bergstrom. Berkeley, CA: Counterpoint, 2024.

Sánchez, Gonzalo J. *Organizing Independence: The Artists' Federation of the Paris Commune and Its Legacy, 1871–1889*. Lincoln: University of Nebraska Press, 1997.

Santos, Boaventura de Sousa. *Epistemologies of the South: Justice against Epistemicide*. London: Routledge, 2014.

Sartre, Jean-Paul. *Critique of Dialectical Reason: Theory of Practical Ensembles*. Vol. 7. Translated by Alan Sheridan-Smith. London: Verso, 2004.

Sartre, Jean-Paul. *Search for a Method*. Translated by Hazel E. Barnes. New York: Alfred A. Knopf, 1963.

Schmukalla, Magda. "Artistic Ruptures and Their 'Communist' Ghosts: On the Post-Communist Condition as Threshold Experience in Art from and in Eastern Europe." PhD diss., Birkbeck, University of London, 2017.

Schneider, Rebecca. *Performing Remains: Art and War in Times of Theatrical Reenactment*. Abingdon, UK: Routledge, 2011.

Scott, David. "Black Futurities Past and Present: Thinking Reparations Through." Paper presented at "Colonial Repercussions: Sara Ahmed and David Scott, Opening Plenary Session," Akademie der Kunste, Berlin, June 23, 2018. Posted by Akademie der Kunste, June 23, 2018. YouTube. https://www.youtube.com/watch?v=OlzDe2rgfzs (1:44–2:25).

Scott, David. *Conscripts of Modernity: The Tragedy of Colonial Enlightenment*. Durham, NC: Duke University Press, 2004.

Scott, David. *Omens of Adversity: Tragedy, Time, Memory, Justice*. Durham, NC: Duke University Press, 2014.

Sekula, Allan. "The Body and the Archive." *October* 39 (Winter 1986): 3–64.

Sells, Mike. *Avant-Garde Performance and the Limits of Criticism*. Ann Arbor: University of Michigan Press, 2005.

Şerban, Oana. "The Critical Theory of Artistic Capitalism." *Hermenia* 18 (2017): 22–33. https://hermeneia.ro/wp-content/uploads/2017/05/03_Serban-Oana.pdf.

Sharma, Sarah. *In the Meantime: Temporality and Cultural Politics*. Durham, NC: Duke University Press, 2014.

Shklovsky, Viktor. *Khod Konia* [Knight's move]. Berlin: Gelikon, 1923.

Sholette, Gregory. *The Art of Activism and the Activism of Art*. London: Lund Humphries, 2022.

Sholette, Gregory. *Dark Matter: Art and Politics in the Age of Enterprise Culture*. London: Pluto Press, 2010.

Sholette, Gregory. *Delirium and Resistance: Activist Art and the Crisis of Capitalism*. Edited by Kim Charnley. Foreword by Lucy R. Lippard. London: Pluto Press, 2017.

Sholette, Gregory, and Todd Ayoung. "A Counter-Progressivist Turn?" *e-flux notes*, February 26, 2023.

Shor, Ira. *Critical Teaching and Everyday Life*. Montreal: Black Rose Books, 1980.

Simoniti, Vid. *Artists Remake the World: The Rise and Fall of Artistic Autonomy*. New Haven, CT: Yale University Press, 2023.

"SJMA Presents New Commission by Trevor Paglen," San José Museum of Art press release, November 5, 2021. https://sjmusart.org/press-release/sjma-presents-new-commission-trevor-paglen.

Slate, Michael. "Hundreds Trace the Path of the 1811 Slave Rebellion in Louisiana." *The Michael Slate Show*, KPFK 90.7 FM, November 11, 2019.

Sosnovskaya, Olia. "Future Perfect Continuous." *Zeitgeister* (Goethe-Institut), November 12, 2020.

Spivak, Gayatri Chakravorty. *Outside in the Teaching Machine*. New York: Routledge, 1993.

Steyerl, Hito. "A Tank on a Pedestal: Museums in an Age of Planetary Civil War." *e-flux* 70 (February 2016). https://www.e-flux.com/journal/70/60543/a-tank-on-a-pedestal-museums-in-an-age-of-planetary-civil-war.

Streeck, Wolfgang. *Taking Back Control? States and State Systems after Globalism*. Translated by Ben Fowkes and Joshua Rahtz. London: Verso, 2024.

Strotsev, Dmitriy. "The Art of Popular Disobedience." *COLTA*, December 10, 2020. https://www.colta.ru/articles/specials/26156-dmitriy-strotsev-fenomen-belorusskogo-protesta.

Strożek, Przemysław. "Futurist Responses to African American Culture." In *Afromodernisms: Paris, Harlem, and the Avant-Garde*, edited by Fionnghuala Sweeney and Kate Marsh, 43–61. Edinburgh: Edinburgh University Press, 2013.

Szreder, Kuba. *The ABC of the Projectariat: Living and Working in a Precarious Art World*. Manchester, UK: Manchester University Press, 2021.

Szreder, Kuba. "The Authoritarian Turn: On the Crisis of the Polish Institutions of Contemporary Art." International Committee for Museums. March 6, 2023. https://cimam.org/news-archive/the-authoritarian-turn-on-the-crisis-of-the-polish-institutions-of-contemporary-art/.

Tafuri, Manfredo. *Architecture and Utopia: Design and Capitalist Development*. Cambridge, MA: MIT Press, 1979.

Táíwò, Olúfẹ́mi O. *Elite Capture: How the Powerful Took Over Identity Politics (and Everything Else)*. Haymarket Books, 2022.

Takayama, Akira. Interview by Mikala Tai. *Ocula*, April 17, 2018. https://ocula.com/magazine/conversations/akira-takayama/.

Talbot, William Henry Fox. *The Pencil of Nature*. London: Longman, 1844.

Tatlin, Vladimir, et al. "The Work Ahead of Us." In *Russian Art of the Avant-Garde: Theory and Criticism, 1902–1934*, edited and translated by John Bowlt, 205–207. New York: Viking, 1976.

Taws, Richard. *The Politics of the Provisional*. University Park: Pennsylvania State University Press, 2013.

Theodoropoulou, Vanessa. *Le monde en situation: la révolte sensible de l'Internationale situationniste*. Dijon: Les presses du réel, 2023.

Theodoropoulou, Vanessa. "Sur la figure du palindrome (et autres figures labyrinthiques dans l'œuvre de Guy Debord)." In *Lire Debord*, edited by Emmanuel Guy and Laurence Le Bras, 389–399. Paris: L'échappée, 2016.

Thomas, Édith. *The Women Incendiaries: The Inspiring Story of the Women of the Paris Commune Who Took Up Arms in the Fight for Liberty and Equality*. Translated by James Atkinson and Starr Atkinson. Chicago: Haymarket Books, 2007.

Thompson, Nato, ed. *Living as Form: Socially Engaged Art from 1991–2011*. New York: Creative Time; Cambridge, MA: MIT Press, 2012.

Tomii, Reiko. *Radicalism in the Wilderness: International Contemporaneity and 1960s Art in Japan*. Cambridge, MA: MIT Press, 2016.

Toufic, Jalal. *Forthcoming*. 2nd ed. London: Sternberg Press, 2014.

Toufic, Jalal. *The Withdrawal of Tradition Past a Surpassing Disaster*. Beirut, Lebanon: Forthcoming Books, 2009.

Tronti, Mario. "Factory and Society." In *Workers and Capital*, translated by David Broder, 12–35. London: Verso, 2019.

Trotsky, Leon. *History of the Russian Revolution*. Chicago: Haymarket Books, 2008.

Trouillot, Michel-Rolph. *Silencing the Past: Power and the Production of History*. Boston: Beacon Press, 1995.

Trump, Donald J. "Promoting Beautiful Federal Civic Architecture." Memorandum for the Administrator of the General Services Administration, The White House, January 20, 2025. https://www.whitehouse.gov/presidential-actions/2025/01/promoting-beautiful-federal-civic-architecture/.

Tucker, Robert C., ed. *The Marx-Engels Reader*. 2nd ed. New York: W. W. Norton, 1978.

Tunalı, Tijen, and Alla Myzelev, eds. *Contemporary Arts across Political Divides*. London: Bloomsbury Academic, 2023.

Tunalı, Tijen, and Brian Winkenweder, eds. *The Routledge Companion to Marxisms in Art History*. New York: Routledge, 2025.

United States. White House. "National Security Strategy of the United States of America." December 4, 2025. https://www.whitehouse.gov/wp-content/uploads/2025/12/2025-National-Security-Strategy.pdf.

Vainshtein, Olga B. "Designing the Future: Constructivist Laboratory of Fashion." In *Fashion and Modernism*, edited by Louise Wallenberg and Andrea Kollnitz, 101–124. London: Bloomsbury, 2019.

Van den Berg, Karen, Cara M. Jordan, and Philipp Kleinmichel, eds. *The Art of Direct Action: Social Sculpture and Beyond*. Berlin: Sternberg Press, 2019.

Varoufakis, Yanis. *Technofeudalism: What Killed Capitalism*. 2023; Brooklyn, NY: Melville House, 2024.

Verhagen, Marcus. *Viewing Velocities: Art and the Practice of Speed*. London: Verso, 2021.

Virno, Paolo. *A Grammar of the Multitude: For an Analysis of Contemporary Forms of Life*. Translated by Isabella Bertoletti, James Cascaito, and Andrea Casson. Los Angeles: Semiotext(e), 2004.

Vishmidt, Marina. *Speculation as a Mode of Production: Forms of Value Subjectivity in Art and Capital*. Leiden: Brill, 2018.

W.A.G.E. (Working Artists and the Greater Economy). *FAQs*. Artists & Activists series, no. 17. New York: Printed Matter, 2012.

W.A.G.E. (Working Artists and the Greater Economy). "W.A.G.E. Certification." Accessed December 27, 2025. https://www.wageforwork.com/.

Walworth, Catherine. *Soviet Salvage: Imperial Debris, Revolutionary Reuse, and Russian Constructivism*. University Park: Penn State University Press, 2017.

Watkins, Peter, director. *La Commune (Paris, 1871)*. 13 Production, 2000. 345 min.

Weibel, Peter, ed. *Global Activism: Art and Conflict in the 21st Century*. Cambridge, MA: MIT Press, 2015.

West, Cornel. *The Cornel West Reader*. New York: Basic Civitas Books, 1999.

Williams, Raymond. *The Long Revolution*. Harmondsworth, UK: Penguin Books, 1965.

Wollstonecraft, Mary. *A Vindication of the Rights of Men, in a Letter to the Right Honourable Edmund Burke; Occasioned by His Reflections on the Revolution in France*. London: J. Johnson, 1790.

Wright, Stephen. *Toward a Lexicon of Usership*. Eindhoven: Van Abbemuseum, 2013.

Yglesias, Matthew. "Trump-Era Politics Is a Surreal Nightmare and We Can't Wake Up." *Vox*, March 30, 2018. https://www.vox.com/policy-and-politics/2018/3/30/17170716/trump-surreal-nightmare.

Zhadova, Larissa Alekseevna. *Tatlin*. New York: Rizzoli, 1988.

Zhang, Gary Zhexi, ed. *Catastrophe Time!* London: Strange Attractor Press, 2023.

Žižek, Slavoj. *Living in the End Times*. London: Verso, 2011.

Žižek, Slavoj. *The Sublime Object of Ideology*. London: Verso, 2009.

Zychowicz, Jessica. "The Global Controversy over Pussy Riot: An Anti-Putin Women's Protest Group in Moscow." *InterDisciplinary Journal of Humanities and Arts* 2, no. 1 (Fall 2012). http://hdl.handle.net/2027/spo.11645653.0002.104.

INDEX